Advance Praise

"*Small Business, Big Change* is a game changer at a time when our world needs new visionaries with a hands-on attitude. Susan Chambers is not only 'right on the money' for eco-conscious small business owners, she is the conscience of our planet speaking in a practical voice that should be heard by all entrepreneurs. Finally the bell is ringing and it says that profitable business and social responsibility are the same enterprise. Don't just read this book…live it."

- Jeffrey Armstrong, Speaker and Author of *Spiritual Teachings of the Avatar, Ancient Wisdom for a New World* (Beyond Words/Simon & Schuster, 2010)

"Being a socially responsible company is vital to being a successful business. Susan Chambers explains and walks you step-by-step through the process of creating a company that aligns with customers' needs. It's an important book that every entrepreneur should read."

- Karl Staib, Author of *Work Happy Now* (2012, WorkHappyNow.com)

SMALL BUSINESS, BIG CHANGE

A Microentrepreneur's Guide to Social Responsibility

Susan Chambers

Night Owls Press

Published by Night Owls Press LLC, San Francisco, CA, 94119, U.S.A., www.nightowlspress.com.
Editor: Genevieve DeGuzman
Production Editor: Andrew Tang
Cover design by Michael Kostuchenko

Library of Congress Cataloging-in-Publication Data:
Chambers, Susan.
Small business, big change: a microentrepreneur's guide to social responsibility/ Susan Chambers.
p. cm.
Includes bibliographic references.

Paperback ISBN-13: 9781937645038
E-book ISBN-13: 9781937645021

1. Business. 2. Green business practices - Case studies. 3. Social responsibility - Case studies.

2012955624

For my family, friends, and teachers who encouraged me to use my love of writing to make a difference, and for all the social entrepreneurs who are changing the business model for the better because they know that how we treat Earth and all her inhabitants matters deeply.

CONTENTS

LIST OF ENTREPRENEURS

From January to July 2012, I interviewed twenty-one microentrepreneurs from a diverse range of industries. Their stories and personal insights on implementing socially responsible practices in their businesses illustrate the triumphs and challenges of transforming a business into a socially responsible one. *Disclaimer:* All information drawn from the interviews, including quotes and case studies, are for informational purposes only. They are snapshots of the people and companies in question. For complete and up-to-date information about the companies featured in this book, please visit their respective websites.

Reesa Abrams, TechCycle3 (techcycle3.com), Santa Cruz, California, USA

Suzanne Akin, Akinz (akinz.com), Fort Collins, Colorado, USA

Toby Barazzuol, Eclipse Awards (eclipseawards.com), Vancouver, Canada

Julie Beyer, For the Love of Food (loveoffood.ca), Vancouver, Canada

Saul Brown, Saul Good Gift Co. (itsaulgood.com), Vancouver, Canada

Melissa Cartwright, Mellifera Bees (melliferabees.com), Vancouver, Canada

James Castro-Edwards, Greenstack Ltd. (greenstack.co.uk), London, UK

Joanne Chang, Nice Shoes (gotniceshoes.com), Vancouver, Canada

Lori Del Genis, Conscious Elegance (consciouselegance.com), State College, Pennsylvania, USA

Jane Faye, Gaia Noir (gaia-noir.co.uk), Glasgow, Scotland

José Alejandro Flores, VOS Flips (vosflips.com), San Antonio, Texas, USA

Juan Gallardo, Greyka (greyka.com), Culver City, California, USA

Hans Hassle, Plantagon (plantagon.com), Stockholm, Sweden

Joseph Hodgkinson, Foda Catering (fodacatering.com), Mountain View, California, USA

Mia Kalef, Emerging Families (emergingfamilies.com), Vancouver, Canada

Joe Staiano, Meaningful Trips (meaningfultrip.com), Seattle, Washington, USA

Kate Sutherland, Kate Sutherland & Associates (katersutherland.com), Vancouver, Canada

Linh Truong, The Soap Dispensary (thesoapdispensary.com), Vancouver, Canada

Troy Van Beek, Ideal Energy Inc. (idealenergyinc.com), Fairfield, Iowa, USA

Nancy Wahl-Scheurich, LittleFootprint Lighting (littlefootprintlighting.com), Santa Cruz, California, USA

Eileen Webb, webmeadow (webmeadow.com), Littleton, New Hampshire, USA

SMALL BUSINESS, BIG CHANGE

A Microentrepreneur's Guide to Social Responsibility

FOREWORD

OVER the past few decades, we have seen an unprecedented alignment of business goals with social and environmental goals. No longer do we think of being "pro-environment" or "pro-local community" as being anti-business. Business and social responsibility can go together.

I saw these dual ideas put into action at Xerox Corporation, where I worked for nearly two decades. With the support of management, I helped implement the Xerox Environmental Leadership Program in 1991, which came to embody the company's commitment to ethical and greener business operations. Expanding over the years, the program helped save Xerox hundreds of millions of dollars, as well as reduced waste and promoted conservation and social responsibility among its employees. I went on to write the *Business Guide to Waste Reduction and Recycling*, a manual oriented to promoting sustainable business practices within Xerox and at other large companies. It provided guidelines for organizing employee teams, identifying source reduction and reuse opportunities, and setting up recycling and resource conservation programs.

My experience working at Xerox, as well as advising and working alongside several environmental and development organizations, including Earth Day 1990 and two San Francisco Bay Area organizations that later merged into Acterra—Peninsula Conservation Center and Bay Area Action— bolstered my belief that social responsibility and good environmental practices are a winning combination for business. More and more, customers are gravitating toward businesses that value social responsibility. Employees are championing social responsibility and green initiatives in the workplace, their enthusiasm translating to better customer service and productivity. At Xerox, I saw individual employees and small teams develop innovative ideas and programs, including designing reusable packaging for new product delivery, launching a cartridge return and remanufacturing program, and pushing "minimum impact" design standards for products, among others. This alignment of values has been a win-win for the organizations I've worked with.

While at Xerox, I worked with the Peninsula Conservation Center (now Acterra) in the early nineties to start a Business Environmental Awards (BEA) program, which offered awards in different categories, including small businesses, to encourage environmental responsibility and sustainable business practices. The BEA program is still ongoing after almost twenty years. Some of the most innovative ideas and results were from dedicated employees at small companies who wanted to make a difference. These included Satellite Telework Centers, for facilitating environmentally efficient telecommuting, and Metro Lighting, where owners and employees pooled their own savings to install solar panels on top of their renovated building.

While major multinationals and large corporations may be moving forward with integrating social responsibility in business operations, it is the small businesses that can have a larger, more far-reaching social and environmental impact. In the U.S. alone, the latest census data shows that small businesses represent 99.7 percent of all employer firms, employing half of all private sector employees.[i] According to the U.S. Small Business Administration, small businesses hire 43 percent of high tech workers, and more than half of these small businesses are home-based. Over the past two decades, small companies have generated 65 percent of net new jobs and created more than half of the nonfarm private sector GDP. Small businesses can have an impact—and solopreneurs and microentrepreneurs have a definite stake in the social responsibility debate.

Susan Chambers' *Small Business, Big Change: A Microentrepreneur's Guide to Social Responsibility* is a timely book that captures these ideas well. It is one of the first books geared specifically toward microentrepreneurs, showing that businesses of *all sizes* can become social change agents. It illustrates that everyday entrepreneurs can actually improve their profitability, as well as customer and employee satisfaction, through efforts to be more green and socially responsible.

Through a sensible, step-by-step, checklist-based approach, *Small Business, Big Change* teaches both aspiring and veteran entrepreneurs how to align their values with their business practices to make a positive difference in the world. It shows how small businesses can adapt and adopt business practices that inject social responsibility into how they deal with their business networks and communities: vendors, customers, employees, contractors, shareholders, and investors. Finally, addressing the concerns and frustrations that owners experience when their ideal vision of what they want to accomplish conflicts with business realities, the book offers a balanced approach: microentrepreneurs will learn to assess what's feasible and what's not, and plan better.

Over the years, the business community has come to realize that interdependence and cooperation is more vital than ever. We are all but cells in the whole body of life and the fabric of the planet. If one group takes more and more at the expense of other groups and interests, humanity as a whole suffers. Working together for the benefit of the wider community is true social responsibility. We often think businesses can only survive by implementing cutthroat competition—survival of the fittest where only profits matter. But really, it is the adaptable that survive; those who excel while cooperating are, indeed, the "fittest."

There is far more to be gained through cooperation as we all work toward achieving mutual goals of sustainable progress. As more businesses, big and small, get "on board," we can all move towards a healthier planet and more vibrant economy.

- Abhay K. Bhushan
Chairman, ASquare Inc.; Board member and Advisor, Pointcross Inc.; and Mentor for StartUP Ventures

INTRODUCTION: CHANGING THE WORLD THROUGH YOUR BUSINESS

IN 2011, I was inspired by a teleseminar offered through Mark Silver's Heart of Business Inc., a mentoring and training company for heart-centered entrepreneurs and small businesses.[1] This particular seminar was about helping "heart-centered" business owners examine and redefine their relationships to money and influence and change their businesses for the better.[2] During the question and answer segment, several participants expressed an interest in learning how they could effect change in their communities through their businesses. Hearing small business owners, many of them solopreneurs, motivated and committed to redefining how they do business intrigued me. Despite the lack of resources, many of these microentrepreneurs believed they could serve as agents of social change—and continue to make a profit. These were bold ambitions and I wondered how many others shared that vision.

At the time, what struck me was that these were individual entrepreneurs—not corporations or large companies—having a candid conversation about social responsibility and its practical applications. For a time, discussions about the social and environmental impacts of business mostly took place in the context of large companies. Corporate social responsibility (CSR) blossomed as a popular field in the 1990s and dominated the conversation on the commitment of business to the environment, consumer and employee well-being, and the health and welfare of local communities.

In retrospect, Milton Friedman was wrong when he first asserted in 1962 that the only social responsibility of a business was to increase its profits for shareholders. Yes, it's true that businesses are expected to make a profit and corporations do have a financial responsibility to their shareholders. But it's also true that entrepreneurs are inspired to start and run businesses for reasons that have little, if anything, to do with the accumulation of wealth for its own sake. For an increasing number of entrepreneurs, a business is as much, or more, about finding a way to express their values and purpose through their work or creating products or services that add social or ecological value—not just economic value—to the world.

We know that businesses don't operate in a vacuum. As much as some economic theorists and our individualist culture would have us believe otherwise, we don't live, or run businesses, in "splendid isolation." We are interdependent with other beings and the planet, and what we do in the course of our lives and our businesses affects others. Most business owners are now cognizant of this fact. They know that destroying the physical or social environment in which they operate, alienating other stakeholders (in addition to shareholders), or causing harm to consumers in the process of generating profit will eventually jeopardize their business' financial and organizational sustainability.

Although the CSR dialogue now increasingly includes small and mid-sized businesses, we still rarely think of the solopreneur or microentrepreneur (businesses employing ten people or less) as having any tangible stake in the CSR debate. This is beginning to change. Increasing numbers of socially conscious individuals are not only starting up microbusinesses but also staking their places at the discussion table.

The Socially Responsible Microentrepreneur

Since the 1990s, there has been a groundswell of concern among businesses of all sizes in becoming social change agents in their community and switching to business practices that are more socially responsible. The kind of serious interest in social responsibility demonstrated by the participants of that Heart of Business seminar is no longer an anomaly.

The rising awareness and drive to be both a good business (profitable) and good business citizen (mindful of its social responsibility and values) is often confounded by the lack of resources and scant knowledge base available to the average microentrepreneur. Too often, microbusiness owners don't have the time to look for the resources that will help them learn what it takes to become a committed and yet pragmatic, socially responsible business. Like the participants in the teleseminar and several individuals interviewed for this book, I'm a socially conscious yet "accidental" microentrepreneur. I'm no stranger to barriers such as a lack of financial resources or time that stymie all small business owners. I know intimately the struggles of staying committed to the principles I believe in and making sure that they inform my business practices. It's not easy, and I don't always manage to execute my social responsibility (S-R) strategies as perfectly or consistently as I'd like.[3] I imagine it's just as difficult for other "small shops" to change their mindset and business practices, too.

The more I thought about it, the more I began to wonder: *What information do forward-thinking individuals need in order to align their business processes with personal values? What parts of the process might be so overwhelming that they deter or discourage small business owners from even thinking about shifting to socially responsible business practices? What resources could small business owners turn to for practical suggestions and encouragement from like-minded entrepreneurs?* The more I mulled over these questions, the more I felt compelled to research and write about how microentrepreneurs could bring about social change through their businesses.

THE IMMEDIATE CATALYST for choosing to write about these issues was my mini "Eureka!" moment upon hearing the participants from the Heart of Business teleseminar talk so frankly about wanting to become social change agents through their businesses, but I've been a staunch believer in socially responsible business for a number of years. The content, philosophical approach, and even the timing of this book were inspired and guided by a series of events and experiences over the last few years that not only brought with them a major shift in my career (and life) path, but also offered an opportunity to reconnect with my earlier aspirations of contributing to social change in the world.

When these shifts began to unfold, I had just finished reading *Governing the World. The ethical imperative* (2010) by my friend Martin De Waele. De Waele called for a new system of governance shaped by cooperation and collaboration rather than conflict and competition—ideas close to my heart. He also advocated for sustainability and the equitable distribution of resources over wealth (and profit) at any cost. Not long after reading that book, I heard about an event called "The Great Turning: An Un-Conference to Be The Change" that brought together community leaders and local and international organizations for an inspiring day of talks and artistic performances around social change.

I followed my intuition and attended, thinking that I might connect with like-minded people and organizations. I was right. One of the outcomes of that experience was that I started volunteering with Be the Change Earth Alliance (bethechangeearthalliance.org), a local nonprofit dedicated to encouraging and supporting individuals to contribute to a more socially just, environmentally sustainable, and spiritually fulfilling world through its program of "Be The Change" Action Circles. Action Circles are discussion groups made up of individuals who agree to meet weekly to discuss readings on the circle's theme and commit to take specific actions to promote the organization's principles.

One of my volunteer projects involved research, writing, and editing work for the *Be the Change Action Guide*.[4] Going through the 500+ actions listed in the publication, I was inspired by the potentially far-reaching power of taking small, humble actions to promote far-reaching, radical change. In addition to the collection of manageable actions and strategies, it also included a compilation of resources on tracking and measuring the impact of those actions.

Volunteering with the Be the Change Earth Alliance, I eventually joined a "What's Your Tree?" Action Circle, a group intended to help individuals identify their life purpose and to discover a path or project that would bring their life purpose into action.[5] Over the course of eight consecutive weeks of participating in this Circle, I not only became more aware of my own personal behaviors that already contributed to creating a more sustainable presence on the planet, I was also inspired to take other actions that would make a difference that I either hadn't thought of or wouldn't have thought to have much impact.

A wonderful experience, participating in the Action Circle made me see first-hand the power and potential of a small group of people supporting and empowering each other. I came away with a much clearer picture of how I wanted to express my purpose in the world—and how I could do that through my own work and livelihood. I started taking on research and editing projects that would help empower individuals to become their own social change agents and that supported organizations committed to social change by helping them tell their stories. I started a blog, *Sage Wit*. Drawing on what I had learned through both research and lived experience, I started writing about how individuals can create positive social, environmental, and economic change in their everyday activities. In fact, the book you hold in your hands started its life on *Sage Wit*. In a two-part post, I came to three basic realizations that eventually formed the core themes of this book:[6]

- Everyone has the capacity to be a change agent and to lead by example.

- Even when we feel compelled to be or to create the changes we wish to see, we can't be effective change agents if we don't know what to do and where to start. (Also, eager to be change agents, we sometimes take on too much, too soon, and burn out, jeopardizing the long-term sustainability of our efforts.)

- We're all social animals and more successful when we join forces with others and work collaboratively to create change.

Later, I came to another realization: We're more motivated to continue with new behaviors when we can see some evidence of their impact, and we're more likely to pay attention and be more mindful when that impact gets measured or tracked.

About the Book

Small Business, Big Change takes these philosophical and pragmatic observations and transforms them into a set of actions that every microentrepreneur can take and make their own. It also explores tried-and-true strategies for making decisions about what to do and where to start, where to find a network of like-minded entrepreneurs, and how to tackle daunting data-tracking tasks. This book was written specifically for microentrepreneurs like you: Socially conscious microbusiness owners who have decided they want to become more socially responsible and are seeking an effective but incremental approach to implementing business decisions and strategies that generate profits, as well as promote the values of sustainability and social responsibility.

> *Small Business, Big Change* is one of the first books developed just for solopreneurs and microbusiness owners on how to incorporate socially responsible and sustainable business practices.

I wrote this book from the perspective that business should put equal weight on "value" and "values" to achieve that triple bottom line: people, planet, profits.[7] A truly vibrant business generates its profits through a combination of "value" and "values." *Small Business, Big Change* shows that you should and can focus on both "value"—by creating goods and services that are useful and have a market—and "values"—by improving the lives of your employees, the life of your community at large, and treading on the planet as gently as possible in the course of doing business. I want you to see that your business should be an extension of your personal values and practices, that your "triple bottom line" is less about the numbers at the bottom of the page and more about building two-way relationships with the people and environment around you. As Mark Silver points out, "It's in your hands to ensure that your business both nourishes and is nourished by each of the three S-R strands—people, planet, and profits—in the triple bottom line."[8]

Even with these high ideals and expectations, I haven't forgotten the concerns—and frustrations—that microbusiness owners experience when their visions of being socially responsible and their financial realities clash. As a microentrepreneur, you may have a smaller operating budget and fewer resources available to you. The emphasis in this book is on balancing the potential costs of engaging in socially responsible business practices with your long-term financial obligations.

Guided by this understanding, *Small Business, Big Change* takes a "start where you are and start small" approach. Many of us have heard of the expression "play big or go home" when it comes to setting and meeting goals, but this is a form of zero-sum thinking that can set individuals up for failure. I'm idealistic but also pragmatic. *Small Business, Big Change* encourages you to move beyond "all or nothing" thinking and to set small, realistic goals or milestones in the process of transforming your business into a socially responsible one. Regardless of where your frustrations stem from, this book offers suggestions to get you thinking about low or no-cost approaches to social giving. For each approach, I'll walk you through the steps to put each one into action.

Most of the ideas and strategies discussed here aren't radically new; they have been tested and put into practice by bigger businesses for years. For the first time, these strategies are tailored in ways that are the most effective and practical for the microentrepreneur. I believe that individuals should be empowered to be the best social change agents they can be. If you've ever felt you lacked the time, money, or resources to adopt sweeping changes, or if you think you're "too small" to make a difference, this book shows how you can have a bigger impact than you ever thought you could by changing your mindset and making just a few tweaks and changes in how you do business.

Here's how the book is structured:

Chapter 1 "Your Business as a Social Change Agent" offers you an overview of the process for identifying reachable goals and setting up a tracking system to measure and analyze their impacts. It then discusses how to gradually adopt socially responsible business practices and processes for each of the main dimensions of your business: the physical environment, your products or services, your business networks (including colleagues, suppliers, professional services, etc.), customers, and employees.

Chapter 2 "Treading Gently on the Planet" focuses on environmental practices that reduce your ecological footprint. These include reducing or eliminating the number of toxic products you use, as well as ensuring that your products and services are made available using ethical and sustainable methods. This chapter takes you through the process of working with others to green your business, including the conversations you'll need to have with your employees, vendors, and customers on making your business practices green.

Chapter 3 "Social Capital and Social Impact on Your Community" considers the social impact of your business and the importance of engaging with your community and supply chains. This chapter shows you how to use your wealth, skills, and influence to make a positive social impact by investing in social or environmental causes, educating overseas suppliers about fair working conditions, supporting other local businesses, partnering with nonprofit or community development organizations, or collaborating with other businesses to solve local concerns or global social problems.

Chapter 4 "People Power – Employees and Business Networks" is all about nurturing your employees and your business colleagues. This chapter outlines some strategies for sharing the wealth with your employees. Chapter 4 also offers some ideas for attending to other aspects of the workplace environment that contribute to employee well-being. We'll also explore opportunities to start collaborative projects with your colleagues—and even your competitors.

Chapter 5 "Value, Values, and Valuing Your Customers" shows you how to strengthen the relationship with your customers or clients through your values. Customers are the backbone of every business so it's vitally important that you not only demonstrate that you care about them and their opinions, but that you include them in the planning and feedback stages of every S-R initiative. Learn how to engage your customers around your business plans and how to create a community among your clients and patrons.

Chapter 6 "When Vision and Reality Collide – Unpacking the First-aid Kit" offers simple problem-solving strategies for those times when reality clashes with your ideals and makes it difficult for you to get an S-R initiative off the ground. This chapter shows you how to fine-tune or rein in your vision for the short term to ensure sustainability over the long term.

Every chapter ends with a "Chapter Checklist" that summarizes the main tips and strategies discussed in the chapter. In addition, throughout the chapters you'll get suggestions for other resources, such as books, websites, and organizations that provide indispensible advice and tips for your journey to becoming an S-R-focused business. Learn about support groups, directories of socially responsible businesses and organizations, Green Business and B Corporation certifications, footprint calculators, and much more. For my personal recommendations for extra reading and research that you can do, consider the "Further Reading" section at the end of the book.

Small Business, Big Change is also more than just a cut-and-dried, how-to guide. Along with sharing my own experiences, I've amassed the advice and wisdom from everyday entrepreneurs who have been successful in implementing socially responsible initiatives in their business operations. Their voices and ideas make this book more than just a conventional field guide to social responsibility.

From January-July 2012, I interviewed twenty-one microentrepreneurs from a diverse range of industries, including catering, holistic health, travel, bee-keeping, various clothing and footwear retail shops, service businesses, small-scale manufacturing, web development, and computer and electronics recycling. Their stories and personal insights illustrate the triumphs and challenges of transforming a business into a socially responsible one. While inspiring anecdotes from all twenty-one entrepreneurs are included throughout the book, in-depth case studies of selected entrepreneurs and their businesses are listed at the end of each chapter.

WELL, YOU'VE WAITED this long to start transforming your business into an agent of social change, so let's move on to Chapter 1. There, we'll go over how you can assess your S-R readiness, set and manage different S-R goals, track and measure your progress and impact, and get the support you need to get started on your S-R journey and transform your business.

Social Responsibility, Ltd.

Here's an overview of social responsibility as a movement in business through the years and a discussion of some of the notable issues that dominate the conversation among entrepreneurs.

The Rise of CSR

Milton Friedman's assertions about businesses being only motivated by profit have been proven to be shortsighted. A number of large companies in the nineteenth century—Cadbury being a well-known example—succeeded in both making a profit and implementing corporate social responsibility (CSR) initiatives that benefited their employees and the communities in which they operated.[9] It wasn't just nineteenth century British Quakers who brought a sense of social responsibility to their businesses, though. A number of American business leaders in the 1950s and 1960s also recognized that their companies had a responsibility toward society and a duty to do good works, usually reflected through some form of corporate philanthropy.[10]

Smaller companies have thrived in this CSR wake. Take a look at companies such as Burt's Bees or Ben and Jerry's in their early days. Burt's Bees started out in the mid-eighties as a two-person operation selling honey, beeswax candles, and lip balm, and upholding a commitment to using natural ingredients and building an environmentally sustainable business. While Clorox bought the company in 2007, Burt's Bees appears to have maintained its commitment to its values and practices. It was one of the companies that helped establish the Natural Seal, a set of independent, rigorous criteria used to assess and certify natural products.[11]

Ben and Jerry's also stayed true to the socially responsible philosophies and practices of its original owners. Since it was first started in the late-seventies, the company has been an outspoken advocate for numerous social justice and environmental issues. It spoke out against drilling for oil in Alaska, supported same-sex marriage, and, most recently, supported the Occupy Wall Street movement.[12] Even after the company was sold to Unilever in 2000, Ben and Jerry's strove to maintain its independence and commitment to its mission. It established an independent Board of Directors empowered to uphold its commitment to social and environmental issues, product quality, and sustainable economic growth. In 2012, the current board started advocating for the company to become a certified B (Benefit) Corporation. This change in business structure requires a company to fulfill a social purpose beyond fiduciary responsibility to shareholders, to set out its social and environmental goals within the company's bylaws, and to publish an annual benefit report that evaluates its performance against its stated goals.[13]

Is it inevitable that independent, socially responsible businesses that become wildly successful will be bought out by multinational companies? Not always. Sometimes you see the inverse occurring. In a sort of "reverse" buy-out, Nature's Path Organic Foods, a British Columbia-based business that started in 1985, actually bought back its previous company from a multinational corporation.[14] More than twenty-five years after its inception, Nature's Path has grown from a small, family-run business to a larger enterprise with just under 400 employees in several locations throughout North America. Not only has Nature's Path remained an independent company that is still owned by the same family, but it has also stayed true to its original values on environmental sustainability and social responsibility.

A Demand for Social Responsibility

As the environmental damage and economic injustices that have been inflicted in the name of economic expansion and profit-seeking have come to light over the past few decades, it's no longer just a few environmentalists and social activists who are making waves. Investors, shareholders, and consumers are also demanding accountability. Now that consumers and investors can readily find out about a company's CSR behavior and "vote with their wallet," many are choosing not to support businesses with poor CSR track records—even if those businesses have a great performance record in terms of maximizing profits for shareholders. Corporations are now expected to take steps beyond the minimum legal requirements to reduce environmental damage and to contribute to the common, social good in the communities where they operate.

Today, customers, investors, and even shareholders have increasingly come to expect that value in the form of profits is only one dimension of a vibrant business. These days, when ethically-minded stakeholders see concerns over profit riding roughshod over human rights and environmental considerations, companies are likely to find themselves on a boycott list—losing profits, face, or both. Between 2009 and 2010, a well-known brand of undergarments lost $50 million in sales after college students (and their institutions) boycotted it for closing a Honduran factory that unionized. After the year-long boycott, the company reversed its decision, reopened the factory, and rehired all of the workers.[15]

A paper products company also bowed to pressure from environmental groups, consumers, and shareholders to stop buying pulp from timber companies that were clear-cutting original growth, boreal forests. In response to five years of pressure, the company agreed to revise its procurement and environmental policies and practices.[16]

The Business Case for Social Responsibility

The connection between being a good corporate citizen (or not) and financial performance didn't go unnoticed by business supporters. Since the nineties, business advocates have increasingly framed the rationale for adopting CSR strategies as a business case by linking social performance to financial performance.[17] To show the connection between social and financial performance, many companies focused on translating socially responsible initiatives into publicly documented, measurable outcomes or performance indicators.

Skeptics and ardent free-market economists challenged the business case for the value of integrating CSR activities into a firm's business practices. By 1997, researchers were finding a positive relationship between corporate social and financial performance.[18] A 2003 analysis of the research in this area reported a statistically significant relationship between social and financial performance.[19] While we can never be sure what motivates corporate executives to implement and report on CSR actions, many clearly decided that it was in their best interest to dive into CSR activities. There has been a sharp increase in CSR reporting across all industry sectors, from less than 100 reports in 1992 to roughly 1,800 reports produced globally in 2003. In 2010, just under 5,000 reports were produced globally by corporations across all industry sectors.[20]

Promoting "doing good" as a way of doing well financially clearly worked as a driver to get more corporations involved in CSR, but it had some unintended consequences, too. The emphasis on tying corporate social performance to financial performance inadvertently resulted in spending more time analyzing the impact of the corporation's social performance on its financial performance, rather than on the community or environment.[21] The drive to improve or repair an image problem that affects financial performance has also given rise to "CSR-washing," a ploy that often results in yet more damage to customer and stakeholder relationships.[22]

Value and Values: A New Role for Business

In an ideal world, the goal of CSR reporting isn't just about getting the numbers at the bottom of the page to "look good" because it's an opportunity to improve a corporation's public relations image, to be "trendy," or even to become more profitable. While the public relations image and financial bottom line are important facets of a company's performance, business owners sometimes forget that embracing and practicing principles of fairness and sustainability is the *right* thing to do.

Individuals such as Paul Hawken—an environmentalist, serial entrepreneur, and author—recognized that business people have a critical role to play in not just minimizing but preventing, where possible, the damaging environmental and social impacts of commerce. Far from narrowly defining the purpose of business as just a way of making money for the owners and shareholders, Hawken argues that businesses *should* be focused on improving the well-being of humans and restoring ecosystems.[23] A well-known corporate executive who "got it" and subsequently championed Hawken's argument is Ray Anderson of Interface Inc. As the story goes, after receiving and reading a copy of Hawken's book, *The Ecology of Commerce*, Anderson not only redesigned the manufacturing processes to make his company's product, carpet tiles, more earth-friendly, he also became an active spokesman for sustainable business and industry practices.[24] Another business that was directly influenced by Paul Hawken's philosophy is the Vancouver-based microbusiness, Saul Good Gift Co., a company that specializes in creating gift baskets from sustainable, mostly local products.[25] Saul Brown, the entrepreneur who founded the company, cites reading Hawken, as the inspiration for enrolling in the Sustainable Business MBA program at the Bainbridge Graduate Institute and subsequently founding his company.[26]

From large, national corporations to local microbusinesses, increasing numbers of socially responsible entrepreneurs are turning their backs on the old way of doing business. These entrepreneurs go into business with the firm belief that companies have a duty to act responsibly and be a part of the solution, not the problem. Socially responsible entrepreneurs are at least equally concerned with creating long-term value for their communities as they are about profits and increasing the value of their companies. They have pushed for—and won—changes in legislation that allow them to restructure their companies as B (Benefit) Corporations so that they aren't limited to making decisions based on whether the results will improve the wealth of shareholders. They have demonstrated that "doing well by doing good" isn't only viable, but is also the best way to do business. They have also had the last laugh on Friedman's assertions about the purpose of business.

ONE: Your Business as a Social Change Agent

SOME individuals, it seems, come into the world hard-wired to bring about social change, whether through their personal or professional activities, or both. For some people, those activist tendencies are awakened gradually; in others, the "on" switch is activated early in life. Kate Sutherland, an organizational and community development consultant, facilitator, and author who lives and works in Vancouver, has self-identified as a change agent for most of her life, but has only come to identify herself as a business person in recent years. Initially, Kate thought she would be able to help create changes by applying her study of economics to community development work, but in practice she found herself on a different path. When asked about what inspired her to start a socially responsible business, she replied that while the passion was there (she's been involved in projects that focus on food security, recycling, sustainable living, and citizen engagement initiatives), her interest in connecting her personal interests to business came later. "I've been interested and involved with trying to figure out how to change the world, make changes for the better, since I was a teenager," says Kate. "But what has been interesting is learning to see myself as a business person. I've come to see a positive role for business. I can see a synergy between social purpose and business."

Each of the microentrepreneurs interviewed for this book stepped into their roles as entrepreneurial social change agents in different ways. Some, like Kate, have always seen themselves as social change agents and made deliberate choices to incorporate their social activism into their paid work. Some, such as Julie Beyer, the founder of For the Love of Food, started out as a socially conscious, accidental entrepreneur. Julie's interest in transforming the global food system was first sparked while studying economics and international development, but she thought she'd be making those changes in a detached kind of way through policy work. Julie's love of delicious food was ignited when she studied abroad for a year in France. A stint of volunteering on an organic farm in Turkey helped her to see first-hand the connection between her food choices and the food system, and their implications for small-scale farmers, but it wasn't until she returned to Canada that she figured out what she wanted to do. A debilitating illness that included symptoms of severe food allergies and a hypersensitivity to food additives and pesticides sparked her four-year journey of holistic healing that included embracing a 100% organic, whole foods lifestyle and a commitment to cultivating a love of healthy food.

Along the way, Julie discovered she had a natural talent for combining flavors and making healthy food taste delicious. She developed a passion for teaching people how to make healthier food choices and to cook with organic and sustainably produced whole, plant-based foods and eventually launched For the Love of Food. Julie also makes and sells her GLOW product line of sweet and savory treats made from high quality, raw, organic ingredients. Julie laughs at the irony in her radically revised approach to transforming the global food system. "I never intended to start a business, let alone teach people how to eat and cook healthfully," says Julie. "[When I was growing up], I used to be teased for my lack of cooking skills."

Unlike some of the entrepreneurs in this book who started from day one as a socially responsible business, Toby Barazzuol started Eclipse Awards, a company that creates recognition awards for corporations, nonprofits, and other organizations, as a regular business. The catalyst for transferring his personal interest in sustainability and social responsibility (S-R) to his business operations was nothing smaller than the 2010 Winter Olympic Games. Back in 2002, when local businesses started hearing that Vancouver might be hosting the 2010 Winter Games, they also heard that companies bidding for contracts would be asked about their sustainability practices. Toby started talking to other people about sustainability, as well as reading Paul Hawken's books. What he learned changed everything. A couple of years later, he launched Eclipse Award's S-R transformation starting with green energy certifications. Eclipse Awards is well into its S-R journey and Toby continues to find new ways to refine or expand his S-R practices.

Saul Brown, the owner of Saul Good Gift Co. in Vancouver, and Hans Hassle, the CEO of the Swedish company Plantagon, were fully aware of the power (and responsibility) of business to create positive social changes. Each of these individuals drew from both their knowledge of sustainable business practices and their personal desire to use business as a force for good when they set up their companies. From the start, Saul structured his company as a B Corporation, which required him to meet certain standards as a socially responsible business. He later pursued certification through B Lab (bcorporation.net). Hans and the other directors of Plantagon established a unique governance structure that they refer to as a "companization." The companization brings together two organizations—one nonprofit and one for-profit entity—to ensure both commercial and sustainability concerns are addressed in tandem. Both Saul and Hans have a clearly established social mission as well as a set of values and practices that have been built into the bylaws and charters of their companies.

Whether you're just starting a business or have been running a business for several years—and whether you began with clear intentions or have been an S-R advocate all your life—it's never too late to start the process of transforming into a socially responsible business. You certainly wouldn't be the first business owner to realize, mid-course, that it's time to make a change. While it may be true that the best time to plant a tree is twenty years ago, unless you're literally chopping down the last tree, it's never too late to plant that new tree.

You might even discover that you already have one or two tiny seedlings (S-R practices) in place; it's just that you never thought of them as socially responsible actions, or perhaps you dismissed them as too small to be of consequence. If you've already adopted a policy of going paperless, banished plastic water bottles from your office, and switched to either compact fluorescent or LED light bulbs, then take a minute to congratulate yourself for being further along in the game than you thought, and having a smaller carbon footprint! If you already make a point of supporting other local businesses, participate in projects that improve and add long-term value to your community, or have found other ways to nurture your customers, employees, vendors, and suppliers, you're already engaging in socially responsible business practices.

However and whenever your business came into existence, it can be your vehicle to helping create a more environmentally and socially sustainable world. My guess is that since you've picked up this book, you already knew this at some level and now you're ready to act on this realization.

Changing the World One Person and Business at a Time

"To be successful, I have to have a narrow focus on maximizing profits with no role for S-R..."

"Going 'green' means going broke..."

"My business is too small to make a difference..."

More and more individuals and businesses are recognizing that old paradigms and beliefs that have shaped the marketplace—like the ones cited above—are no longer working. At the same time, we're also realizing that if we want a more socially just and environmentally sustainable presence on this planet, it's no good waiting for others to step up to the plate and do the work for us. The reason Gandhi's admonition that "we must be the change we wish to see in the world" is so often quoted by people interested in social change is because it reflects a simple truth: If we want to bring about positive change in the world, we must consistently engage in actions and behaviors that will produce those desired outcomes.

So, wherever you are with your business, know that you've taken that crucial first step. You are to be lauded for choosing to align your business practices with your personal beliefs, and recognizing that there is an opportunity to use your business to influence and inspire others to create positive changes in the world.

Yes, it may seem daunting at first. Thinking of yourself as just one solopreneur or microbusiness owner acting alone can leave you feeling like you have little influence to bring about any large-scale changes. However, if you step back to gain perspective, you'll see that you don't have to single-handedly inspire others to be social change agents.

> **Taking a Good Hard Look:**
> - Current S-R status and goals: *Where are you now, and where do you want to go?*
> - Social costs of your S-R goals: *What's feasible?*
> - Impact on your stakeholders: *Will they support your practices?*

According to research on social networks, individuals have three degrees of influence, or at least among the people they know and interact with on a regular basis.[1] If this is the case, then as microbusiness owners you're well placed to lead social change within your communities because there are ripple effects to the good you can do.

Changing the world is a major endeavor that requires us to actually do the change-making work before we can inspire others. As helpful as our business or personal networks might be for expanding our ability to influence and inspire others to adopt socially responsible practices, we still have to make the decisions about what practices we want to adopt and then integrate them into our business and personal lives. So, where do we start when there is so much to be done?

As one person or business, you can only take on so much without the risk of either feeling overwhelmed, disillusioned, or burnt out, or jeopardizing the long-term sustainability of your business enterprise. If you want to avoid these hazards and be a successful, socially responsible business over the long term, step back and consider these four tenets, which we'll go into in more detail:

- Start from where you are.

- Take small, steady steps.

- Find simple ways to track changes and celebrate successes.

- Find and maintain a network (personal and business) of kindred spirits for mutual support and collaborative projects.

Your S-R Assessment Process: Getting Started from Where You Are

If you're reading this heading and breaking out in a cold sweat because "assessment" sounds too much like "evaluation" or "test," you can relax. As we walk through this section, you'll be asked to answer a series of questions and take a good hard look at your business and its capacities. There are no right or wrong answers to these questions. The goal is to determine your starting point in your journey to transforming your business into an S-R focused one.

As outlined in the Introduction, S-R business practices encompass three broad strands—social (people), environmental (planet), and economic (profits—or, redefined more broadly, prosperity). Table 1-1 gives you an idea of the types of considerations included in each strand.

Table 1-1: The S-R Strands

S-R Strand	Considerations
People (Social Impact)	• You, your employees, and your contractors • Suppliers, vendors, and other professionals in your business network (e.g., accountants, banker, lawyer, colleagues, and competitors) • Customers and clients • Communities • Shareholders, investors, and grant agencies • Overseas suppliers and their workers
Planet (Environmental Impact)	• Regulations and minimum standards • Water and energy use • Materials and supplies (non toxic, sustainable) • The three R's: Reduce, reuse, recycle (in that order) • Packaging and plastic • The zero-waste challenge • Eco-footprints of your suppliers and vendors
Profits/Prosperity (Economic Impact)	• A living wage • Employee benefits • Recipients of financial or in-kind donations • Opportunities for disadvantaged groups • Local economy and community revitalization • Global economic and social development issues

In practice, these considerations aren't neatly and arbitrarily divided into the three discrete strands listed above; there is often some dove-tailing or overlap between them. For example, the financial success of your company (profits/prosperity) will usually drive how you can "give back" to the community or share the wealth with your employees (people). More details about these S-R practices are presented in Chapters 2 to 5, alongside real-life examples that have been field-tested by the microentrepreneurs interviewed for this book.

S-R Status: Where Are You Now, and Where Do You Want to Go?

The first step of your S-R assessment is to conduct a mini organizational appraisal and determine your readiness and capacity. Do you have the resources and skills or knowledge to put your plan into action? The S-R Readiness Assessment Form (refer to "Tool 1" at the end of this chapter) is a valuable tool for establishing your level of readiness from a personal and business standpoint.

The S-R Readiness Assessment Form will help you do the following:

- Clarify the reasons why you want to integrate S-R practices into your business processes.

- Take stock of your various "capitals" that include the financial, material, human, intellectual, and social resources available to you through your business.

- Identify your stakeholders and how they will be affected by your business decisions around S-R initiatives.

- Establish a starting point from which you can begin to track and measure the impact of your S-R practices.

After completing the Assessment Form, the next step is to identify your starting point. The S-R Inventory Form (refer to "Tool 2") helps you identify what you're currently doing or not doing in the S-R space:

- Take stock of the S-R practices that you already have in place.

- Determine the S-R practices that are relevant to your business or sector that you haven't yet implemented.

Go through the S-R Inventory and answer the questions based on what you're actually doing (or not doing)—not what you think you should be doing, or would like to be doing. Again, there are no correct or incorrect answers to the items in this inventory. Your goal is to gather information so that you can make decisions and set priorities as we move through the book.

Give yourself ample time to complete both forms with care. Remember, not all of the items in each area will apply directly to your business. Depending on how far you want to extend your influence, these suggestions may offer ideas on conversations about business practices you should be having with your customers, employees, suppliers, vendors, and other members of your business network.

Social Costs of Your S-R Goals: What's Feasible?

Now that you've assessed the current S-R status of your business, it's time to start making some decisions. First, consider the resources that are available to you and compare them to the potential expenses (time and money) of implementing various S-R practices (your "social" costs). What are your social costs? A "social cost," for our purposes, refers to any additional costs that are above or beyond your normal business costs and are incurred specifically as a result of the S-R practices you've taken on which reflect your values, vision, and mission.[2] Your social costs for implementing certain S-R initiatives might include: the dollar value equivalent for hours spent volunteering or participating in other community engagement projects; the cash value of in-kind donations or services donated to community organizations; discounts on products or services that you offer for certain groups; or a higher price tag on some of your business activities or operational processes that are tied to your vision and mission.

In particular, when looking at your social costs, remember the time you and/or your employees spend volunteering or participating in community events is time that you're not engaging in work that generates revenue for your business. Consider the trade-offs (e.g., limiting your business hours) and the potential benefits (e.g., generating goodwill and potentially more business in your community) when evaluating what's feasible for you and your business. You also need to know how much time to devote to tracking and reporting various S-R practices. We'll discuss tracking and reporting issues in detail in a later section. Linh Truong is the owner of The Soap Dispensary, a store that provides refills of eco-friendly cleaning products for body and home and also sells the materials for D-I-Y eco-friendly cleaners. In running her business, Linh is committed to reducing packaging and reusing plastic containers, but this comes at a cost. Because she sends product containers back to her suppliers for refilling, she's responsible for ensuring that the containers are thoroughly washed and cleaned. This means she uses more water than she might otherwise use and therefore pays a higher utility bill for water. She also takes on the responsibility of recycling whatever packaging can't be reused or repurposed to further reduce waste. Since commercial properties in Vancouver must pay for recycling services, it means she's paying a cost that's directly related to ensuring that her business operations are aligned with her mission and values.

Identifying and measuring your social costs may all seem a bit abstract to you, so let's walk through an example using a five-step process that was designed by two consultants for Demonstrating Value (demonstratingvalue.org), a research initiative led by Vancouver-based Vancity Community Foundation.[3] To keep it simple, we'll use Linh's S-R strategies related to reducing waste as an example.

> Step 1: Review your business activities and accounts and identify which costs are directly related to your mission and S-R strategies.

What are the social costs for Linh? Linh's higher water utility bill and recycling fees are directly related to her mission and S-R strategies.

Step 2: Assess the importance of each cost in terms of your financial resources and their importance to your S-R objective. Rate it as "high," "medium," or "low."

It's highly important to Linh to align her operational practices with the type of business she's running. It wouldn't make much sense to operate a refill store that encourages people to reuse (rather than recycle) their plastic dish or laundry soap containers if Linh didn't also reuse the product containers from her suppliers. Since she's also committed to reducing waste—either by reusing packaging or recycling as a last resort—and she doesn't want to pass along that responsibility to her customers, she's absorbing that cost.

Step 3: Decide on a method to quantify and track your social costs and determine whether there are other related costs that should be tracked.

Table 1-2 looks at Linh's social costs and determines their potential impact and relevance, specific ways to measure the impact, and whether the method is a reliable and feasible option.

Table 1-2: Deciding What Social Costs to Track

Social Cost:	Impact (high, medium, low):	Measure:	Reliable (Y/N?)
Water utility bill for washing reusable containers from suppliers	High – directly related to company's vision and mission to reduce the use of disposable containers	Track water utility bill and compare to average utility bills for similar types of stores that don't share mission	Yes, if comparable data can be found
Recycling fees for responsibly disposing packaging that can't be reused	High – directly related to company's vision and mission to reduce waste going to landfills	Track recycling fees, benchmark against any available data for comparably sized companies	Yes, if comparable data is from a reliable source

Step 4: Identify whether there are any challenges with the measurements you have decided to use.

Linh will need to consider her measurements and indicators. Are they valid and reliable? That is, do they measure what they're supposed to measure and can they be tracked and recorded consistently? If Linh has identified some challenges, how will she resolve them? In order for a measure or indicator to be a valuable decision-making tool, it has to be useful, relevant, reliable, and easily tracked.[4]

> Step 5: Decide which costs you want to include in your financial tracking and, if necessary, work with an accountant or bookkeeper to help you set up your spreadsheet accurately.

Linh also needs to keep in mind that she's tracking social costs in terms of their materiality (i.e., whether the costs are sufficiently important to her mission and financial analyses that they should be tracked or reported), reliability, and complexity. The absence, presence, or mis-statements about the data could influence business decisions based on the information gathered. Keep it simple, check the data, and make it easy to read for everyone concerned.

Impact on Your Stakeholders: Influence and Support

In addition to making note of the social costs that your business will incur, spend some time identifying which of your various stakeholders (e.g., your customers, employees, suppliers, investors/funders, regulatory bodies, etc.) are likely to be most interested in what you plan to do. What is important to them? Which group(s) will be most affected by changes to your business practices? Which of these group(s) has the most influence over and support for your successful transition to a socially responsible business?

With all of these dimensions and potentially competing interests to consider, you might be wondering how you'll ever establish any priorities for making decisions about which S-R actions you should adopt. One approach to solving these problems is to create some matrix-type charts to examine where your interests intersect and where they diverge. For example, if you wanted to choose S-R initiatives that are important to both you and your various groups of stakeholders, you might create a matrix where the X- and Y-axes represent "importance to stakeholders" and "importance to business success," respectively.[5]

What happens if what's important for one group of stakeholders (and for your business) clashes with the interests of a key stakeholder group whose influence has major implications for the success of your business? For example, are your customers willing to absorb a price increase in your products if you start offering or producing more eco-friendly options? Since your customers are vital to your financial sustainability, they wield a lot of influence over which practices you might be able to realistically implement.

One approach to solving your dilemma would be to use the same kind of matrix diagram, described above, to plot the relative levels of support and influence of various groups of stakeholders. Imagine the relationship between support and influence as coordinates along two axes: the horizontal axis represents a stakeholder's level of support and the vertical axis represents a stakeholder's influence on one's S-R business practices. Ideally, you want the stakeholders who have the most influence over the success of an S-R strategy to also show an equally high level of support for that same strategy.

To make this concept easier to grasp, let's walk through a couple of examples and see how they look in graphic form.

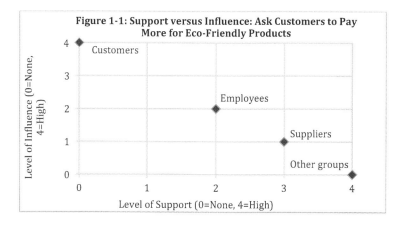

various, captions within figure:
Figure 1-1: Support versus Influence: Ask Customers to Pay More for Eco-Friendly Products

Figure 1-1 illustrates a possible worst-case scenario: Your customers, one of the most critical stakeholders for any company, don't support your proposed strategy to offer more eco-friendly products at a higher price point. In this case, your customers have a lot of influence over the success of your proposed S-R strategy. As they say, "if customers won't buy, the strategy won't fly."

If all of your customers feel the same way, you'll probably want to think twice about implementing this particular strategy. If only a few customers feel that way, and you aren't revenue-dependent on them (i.e., most of your business revenue *doesn't* come from those customers), you might choose to risk losing those customers. But if most of your customers or clients feel uncomfortable with the price increases, you might be less inclined to follow through with an S-R practice that might jeopardize a major stream of income.

To make an S-R practice succeed, it may just be a matter of adjusting it so it's more palatable to customers. In the example above, maybe you consider offering discounted, introductory trials of the eco-friendly products to show customers they're getting more value for their money. Perhaps, you increase prices by smaller increments (e.g., increase the price by 5% instead of 10%), or reach out to customers about why you're increasing prices to provide them context and to ease possible "sticker shock." Maybe you consider talking to your suppliers to get better deals on materials or supplies to lower some of your business costs. Whatever you ultimately decide to do will depend on your business needs and clientele. Talk to your stakeholders, get feedback, and integrate S-R practices with their needs in mind. Patience and a willingness to make changes gradually and involve your stakeholders early on will help you avoid disrupting existing relationships that could adversely affect your business.

Let's look at another example. Figure 1-2 shows you how the support of one group of stakeholders is negated by the influence of another group of stakeholders. In this chart, we have a hypothetical, socially responsible owner of a small, take-out food stand or café who would love to have people bring their own reusable containers as a strategy for reducing the amount of plastic and Styrofoam containers that are typically used for orders.

In our hypothetical case, customers support the idea wholeheartedly, while the Health Department is less enthused. Health code regulations regarding potential food contamination just don't allow vendors to sell food to customers using their own containers.[6] Unfortunately, the Health Department's influence over the café owner's ability to stay open and do business will probably be the deciding factor in this case.

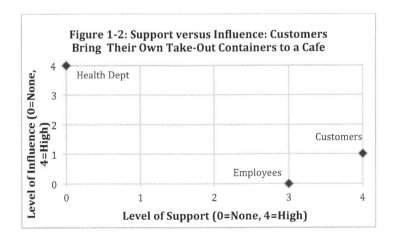

Figure 1-2: Support versus Influence: Customers Bring Their Own Take-Out Containers to a Cafe

Start Small and Progress Steadily

By now, you've assessed your S-R status, determined the level and availability of resources that are realistically available to you for adopting various practices, and identified which of your various stakeholders will have the most influence on your ability to successfully start implementing them. Congratulations on making it this far through the process.

At this point it's normal to feel a little overwhelmed by so much information. You may need to take some time to sit with the knowledge and observe what thoughts or concerns emerge. Once you've digested the information and have a clear-eyed view of what you can realistically accomplish, use what you've learned about your business and your own mindset about S-R to identify some "big picture" objectives or actions to help guide you through the transition.

Setting Time-Specific Goals

If you're feeling really enthusiastic and excited by the process, you may be tempted to take on a lot of S-R related projects or practices all at once. In reality, slow and steady implementation makes more sense. In Chapters 2 to 5, as we go through each of the relevant thematic areas of social responsibility, I'll recommend classifying your goals into three time periods: short term (within three months); medium term (within one year); and long term (more than a year). As you consider the different activities in each chapter, choose two (no more than three) S-R practices for a particular time period that would be the easiest and most cost-effective to implement.

Here are examples:

Within 3 months:

- Replace all plastic bags with reusable or recyclable paper bags.

- Reduce the amount of paper used by 500 sheets.

Within 1 year:

- Start volunteering at the local community center two days a month and implement a discount program for customers who volunteer with you.

- Switch to suppliers who use recyclable and biodegradable materials.

Long term:

- Donate 2% of profits to a local charity.

- Make your commitment to social responsibility official and become a certified B Corporation.

Armed with a few tangible goals, you can now focus on the steps and practices to meet those goals and make your transition to a socially responsible business an easier one. Starting with a limited number of S-R practices that are "low hanging fruit" may not feel like you're doing anything dramatic or making a significant difference, but it's important to stay focused on the value and benefit of gradually shifting. The "small, slow, and steady steps" approach advocated here will prevent you from getting overwhelmed, burning out, or overextending your financial resources. Focusing on just a small number of new initiatives is also less likely to disrupt your current business processes. Also, early successes are critical in encouraging you to reach for bigger goals over time. There is nothing like a few early successes to boost your enthusiasm and motivate you to stay on the S-R path. By giving yourself achievable targets, you win small victories that will give you more confidence as you ramp up to your bigger, medium- and long-term goals.

Ways to Track and Show Your Progress and Celebrate Successes

The next step is to track your progress over each time period and observe your results. Tracking progress on a specific set of indicators and measures can be a daunting prospect for small businesses. The bias can probably be attributed to the fact that corporate social responsibility (CSR) tracking is highly complex. A Canadian study found that owners of small- and medium-sized businesses are inclined to perceive CSR reporting as a highly formalized process and something only done by large organizations.[7] It isn't an entirely implausible view. Triple bottom line reporting through organizations such as the Global Reporting Initiative (globalreporting.org) imposes rigorous data quality standards and extensive reporting requirements. At its most onerous, triple bottom line reporting often involves collecting information on fifty or more performance measures across multiple dimensions of social responsibility, including human rights, the environment, labor practices, and the social and economic impacts on communities.

The level of reporting is both time and labor intensive—even for some medium and large businesses that can afford to hire staff just to track the information and produce the analyses for reports. It can be a lot for a small business to handle, and it's often well beyond the capabilities of most microbusinesses. In fact, only two of the entrepreneurs I interviewed for this book had implemented formalized approaches to tracking their S-R performance, and only one company participated in an external CSR reporting program.

Despite the challenges, there are big benefits for small businesses that make the effort to track the impact of their S-R practices. First, developing a method for tracking your information that's easy, effective, and time-efficient will ensure that you're less likely to abandon your S-R practices. Second, without a tracking system, there's no way of demonstrating—even if only to yourself—that your S-R initiatives are making a difference on your triple bottom line.

The complexity of the information you collect, your tracking system, and your method of demonstrating your successes should be guided by the following considerations:

- **Data analysis:** What is your aptitude for and comfort level with defining, identifying, and tracking valid, reliable indicators? Does the information you're collecting actually measure what you're trying to show?

- **Data management:** What is your aptitude for and comfort level with using spreadsheet programs (e.g., Microsoft Excel) or relational databases (e.g., Microsoft Access) to store the data and produce the charts or tables that tell the quantitative story?

- **Time commitment:** Do you have a sense of how much time you'll realistically have to set up and maintain your data collection process on a regular basis, and then create an effective way of sharing the results with your stakeholders? It can often take up to ten to fifteen hours just to set up and organize the underlying tables. This is all the more reason to keep things simple and choose only a few S-R strategies to track at first.

If you're beginning to think that maybe this is far too much work after all, please don't despair. Yes, it takes some time and effort to set up and maintain any kind of tracking system, and the process does pose challenges—or learning opportunities, depending on how you like to frame these experiences.

Setting up a tracking system may take some time upfront, but once you have it in place, you'll find it's just a matter of updating your tracking sheet on a weekly or monthly basis.

Types of S-R Tracking Systems

Many organizations struggle to effectively track and communicate their financial and business performance, let alone their social impact on their communities. To simplify things, we'll focus on three specific methods:

- **Method 1:** Using Demonstrating Value Initiative's tracking tools (a ready-made framework for your performance snapshot).

- **Method 2:** Designing customizable spreadsheets (creating your own performance snapshot from scratch).

- **Method 3:** Collecting stories and anecdotes (going beyond quantitative indicators).

Whatever approach you use to track and share the results of your S-R strategies, there are some important details you'll have to attend to before you create a single table or chart:

1. **Narrow down your list of S-R goals or practices that you want to track.** Take the results of your organizational assessment (from the S-R Readiness Assessment and S-R Inventory forms you completed) and the S-R strategies you've decided to implement (along with any notes you've made on what you can realistically undertake with your current resources) and decide on one or two activities in each major strand—people, planet, and profits/prosperity—that you want to track. It may not seem like very much data to track, but when you're already busy, even finding the time to track a few simple indicators can be a challenge.

2. **Translate your S-R goals or practices into specific indicators.** Indicators are defined as measurable information that can be documented and tracked on a consistent basis. Make sure you choose indicators that provide you with relevant information. According to Bryn Sadownik, author of *The Demonstrating Value Workbook: An Activity Guide to Tracking and Expressing Your Organization's Success* (2011), good indicators should be:[8]

    - Reasonable to collect;

    - Easy for you to interpret and explain to others;

    - Relevant, showing qualitative and quantitative changes;

- Precise and reliable; and

- Comparable to an existing set of data.

Be sure you understand how to correctly calculate the indicator or measure in question. If the indicator combines data from other sources, make sure the sourced information is also reliable. Sources from government agencies, university departments, or other well-known organizations are your best bet.

If you're spending too much time trying to track down a reliable source of information, or if the indicator is too complex, consider finding a simpler indicator. Also, if you must make some assumptions in your calculations, be sure to clearly note those assumptions in your tracking efforts.

If you're unsure how to turn your goals or strategies into measurable indicators, check out some of the resources on indicators in the *Demonstrating Value Workbook*, or visit the Proving and Improving website (proveandimprove.org). This UK-based organization provides examples of indicators and walks you through the processes of choosing what to measure and how to measure your impact.

3.   **Decide how often you'll track your indicators and create a report that can be easily updated.** How frequently will you need to collect information and how often do you want to report that information? Be aware that tracking your progress and reporting on your impact are two different activities, so make sure you choose time intervals that make sense for what you want to show. For example, you might collect data on a daily or monthly basis, but only show the results of your actions on a monthly, quarterly, or annual basis.

Method 1: Demonstrating Value Initiative – Using a Ready-made Framework

If this is your first foray into any kind of systematic information gathering activity, it may be useful to start with a ready-made framework that walks you through the process of identifying your information needs and developing valid, reliable indicators to measure your company's performance along various dimensions. There are several user-friendly resources available both online and as print publications that can help you with the process of identifying what you want to track and how to record that information. One resource that I recommend and have seen used to good purpose by various social enterprises in Vancouver is the Demonstrating Value Initiative (demonstratingvalue.org). The Initiative evolved out of a two-year collaborative research program, led by the Vancity Community Foundation (vancitycommunityfoundation.ca) in Vancouver.[9] It asks social enterprises and other organizations with a clear social mission, "What do you want to know and show?" The Framework is conceptualized as two "lenses": the information needs of the organization and the types of information that might be produced for various groups of stakeholders based on the information that would be useful to them.

We'll focus on how to use the Initiative's tools here. Demonstrating Value Initiative's "Snapshot" tools under the Demonstrating Value Framework show you how to track your financial and operational performance, business growth, and organizational sustainability (e.g., number of employees, turnover rate, benefits offered, and employee recognition programs)—alongside the impact of your S-R initiatives. The beauty of the Framework and its accompanying tools is in its flexibility. With a few tweaks, microbusiness owners can track the progress of their S-R initiatives and make better financial, strategic, and operational decisions. Although the material on the site has been developed with social enterprises and nonprofits in mind (hence, the references to grants, donations, and board development related indicators), the information can be easily adapted for a for-profit, business context. Also, if you choose to have your company independently recognized for its commitment to socially responsible practices—whether by B Lab (bcorporation.net), which facilitates B Corporation certification, or through Green America (greenbusinessnetwork.org), which offers a Green Business Certification—then the Demonstrating Value Framework can help you organize and document the information you'll need to provide.[10]

Let's get started. First, download the activity guide, *Demonstrating Value Workbook: An Activity Guide to Tracking and Expressing Your Organization's Success*.[11] The workbook guides you through a five-step process that will help you identify your audience, develop key indicators, and design your snapshot. A snapshot is a kind of summary report of your business. Worksheets for identifying and defining your indicators, for noting where and how you'll track data, and for mapping out the main sections of your snapshot report (e.g., people, planet, profits/prosperity, business performance, financial performance, etc.) are also included. You'll learn how to identify quality indicators using a set of criteria as well as how to create an engaging, easy-to-read snapshot for your stakeholders.[12]

The workbook also includes a wealth of examples for how to organize your information to share internally and with others. While there are currently no downloadable templates, it's possible to view examples of various snapshots in either interactive (on the Web) or document (as PDF files) formats.[13] Peruse these sample snapshots and get ideas on how to organize the sections of your snapshots in visually pleasing and informative ways.[14] Choose one or more of the examples as models for the design of your own mini snapshot and the type of information you might want to include in your snapshot. Finally, while you read through the workbook, be sure to check out Demonstrating Value's many other resources and tools (demonstratingvalue.org/tools-and-resources).

Method 2: Designing Your Snapshot from Scratch

You can develop your snapshot in almost any kind of software that allows you to create (or import) tables, charts, and text—whether that be a word processing, spreadsheet, or reporting (e.g., SAP Crystal Reports) program. Some questions that might shape your choice of software are:

- What software program am I most comfortable using right now? Most people will have access to Microsoft Excel or a similar program. This is the most versatile program to manage data and to produce graphic charts and tables.

- How much data will I have to copy and paste from other sources of information—and will I have to first do something with that information if it's in a raw, unusable format? If you're versed in using CSV files, you can easily import raw data sets into a program; otherwise you'll have to manually input the information into your spreadsheet.

- What information do I want to collect and for what purpose(s)? What is the simplest, most accurate and effective format for conveying the results of my S-R strategies with various stakeholders? Your audience will often determine how you'll present the information.

Devising Indicators and Collecting and Tracking Data

Let's consider an example. Say, you own a retail shop called "Eco-Friendly Refill Store" that sells refills for eco-friendly household and personal cleaning products. You've decided that one of your S-R goals is to encourage customers to reduce the amount of disposable plastics in their lives through reusing and refilling their plastic detergent or shampoo bottles. You decide on an indicator: the number of bottles that are brought to the store for refills, by customer. How do you go about tracking and collecting data for this indicator?

At The Soap Dispensary, a real store with similar goals, owner Linh Truong automatically records the number of containers brought back for refills as part of the financial transaction when customers are paying for their refills. In this way, she's able to track the total number of refills every month. The software she uses also records the number of new (reusable) bottles purchased each month, as well as the type of product sold (cleaners, personal care products, and raw ingredients for D-I-Y cleaners), so Linh could, if she chose to do so, track several indicators over time to see if any clear trends emerge. For example, it might be interesting to track whether the number of reusable bottles decreases over time as repeat customers get into the habit of reusing the containers they have on hand.

As mentioned earlier, we know that Linh has social costs from her commitment to reusing the containers she gets from her own suppliers and from recycling packaging (if it can't be reused or repurposed) that other refill stores might not incur. How might she take into account these extra expenses? To track these social costs, Linh might consider tracking how much water she actually uses to wash her and her customers' containers prior to refilling them, or recording how little waste her company generates.

What else might you want to track as the owner of our fictitious eco-friendly refill store? In addition to showing how many bottles were diverted from the landfill or recycling stream, you might want to share some additional information that puts your numbers into a context that people can relate to easily. If it were easy to find the data, you could track how much embedded water or fossil fuel is saved by reusing the plastic containers rather than recycling or disposing of them. You could frame it this way: "400+ bottles that we saved from the waste or recycling stream conserved water equivalent to "x" number of 10-minute showers and saved enough fossil fuels to fill up the gas tanks of "y" number of cars. With research and a little creativity, you could present your information in a variety of compelling ways and interesting contexts.

Like The Soap Dispensary, if our hypothetical refill store seeks to connect with and educate the community by offering workshops on a monthly basis, then we would probably want to track how many workshops we offer on a monthly or quarterly basis and how many people attend. If our hypothetical store occasionally donates the proceeds of a workshop or a percent of annual profits to mission and value-aligned nonprofits, then you could mention that you supported "x" number of nonprofit organizations, or that you donated "y" percent of your net profits to these nonprofits throughout the year.

When presenting your data, you'll have to decide how comfortable you are sharing your financial information publicly and whether the recipients of your financial or in-kind donations are comfortable being publicly identified by name. Be sure to look into any state/provincial information privacy laws that govern both how you store information and what you share publicly. Obviously, for tax reasons, you'll need to keep a detailed record of donations, but for your snapshot you could choose to either list a total amount donated throughout the year or break out the recipients by type and percentage only (e.g., environmental 15%, anti-poverty 15%, etc.).

If, at this point, you're thinking, "This is all very nice, but I don't see how this helps me figure out how to devise indicators for my company," don't worry. I'm about to bring this back to a more general set of guidelines for you. Most of your environmental and financial indicators will involve showing an increase or decrease in some quantity, so you'll need to start with a base—where you are now—and track the increases or decreases. For example, if you want to decrease the amount of electricity your business uses, start by looking at how many kilowatt-hours you average and how much you pay in electricity costs on a monthly basis. Those are your base numbers. Then, track how many kilowatt-hours you save by taking particular measures: shutting off all of the electronic devices at the end of the day; switching off your computer at the end of the day or during lunches; or switching to energy saving appliances. Likewise, track how much money you save during the same time period. Ideally, both your kilowatt-hour usage and electricity bill should be decreasing relative to your base measure. If you're really meticulous, introduce initiatives one-by-one on a rolling basis and track the incremental decreases in kilowatt-hours and costs.

Don't forget to measure and track other S-R initiatives related to people and profits/prosperity. Indicators in these areas are less commonly collected and tracked but are no less important. How do you reach out to the community? Do you make your space available for workshops (or teach the workshops yourself)? Do you participate in committees that help to revitalize your community or find solutions to social problems or social injustices? Do you help organize or contribute to community events? If so, make a note of them and what the event or committee achieved. At the very least, you want to internally track how many hours you're devoting to these activities in comparison to how much time you're devoting to running and building your business and show how your business is adding value to the community through these activities. If, like some of the entrepreneurs interviewed for this book, you've publicly declared an intention to donate x% of your annual gross income or net profits to nonprofits or NGOs, then it's fair to expect reporting that shows how you've followed through on your promise or fell short.

Some of the indicators related to community and prosperity may be easy to track as quantitative measures, but others might be a bit trickier to compute on a spreadsheet. As you'll see further along in this chapter, not all of your indicators have to be expressed as a chart or table. Sometimes, a short narrative or anecdotal summary is your best choice.

Presenting Your Data

After a significant period of data collection, it's time to format and present your information. Sometimes, it's difficult to see a trend on a month-to-month basis, so you may want to wait until you've accumulated data over several months. Let's go back to our indicator on the number of containers saved from the landfill or recycling bin. For Linh, while the data on the number of bottles clients bring in for refilling is automatically collected on a day-to-day basis, reporting shouldn't be at the daily level. It would make more sense to aggregate (sum up or combine) her data at a monthly or quarterly level and share the information with interested stakeholders on a quarterly or semi-annual basis.

Let's look at some hypothetical numbers. Table 1-3 shows quarterly aggregated data on the number of bottles that customers diverted from the landfill and recycling stations by choosing to reuse and refill the bottles.

Table 1-3: Quarterly Aggregated Data

Plastic Containers Customers Diverted from Landfills and Recycling	
Quarter	**Total Number of Bottles**
Q1	800
Q2	1,100
Q3	1,200
Q4	1,100

Note: The data presented here is fictitious and is provided for illustrative purposes only.

After the data collection and analysis, it's time to transform your raw data into readable, visually appealing charts. Figure 1-3 shows the same data broken out on a monthly basis as a trend report over one year.

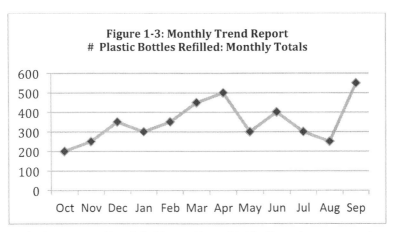

Figure 1-3: Monthly Trend Report
Plastic Bottles Refilled: Monthly Totals

Note: The data presented here is fictitious and is provided for illustrative purposes only.

Preparing a Report: An S-R Performance Snapshot

Once you have several indicators, you may want to start preparing a performance snapshot. A fairly comprehensive performance snapshot includes one or two key indicators reflecting your company's performance on each of the three main S-R strands: people, planet, and profits/prosperity. In addition to using charts and graphs to summarize your outcomes, you may also include other ways of conveying information about your company's S-R activities and its positive impact on the community, such as posting some photos of community events that you sponsored, or adding a list of specific S-R accomplishments.

Figure 1-4 is a sample snapshot for our fictitious company, Eco-Friendly Refill Store. It shows several simple indicators that highlight the impact of S-R practices for customers and community partners, including: the number of containers used for refilling (planet); the number of workshops offered for the community (people); and the number of donations to aligned nonprofits (profits/prosperity).

How time-consuming was this exercise? Putting together the snapshot took me approximately two and a half hours. This included choosing my indicators, generating the data for my indicators, and designing the charts from the raw data in my spreadsheet tables. In reality, though, it would take much longer to prepare a real snapshot since choosing your indicators and collecting actual data may take several more hours to several days depending on your research efforts. In fact, my ambitious plan to document the amount of water and energy embedded in plastic bottles and the carbon emissions produced in the recycling process added a few more hours onto the project.

Unfortunately, a web search yielded no ready, reliable source of information about those indicators. (In fact, the indicators are left blank in Figure 1-4).

Figure 1-4: S-R Performance Snapshot

Note: The data presented here is fictitious and is provided for illustrative purposes only.

The charts on the snapshot (Figure 1-4) were generated from tables on a spreadsheet database created in Microsoft Excel. Figure 1-5 shows a screenshot of the spreadsheet database I used for the S-R performance snapshot for our Eco-Friendly Refill Store example.

Figure 1-5: Database for the S-R Performance Snapshot

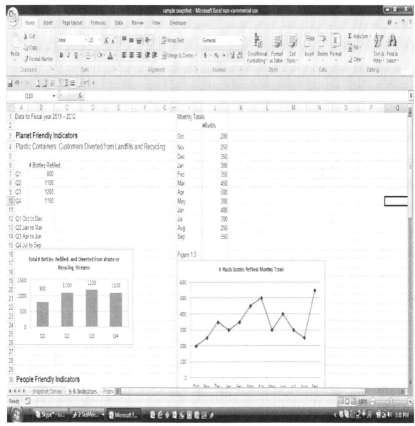

Note: The data presented here is fictitious and is provided for illustrative purposes only.

Tracking Indicators –
Challenges and Considerations

Be realistic about the indicators you plan to use. Sometimes, what seems like a useful indicator, in theory, proves to be a highly challenging indicator to track, in practice. As a general guideline, the more work you have to do to either find a reliable source of information that will serve as a benchmark, or transform your raw data into a usable indicator, the more likely it is that you'll find it too time-consuming and frustrating to use on a regular basis. You may end up abandoning that particular indicator (which may be a good idea), or giving up entirely on tracking any of your indicators (not such a good idea). This isn't to say that you should steer clear of using any indicators for which it's a challenge to find the data you need, but you may want to assess whether the importance and usefulness of the data justifies the amount of work required to obtain or calculate the information.

While it would have been great to be able to show in our hypothetical example how much embedded water was saved through reusing plastic containers, an extensive (and extended) search on the Web yielded little in the way of reliable information for plastics other than water bottles. Also, since bottles for shampoo, laundry detergent, liquid soaps, etc. come in a variety of shapes and sizes, not to mention different densities of plastic, there isn't an easy way to calculate an accurate savings number.

A valid and reliable formula for calculating the information we want to know probably exists out there, but the question then becomes: How much time do you want (or can you afford) to spend trying to locate that one piece of valid, reliable information? Alternatively, the information for plastic water bottles could be used as a proxy measure as long as you make it clear in your snapshot that it's a proxy measure and not a precise one.

Be choosy about your data sources. As you search the Web for data, remember to check the integrity of your sources. Good places to start looking for high quality information include government agencies, universities, and well-known, reputable organizations.

Prioritize what you plan to collect. In the *Demonstrating Value Workbook*, make use of a matrix (p. 25) that can help you prioritize what information to collect based on the importance of the information (high, medium, or low) and the difficulties in collecting the information (easy, feasible, or challenging). If an indicator is critically important but data is difficult to collect, see if there's a more feasible alternative that will meet the same need. Conversely, if an indicator is interesting but not important to use—a "nice to have"—but data is easy to collect, go ahead and track it.

Bottom line—keep it simple. Start with the information you're already collecting (or could easily collect) for the indicators that are important for showing how you're making a difference with your S-R actions and affecting your business and financial performance.

Tips for Creating Graphic Charts

Individual charts can also be copied or exported as individual image files from Microsoft Excel and published in a variety of forms, such as on your website or in your company newsletter. Always keep your spreadsheet handy; it will become your database for all of your S-R tracking efforts going forward. When updating your performance snapshot (Figure 1-4) for future reporting periods, you'll revisit your database (Figure 1-5) and make your updates.

Always give careful thought to the best way to accurately show your results in a graphic format. There are so many options—from simple, two-dimensional bar charts or pie charts, to complex, three-dimensional bubble charts that compare three sets of values—it's easy to inadvertently distort the data picture if we select an inappropriate scale or chart. Choose a format that accurately portrays the data and is easy for most people to understand. Label the elements on your charts, including the axes and data points, as appropriate. For more information about good design practices for charts and tables, consult the online resources suggested in the *Demonstrating Value Workbook*, such as "Using Graphs" (Statistics Canada) and "Put the Art in Charts" (Adobe Illustrated), as well as Stephen Few's *Show Me the Numbers: Designing Tables and Graphs to Enlighten* (2004).[15]

Method 3: Collecting Anecdotes and Stories

Your S-R performance snapshot doesn't have to be told only in graphic charts and tables. If you're intimidated by number crunching, remember that not all of your reporting has to be in numeric form. Numbers only ever tell part of the story; narratives, however, give your S-R reporting a human touch that will likely engage more stakeholders than will quantitative data on its own.

Here are some specific suggestions for finding and generating relevant content:

Sharing the Press from Others

Find anecdotes published elsewhere about your company's participation in events or projects that make a positive difference to your community. If one of your Facebook friends or Twitter followers has written a particularly compelling comment that speaks to your S-R practices, ask for permission to include the comment on your snapshot.

Keep in mind, however, that sharing laudatory anecdotes or stories from external sources is, at some level, a form of marketing for your company. To avoid inadvertently exploiting some of your community ties, make sure that others involved also get a huge, positive PR boost from the anecdotes you choose to share with the public. Toby Barazzuol from Eclipse Awards advises that it's best to be discerning about how often you include these kinds of anecdotes in your blog or other social media communications. However, there are no hard and fast rules about how often is too often; it's more about knowing your audience (e.g., your target clients) and being able to put yourself in their shoes than arbitrarily choosing a schedule.

Using Social Media Strategically

Blog, post, or tweet about issues and local organizations that are relevant to your S-R strategies. Aim to publish a blog post at least twice a month (weekly is best) and to tweet a few times per week (daily is ideal). While frequency and consistency is important with your social media interactions, aim for quality and authenticity. Webmeadow, a home-based (or more accurately, farm-based), solar-powered website development company, writes about web design alongside renewable energy and sustainability issues on their blog. Owners Eileen Webb and her partner also feature a counter on their website that displays the amount of solar power generated from their solar panels—a nice, quantitative indicator that highlights their S-R progress alongside their stories and commentaries.

Post photographs or videos of community and S-R related events on social media channels. VOS Flips, a company that designs eco-friendly footwear, posts photos from various community events on its Facebook page. Eclipse Awards, which designs recognition programs and awards for organizations, has featured videos on its company blog that show inspiring scenes from its community engagement activities and events recognizing front-line, grassroots, social change agents. *Reminder:* Ask for permission before you post photos or videos of other people. This is especially important if you're posting photos of minors.

Taking Stock of Your Progress

At the end of your first reporting cycle, you may see some positive results, or you may not. If one of your S-R practices has made a positive difference to people or the environment, share your success and celebrate. This might be another point in your S-R journey where you're tempted to become more ambitious in your efforts to implement new or more complex levels of S-R reporting. I'd suggest maintaining your existing course and waiting until another cycle of reporting is finished before adding new S-R goals.

If you fell short of meeting a goal or had difficulties consistently following through on a new S-R practice, exercise the same compassion and patience you'd show to someone else in the same boat. Rather than berating yourself for not meeting your goal, ask yourself what did go well, and then engage in a nonjudgmental assessment of what didn't work, why it didn't work, and what support you need to succeed the next time around.

Here are a few questions to consider:

Had you underestimated how long it would take to implement the S-R practice?

Adjust the timeframe for your goals (see the earlier section, "Setting Time-Specific Goals"). For example, turn a short-term goal into a medium-term goal. Say you started with the immediate goal of leaving early on Fridays to volunteer at the local community center. Later, you realized you didn't have the operating capacity to leave your store before 4 p.m. because that's when you received the most customer walk-ins.

Now, on second thought, maybe you're better off waiting a year to adjust your store hours and schedule. A longer timeframe may be just what you need to let your customers know that you're planning on changing your store hours. You can also get feedback and experiment with other days of the week and times. Maybe you find you're less busy in the mornings and it makes sense to adjust your store hours to open later in the day, leaving you time to volunteer in the mornings.

It takes time to test and establish new behaviors or practices as habits. It may take six months to a year before you can reasonably expect to see results. Re-evaluate your timeline as needed to fully and successfully integrate S-R practices into your business processes, or revise a goal to be more modest.

Was the S-R initiative more expensive to implement than you thought?

Explore other, less expensive options for achieving the same result. Factors that have to be considered in your cost calculations—such as buy-in from influential stakeholders, time to change suppliers or to source more people/planet friendly materials—can often make the process more complex. In fact, a recurring theme echoed by many of the entrepreneurs I interviewed was that it takes more work (at least initially) to set up processes the S-R way. The extra work upfront, though, will often pay dividends in saved time later.

Did you meet with resistance from a key stakeholder?

Involving stakeholders early on is always helpful and appreciated (refer back to the section in this chapter, "Impact on Your Stakeholders: Influence and Support"). Perhaps you need to have a discussion with your customers or your vendors to get them on board. Or, maybe you need to launch an awareness-raising campaign first to get people excited about the social cause or environmental issue you're championing.

Are you trying to implement too many new behaviors at once?

Remember, "slow and steady" wins the day when it comes to making S-R changes in your business. Don't bite off more than you can chew. Repeat after me: "It's not an all-or-nothing proposition." Stay mindful of your goals, your time, and your resources, and adjust your S-R plans accordingly.

Still feeling overwhelmed? In Chapter 6, we'll go over in more detail how to tackle some of these challenges you'll encounter along the path to becoming an S-R business. We'll help you modify your S-R goals in ways that respect your concerns about financial sustainability and continue to help you make strides towards becoming more socially responsible business.

Establish and Maintain Your Network of Like-minded Changemakers

While business culture may predominantly celebrate and perpetuate an ethos of "rugged individualism," the reality is that we're social creatures. We function better when we can call on a network of like-minded individuals for mutual support, encouragement, and the opportunity to learn through shared experiences. Connecting with others who share similar values and goals not only helps you to stay engaged with developing a socially responsible business, but also provides opportunities to collaborate on projects and "share the wealth."

Ideally, it would be great if small and microbusiness owners with a social conscience could find other like-minded entrepreneurs in their communities to start groups, plan community engagement projects, or just meet to share ideas, resources, and offer mutual encouragement and support. You don't even need a large group or grandiose movement behind you. A small group of thoughtful individuals (say, up to a dozen people) committed to the same changes you want to see in the world can be a wonderful source of support.

The only challenge might be figuring out *where* to find your group of committed citizens and kindred spirits, and, admittedly, this is probably easier to achieve in urban areas than in rural locales. Connecting with other business owners will help you find or create a group of thoughtful and committed citizens who will provide the support and encouragement to push you forward along your S-R path. In fact, just by reaching out to others, you may also achieve one of your S-R goals, whether it be promoting community engagement or giving back to the community in some way.

Here are some groups you should consider:

Business Associations

Start with looking at existing business associations. While you may think that folks with somewhat traditional outlooks on business and the economy populate these organizations, it doesn't necessarily mean they don't care about social and environmental issues. Find out how the group understands principles of social responsibility and what kind of community development projects they support. Then, decide whether there is a "good enough" fit for you and your business.

BALLE (Business Alliance for Local, Living Economies)

BALLE (livingeconomies.org) is dedicated to empowering local, independent businesses to make a positive difference in their communities through community-building around environmental and social justice issues. Currently, the BALLE network has eighty community networks across thirty states in the U.S. and three Canadian provinces. If you don't have a regional network in your area, check the BALLE website for detailed information about starting one in your area.

Coworking and Collaborative Workspaces

Coworking spaces (wiki.coworking.com) are a fairly new phenomenon in which independent workers, startups, and freelancers share mostly open-plan office space and equipment. The spaces are also a great place to meet new people, join or create a community of like-minded individuals, and most importantly, to share ideas and inspiration—collaboration at its best.[16] For S-R solopreneurs or small business owners who are tired of working in isolation and unable to find their "tribe" elsewhere, collaborative workspaces might be just the place to find a much-needed support network.

Community Centers and Organizations

Other options for starting an in-person support group might include starting an Action Circle or Meetup (more on this in Chapter 3) with friends and neighbors, or connecting with people through community foundations, credit unions, or through your spiritual affiliations (e.g., Unitarian churches often have a social justice committee). You might also consider approaching a local community center and offering to organize a group and tie it to a local grassroots project.

Business and Social Enterprise Social Networks

As long as you have an internet connection, you have options for finding or building communities of like-minded individuals no matter how geographically or socially isolated you are from other people in your region. If most of your business is carried out online, or if you've made numerous social connections online, you might be more likely to find your community on the

Web than in person. Are there like-minded people you've met through Twitter, Facebook, or the blogosphere with whom you would want to collaborate offline? If so, what would stop you from forming an online circle and using something like Skype to hold regular meetings? While it's not exactly the same as all being in the same room, it's a fabulous "next best thing" as you can at least talk to each other in real-time.

You might also want to connect with others through online communities, such as Social Venture Network (svn.org), Social Earth (socialearth.org), Triple Pundit (triplepundit.com), the new economics foundation (neweconomics.org), Social Edge (socialedge.org), 2degrees (2degreesnetwork.com), or i-genius (i-genius.org), all of which focus on S-R issues. LinkedIn also has some good S-R discussion groups, such as the Green Entrepreneurs & Small Business Network.

Business Contacts and Your Personal Network

Last but not least, don't forget to share your vision of becoming a socially responsible business with your employees, customers, vendors, supply chain, and other individuals in your business network. Reaching out to your business contacts demonstrates your regard and respect for them and their roles in helping to make your business successful (we'll look at this in more detail in Chapters 3, 4, and 5). It also makes good business sense from a planning perspective. Presumably these people and organizations do business with you, or work for or with you, because they appreciate the value of your products or services and the values (however clearly or subtly stated) you bring to your business. Whether or not you have explicitly stated your values, there's a good chance that your stakeholders support your business because their values align with yours.

CHAPTER CHECKLIST:

✔ Use the S-R Readiness Assessment Form to find out where you stand in terms of resources and mindset to tackle an S-R transformation in your business. Use the S-R Inventory Form to assess the resources you currently have available to you. Make sure you can confidently answer the following questions:

- What steps or S-R practices can you realistically take on now?

- What practices would you love to adopt but don't currently have the money, human resources, or time to implement?

- What would you need to change in order for you to adopt S-R practices?

- How can you plan or budget for the practices you intend to implement?

- What other resources or support do you need?

✔ Understand how to classify your S-R goals for the short, medium and long terms. Remember to select your goals based on the resources available to you and how your choices might affect or be affected by various stakeholders in your business.

✔ Set up a tracking system that's tailored to your abilities and comfort level with various spreadsheet and graphing software programs.

✔ Find your like-minded networks.

✔ Get feedback from your key stakeholders and talk to them about your vision.

Toby Barazzuol, Eclipse Awards

Location: Vancouver, British Columbia, Canada

Product/Service: Awards and recognition programs for formal and scheduled events at corporations and nonprofit organizations.

Company start date: April 1998

Company website: eclipseawards.com

Bio: Toby Barazzuol is the founder and director of Eclipse Awards. In the fourteen years he has been leading the company, he has combined his dedication to creating meaningful recognition awards and helping organizations create a culture of recognition with his passion for environmental sustainability and community engagement. He currently serves as the Vice-chair of the Strathcona Business Improvement Association (SBIA) and the Chair of the SBIA's Sustainability Committee. In 2012, Eclipse Awards was selected by Small Business British Columbia as "BC's Best Employer."

Inspiration: Toby started Eclipse Awards as a regular business. The catalyst for transferring his personal interest in sustainability and social responsibility to his business operations was nothing smaller than the 2010 Winter Olympic Games. Back in 2002, when local businesses started hearing that Vancouver might be hosting the 2010 Winter Games, they also heard that companies bidding for contracts would be asked about their sustainability practices. Toby started talking to other people about sustainability, as well as reading Paul Hawken's books.

What he learned changed everything. A couple of years later, he launched Eclipse Awards' S-R transformation starting with green energy certifications. Today, Toby has an impressive list of accomplishments. He continues to find new ways to enhance the sustainability of his products, to contribute to his community, and to power up front-line social change agents through his products and services.

Business philosophy: Toby's approach to growing a business and creating value is the antithesis of the usual, short-term (quarterly) focus and emphasis on putting profits over people. At Eclipse Awards, Toby's general S-R philosophy is best summarized as a long-term commitment to creating lasting value for the community and championing the human, social dimensions of sustainability.

Social Responsibility in Action

Overall: From greening the workspace and switching to alternative energy, to being an early adopter of paying a living wage and spending 20% of his time on volunteer activities that bring regenerative, lasting value to the community, Toby has woven S-R initiatives from each of the three strands—people, planet, profits/prosperity—into Eclipse Awards' core philosophy and operating practices.

People: For Toby, the social dimension of sustainability is a key piece for green companies to keep in mind. "We're [engaging] in sustainability practices to create a better life, but why do it if we forget the human element?" he asks.

The core of Eclipse Awards is recognition of people's achievements and efforts through meaningful symbols (awards) and actions—starting with Toby's own employees. In addition to paying a living wage, Toby offers incentives to employees for using environmentally sustainable modes of transit to get to work, including contributing a sum of money toward purchasing an environmentally sustainable vehicle (e.g., an electric scooter or hybrid car) or bike that will be used as the primary means of transportation for getting to and from work.

He also provides bikes, shower facilities, and a fully equipped kitchen for employees. In order to encourage employees to bring their lunch to work, he initiated a "Brown Bag" award, which he gives out every two months. The employee who brings his or her lunch from home most often during that time period is awarded a CAD$300 cash bonus.

Beyond the value of crafting beautiful awards from recycled and reclaimed materials, Toby has incorporated technology into the process of working with customers at each stage of the process to ensure that inscriptions on the awards are correct and that the awards are delivered on time. The customer service goes beyond just selling products; it also includes educating organizations across all sectors on how to effectively use recognition to improve their work culture and contribute to their employees' happiness and quality of life.

Community: Eclipse Awards supports and contributes to its community through initiating or participating in projects that yield long-term, regenerative value and lasting social changes. The company invests time and other resources into creating community gardens and an urban farm, SoleFood Farm (1sole.wordpress.com), a social enterprise that provides training and employment opportunities for inner city residents. Toby also spends 20% of his time volunteering with the SBIA working on projects that contribute to both environmental and social sustainability.

Planet: Toby started his S-R transformation with green energy certifications. Although the company is now 100% powered by alternative energy, he tracks electricity, water, and carbon use and looks for additional ways to reduce the company's ecological footprint. In addition to sharing space and resources (heat, light, and water) with another company, Eclipse Awards is in a building that features a number of green amenities, including: large windows to maximize the amount of natural light coming into the building, and a living, green roof that improves insulation. Staff members also have and tend their own plots on the rooftop garden.

S-R advantage: For employees, being actively involved in following through on the commitment to becoming a socially responsible business increased their level of engagement. However, it was a process. At first, individual employees varied in their levels of buy-in. Now everyone has adopted some elements of social responsibility into their lives.

From a business perspective, using a set of benchmarks to track and measure Eclipse Awards' resource use and carbon footprint helps the company to see what it's actually doing. Says Toby, "When you can see the changes you're making, it's inspiring."

Transformative power of an S-R business: Toby recognizes that while we, as socially responsible entrepreneurs and social change agents, like to think that what we do in terms of our sustainability efforts and community engagement practices means a lot to our customers, it isn't always the case. However, that shouldn't stop S-R entrepreneurs from being true to their values and finding ways to create positive changes in the world.

To raise awareness about sustainability, Toby uses the company blog, *Happiness Delivered*, for personal interactions with clients, and the work he does through the SBIA. He helps his clients and community organizations create goodwill and happier employees by "understanding that it can't just be about recognizing the rock stars; it's also about appreciating everyone and remembering that not all gestures of appreciation have to be through an award or formal event."

One of the most moving examples (posted on the company blog) of the power of recognition was the effect of honoring a local "character" with an award for all of the work he did keeping the green roof and street outside the building tidy. Not only did the recognition change how this individual saw himself, he went on to appreciate others and even asked Eclipse Awards to create an award for a front-line social worker at her retirement party.

Eclipse Awards is also changing perceptions of what is beautiful through its line of green awards made from recycled and reclaimed materials.

Words of wisdom: Be patient about and persistent in realizing your S-R vision. "Becoming a socially responsible company takes time," says Toby. "You can't just flip a switch. We're six years into our S-R journey, and we're still figuring out how to create something of maximum value with minimal resources."

When sharing the stories of others, practice care. "Find ways to create marketing value out of your social commitments, but be discerning about how and where you tell these stories—don't exploit the relationships just to get publicity."

Don't base all of your business decisions on price or cost factors. "The greatest 'a-ha' moments happen when price is third or fourth on the list of priorities for making a decision," he says.

Cherish the good times. "Take time to have fun," advises Toby. "Make sure your people are happy and engaged and that your staff have opportunities to lead fuller, richer lives."

Julie Beyer, For the Love of Food

Location: Vancouver, British Columbia, Canada

Product/Service: Julie teaches people how to eat more healthfully and provides them with practical, delicious strategies for incorporating more organic, plant-based, whole foods into their every day cooking. Julie also develops products designed to satisfy common cravings through healthy and delicious food, including the GLOW collection of gluten-free, dairy-free, and sugar-free snacks made from organic ingredients.

Company start date: May 2009

Company website: loveoffood.ca

Bio: Julie Beyer is a self-taught holistic chef, educator, and creator of the GLOW Collection. Julie's love of delicious food was first sparked when she studied abroad for a year in France. When she returned to Canada after her time abroad, she experienced several personal and health crises. She began a four-year journey of holistic healing that included embracing a 100% organic whole foods lifestyle and a commitment to cultivating a love of healthy food. Along the way, Julie discovered that she had a natural talent for combining flavors and making healthy food taste delicious. She's currently studying to become a registered holistic nutritionist.

Inspiration: Julie defines her work as teaching people how to use local and organic food to make healthy, delicious, whole, plant-based food as a symbol of compassion and love for animals and the sustainability of communities worldwide. Her inspiration for starting her business arose out of a combination of academic, professional, and personal experiences. She first became interested in the global food system after taking some courses in agricultural economics while she was studying for her undergraduate degree in international relations and economics. Upon realizing the far-reaching impact of agriculture and agricultural policies on all facets of the economy, the environment, and the social fabric of communities, she decided she wanted to make a positive change in the world by changing the food system.

Her intention was to create these changes through policy work within the system. But a series of experiences and observations ultimately set her on a different path to creating change. After volunteering on an organic farm in Turkey, and then experiencing a debilitating illness upon her return to Canada that included symptoms of severe food allergies and a hypersensitivity to food additives and pesticides, she decided to try a different path. Julie's mission to promote sustainable economic development, environmental preservation, and the prevention of war over resources remains the same, but now her methods are different. "Now I am being the change that I want to see in the world—and making it delicious," she says.

Business philosophy: The driving force for Julie is an understanding of how much power we have to change the world through the impact of our everyday actions and decisions. "People don't realize how much power they have through their spending patterns." She's passionate about teaching this to others and helping others give back to the community by giving them options to spend their money in ways that makes a positive difference in the world.

"For a while, I had felt that I was wasting my time preparing all my own food in the kitchen and that I was missing out on the opportunity to go out and change the world. Yet, I realized that I was likely [creating] more change for the world [by] spending time in my kitchen cooking my own food everyday than involving myself in politics because I was *being* the change," Julie says. "We truly vote with our dollars, and we have the potential to make tremendous change in the world by being mindful of how we spend our money. It was also interesting to note that people around me started to become very inspired to change their own diets simply by observing me. I realized then the power of Gandhi's quote, 'Be the change you want to see in the world'."

Another way Julie brings social consciousness into her business is by standing behind what she sells. "I have my name on all my products so that people know there is someone standing behind what is being sold to them," she says. "I stand behind my products 150%, and I use the purest and most delicious ingredients. When there is no one standing behind a product, it is easier to lose accountability to the people you serve."

Social Responsibility in Action

Overall: Julie helps both people (e.g., customers and suppliers) and the planet through her focus on using local (when it is available), organic, or fairly traded items in her GLOW collection and her cooking classes. She supports her local economy by choosing to partner with other local vendors and suppliers whenever possible. She gives back to the community by hosting open houses through donations and giving the proceeds to local organizations and by volunteering with local organizations.

People: Julie doesn't yet have paid employees, but she does have interns. (The internships are unpaid positions). She makes a point of giving her interns work that's new, challenging, and meaningful. In return, they learn about healthy food preparation and what it is like to run a business in the holistic nutrition field. Julie also has volunteers who help her out with the website, photography, etc., and she makes sure she gives credit where it's due.

When it comes to suppliers and vendors, Julie has partnered with other local, socially responsible businesses that share her values. Julie explains that she has many clients who want to do good in the world. They, too, want to support local businesses and organic agriculture and to buy ethical products. They value the fact that she has done the research for them, and they trust her knowledge.

Community: Julie gives back to the community by donating time and money to different organizations. She holds open houses for people to sample her product line and learn about all of the nutritional benefits. The open houses are by donation, and she gives the proceeds to various local organizations. Julie also participated in a fundraiser for The World in a Garden (theworldinagarden.wordpress.com), an urban agriculture project that teaches youth and other community members about the nutritional, cultural, social and environmental benefits of a just and local food system.

Planet: Based on her personal experiences and the insights she gained from reading various books (she mentioned authors Michael Pollan and Pema Chodron), she treads as gently as possible on the planet. She's acutely aware of the need to reduce our use of petroleum (whether for fuel or through the use of plastic containers) and finds that trying to choose the most eco-friendly packaging can be a tough decision. Ideally, she would like to go with re-usable containers, but in many cities there are regulations against that for food products. Instead, she chose to go with containers made from renewable, recyclable materials, but notes that even some of the vegetable-based "plastic" containers take energy to produce and only break down in landfills under certain conditions. The available options are sparse right now. "There needs to be more of a concerted effort between government and food producers to find solutions to the problem of waste from food packaging," she says. "The solutions are out there; we just need more motivated, environmentally conscious people to take on this task."

S-R advantage: For Julie, the advantage of running an S-R business is the personal satisfaction she gets from knowing she's making a positive difference in the world. As a business owner, Julie values efficiency. However, she also values quality, and so she won't cut corners or eliminate processes that add value to her products. "It's actually a lot more work. But making products with high quality ingredients and from a place of high integrity makes a difference to people, and in return they're willing to support and pay for such products."

Julie pointed out that as a socially responsible business in the food industry, there are a lot of expenses, so it takes a long time to see a profit and it takes a long time to find trusted suppliers who share her values. On the other hand, she receives a lot of high quality assistance from people in all areas of her business, which has definitely contributed to increasing the productivity of her operation.

Julie looks at her business—and the business of running her business—as a spiritual practice. One of the main benefits of running an S-R business for Julie is that she feels fulfilled and gets a sense of joy in life knowing that she's contributing to changing the world. "Feeling this way is one of the biggest gifts you can ever give to yourself." On a more practical level, Julie asserts that because she does her best to come from a place of love in her business, she receives a lot of free help and miracles in return that positively impact her bottom line.

Transformative power of an S-R business: Both Julie's customers and interns are transformed by her business. Customers get health benefits from eating her food products and learning how to incorporate healthful eating into their lives. Interns not only learn new cooking techniques for preparing ingredients, they also learn more about the S-R philosophy that drives the business and how it makes a difference in the world.

Words of wisdom: First, be aware of whether you're making business decisions from a place of love and generosity or fear. "To clarify, when you make a decision from a place of love, it is because it feels right in your body and you are doing it for the greater good of yourself and the world. For example, offering a 'competitor' a tip because she is also making life-giving products that are helping others. Or, turning down what looks like a great opportunity because you don't have the time or energy for it."

She also notes that "coming from a place of love will always bring you more money if your intention is pure, though often times it will seem counterintuitive. It's easy to make decisions from a place of fear when you're dealing with money questions, but I've had a huge amount of success when I come from a place of love, integrity, and generosity."

Second, Julie advises others to master some practical business skills. "You absolutely need to know who your audience is, what your mission is, and then tailor your services and marketing to your audience," she says. "So many heart-based entrepreneurs want to help everyone because they know their product can help everyone. The truth is, if you don't choose a specific audience to speak to, no one will know you are speaking to them, and you will struggle."

The other piece of advice she gives to entrepreneurs is to effectively market your service to your audience. Not only do you need to know who your market is, but also how to effectively market your product or service to that audience. "You need to understand what their problem is and how you will solve it, and know how you are going to communicate that to them," she says. "There are tons of business coaches and experts now offering workshops for heart-based entrepreneurs, so do some research and find someone who resonates with you. They also offer lots of free material, and I have learned a ton about business through reading blogs and watching free videos online."

Finally, move away from traditional views of selling. "Most conscious entrepreneurs are afraid to promote and talk about their products because they don't want to be sales-y," Julie says. "The good news is that you shouldn't 'sell' your products to make sales. When talking about what you offer, be detached about the outcome. It is really important that you are coming from your heart and sharing what you have to offer because you genuinely care about others' well-being. There will always be enough people who need your divine offering, so if someone doesn't need it, do not take it personally or get worried. So, never sell. Simply share with your heart what you love. You will be amazed at your results!"

Melissa Cartwright, Mellifera Bees

Location: Vancouver, British Columbia, Canada

Product/Service: Locally produced honey infused with spices and herbs

Company start date: January 2011

Company website: melliferabees.com

Bio: Melissa Cartwright is a solopreneur in Vancouver whose business not only evolved out of a hobby but also reflects the meaning of her name: honey bee. Melissa is an urban beekeeper who sells the honey from her bees' hives to local vendors. Prior to starting her beekeeping business, Melissa worked in both event planning and fashion design.

Inspiration: Melissa always knew she wanted to have her own business; she just didn't know what it would be. Her current business evolved out of her beekeeping hobby, which, in turn, was inspired by a book she picked up one rainy afternoon in a small bookstore on one of the Gulf Islands off the south coast of British Columbia. Her fascination with learning more about bees in general and beekeeping, specifically, led her to take a course in beekeeping, and then later to beekeeping as a hobby.

Melissa started out with a background in fashion design, but as much as she loved fashion she had some issues with the environmental aspects of the industry. Whenever she raised the issues with others in the industry, she would get teased about having "hippie" ideals. In retrospect, Melissa can see that her ideals were always socially responsible, although she didn't initially recognize them as such. "I always had the idea that when my generation came of age, we'd be making changes that contributed to a more sustainable way of living," she says.

Business philosophy: Melissa's broad philosophy focuses on the quality of the relationships with the people in her business network (mentors, vendors, other suppliers) and bee-friendly hive management practices (e.g., hives are stationary, bees are stressed as little as possible and get a varied diet). Her philosophy is driven by both the ability to put herself in another's shoes and a habit of thinking ahead. Melissa balances striving to meet her S-R ideals with pragmatism. For example, while Melissa likes to work with local suppliers as much as possible, she has not yet found a local supplier for her packaging (glass jars for the honey), and so the glass jars come from China.

Social Responsibility in Action

Overall: Melissa's S-R strategies include nurturing her business networks, supporting her local economy by choosing to work with local suppliers and vendors as much as possible, and employing bee-friendly hive management techniques that would translate as healthy working conditions for her bees.

People: Although Melissa is currently a solopreneur, she keeps in mind that down the road she might have employees. Drawing on her own experience of feeling under-valued and under-appreciated by past employers, she gives a lot of thought to how she'd want her employees to feel about working with her.

When it comes to her suppliers and vendors, the quality of her interactions with them are important to her, and she looks to see whether their values are aligned with hers, especially with regard to the hive management practices of other beekeepers.

As for her customers, Melissa reports that she has been getting really good feedback on the honey. "Lots of people like the idea of micro-hive honey production that is community-based."

Community: Melissa tends to engage with community members on a one-on-one basis when she's out working with the hives. (She keeps one of the hives on a garage roof in the backyard of one of her vendors.) People often stop and ask her questions, so she invites them to see the hives and turns the interactions into an opportunity to teach them about her bee-friendly hive management practices. For future S-R strategies, Melissa envisions offering educational tours of the hives and giving regular talks about bees.

Melissa contributes to her local economy by supporting other local vendors and businesses as much as possible. When she needs something for her business, she'll try to think of a local supplier to approach first.

Planet: Melissa's commitment to bee-friendly hive management practices that help bees to stay healthy is an important contribution to ecological sustainability. Melissa also supports sustainable farming through her decision to purchase the herbs and spices for her infused honey from a local trading company on Cortes Island that only imports spices from organic, fair trade spice plantations.

S-R advantage: For Melissa, one clear advantage of running an S-R business is that it's more pleasurable so it doesn't feel like work. In addition to knowing that she's making a positive difference in the planet's long-term ecological sustainability, Melissa enjoys engaging with curious passersby and talking to them about the importance of keeping bees healthy.

Transformative power of an S-R business: Melissa noted that, to some extent, her two vendors—small, independent stores who sell mostly local and organic goods—have already tapped into customers with progressive values. She also observed that people who have tasted the honey and heard the explanations about how the products are produced get a better understanding of how to treat bees and why it's important to keep bees healthy.

Words of wisdom: Take the time to cultivate and trust your instincts. "For me, personally, if something doesn't feel good at a gut level, I honor that," she says. "Trust your inner wisdom. Sometimes, I've had to take some time and space to listen to what my gut is saying."

Second, while it's good to have an ultimate goal, it's important to acknowledge that there will be times when you can't make it happen. "There are times when you might have to make compromises on some issues—but never compromise when it comes to your core values or the quality of your product or service."

Tool 1: S-R Readiness Assessment Form

This assessment tool has been adapted from the "Organizational Assessment Tool" featured by the Demonstrating Value Initiative (demonstratingvalue.org). In addition, I've added a couple of questions about your motivation for and commitment to transforming (or building) a socially responsible business.

My Personal and Business Motivations

The driving force behind your decision to become more socially responsible can bolster your commitment when obstacles or challenges arise. Are the motivational drivers behind your decision to incorporate S-R practices into your business mostly internal (proactive—you decided on your own) or external (you're responding or reacting to outside influences or factors)?

Examples:

Person 1 (internally motivated): I want to express my values through my business practices and contribute something of lasting value to my community and local economy.

Person 2 (externally motivated): I know becoming more socially responsible in my business practices would really go over well with some of my customers—and it might expand my share of the market. Some of the planet friendly practices would definitely produce savings down the road, too. If some of the strategies don't work out, or are too difficult to implement, I'll just go back to the old way of doing things.

The S-R Readiness of My Business

Consider the following dimensions of your business. To what extent do/will they facilitate your ability to transform your business? Rate each dimension on a scale of 0-4, where 0=not at all and 4=completely. If any of the dimensions aren't applicable to you, write "N/A" next to the rating. State the reason for your rating, and list one action you could take to change or enhance this situation.

a) **Level of commitment** to transforming your company into an S-R business

    Example:

    Rating: 3

    Reason: I really want to use my business to make a positive difference, and for now I can commit to taking on some of the simpler, less expensive strategies as I am just starting out. I can't predict what will happen in the next couple of years and how that will affect long term commitment to the process.

    Action: Complete this S-R Assessment Form, make note of the resources I currently have available to me (especially financial data—actual and projected income, etc.), and let this information guide which S-R actions I can reasonably take on this year, and which actions I will have to budget for in the longer term.

b) **Employees** (How involved are employees in your S-R vision?)

    Example:

    Rating: 3

    Reason: I have two employees. While one person is all for transforming the operation into an S-R business, the other person seems to be lukewarm to going in this direction.

    Action: Talk to the less enthusiastic employee and find out about her concerns and/or assumptions about how the S-R transformation will affect her workload or activities in the office. Find out what would inspire her to feel more engaged in the process and how we can make that happen.

c) **Business advisors** (e.g., accountant, lawyer) or **Board of Directors**, if applicable (To what extent are advisors on board with your S-R vision?)

    Rating:

    Reason:

    Action:

d) **Strategic plan** (An up-to-date planning document to guide your company's development goals and S-R transformation process.)

Rating:

Reason:

Action:

e) **Operational systems** (Adequate systems to track projects, inventory, finances, etc.)

Rating:

Reason:

Action:

f) **Technology** (Computer technology and software assets to meet your business and S-R tracking needs.)

Rating:

Reason:

Action:

g) **Financial sustainability** (The short- and long-term financial stability and growth of your business and how this impacts your S-R plans.)

Rating:

Reason:

Action:

h) **Social capital, business-related** (The number and quality of relationships you have with customers, suppliers, business organizations, etc.)

Rating:

Reason:

Action:

i) **Social capital, S-R related** (The relationships you already have in place with organizations and other businesses that share your S-R mission and vision.)

Rating:

Reason:

Action:

j) **Community leadership** (Demonstrated ability to take the initiative and use your expertise to advocate for a community group or contribute to solving a local problem.)

Rating:

Reason:

Action:

k) **Product or process innovation** (Ideas or inventions that you have developed in relation to your products/services and business processes that yield blended returns.)

Rating:

Reason:

Action:

l) **Brand strength** (The ability of your brand to clearly convey to customers, other businesses, and the community what you are about; your business' image and reputation in the community.)

Rating:

Reason:

Action:

Tool 2: S-R Inventory Form

Find out what you're already doing that aligns with the three Ps of social responsibility: people, planet, and profits/prosperity. Answer the questions based on what you're actually doing, or have in place right now—not what you wish might be the case. Treat the results of this S-R inventory as useful information that will help you shape your strategies, rather than as a judgment about the extent of S-R activities you're currently engaged in. Indicate "Never," "Sometimes," "Always," or "N/A" for each statement below:

What We Do for Our Community and Business Networks ("People"):

We pay our employees a living wage.

We pay for health insurance for our employees.

We screen our suppliers to ensure they meet fair labor standards.

We provide our employees with ample training opportunities.

We participate in community engagement projects.

We support local nonprofits.

We believe in a high level of customer service.

We pay our suppliers promptly.

We support local businesses.

We partner with or hire local suppliers and vendors.

What We Do to be More Green ("Planet")

We use reusable plates and cutlery.

If we must use disposable plates, etc., we make sure they're ecofriendly (e.g., made from sustainable materials, fully biodegradable, etc.).

We drink filtered tap water.

We use travel mugs and reusable water bottles when we're out.

We have reusable mugs and glasses.

We use eco-friendly cleaning supplies.

We turn computers and other electronics off at the end of the day.

We use rechargeable batteries.

We unplug rechargers not in use.

We set the printer to double-sided.

We recycle or refill toner and ink cartridges.

We use alternative energy.

We buy carbon credits if we must fly.

We use office supplies made from recycled materials.

We use vegetable-based ink for printing.

We periodically complete an energy audit.

We find ways to reduce the use of heating and air conditioning.

We encourage telecommuting on a regular or part-time basis.

We minimize our air travel.

Our supplies are made from non-toxic goods.

We have reduced our packaging.

We participate in zero-waste challenges.

We have reduced our water use.

We have installed low-flush toilets.

We screen our suppliers for environmental standards.

What We Do for Our Business ("Profits/Prosperity"):

We donate in-kind goods and services.

We offer high quality products or services for good value.

We implement a profit-sharing program with our employees.

We make purchasing decisions based on economically and environmentally sustainable criteria.

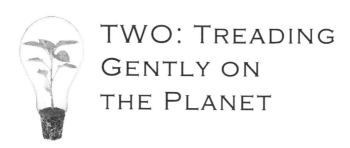

TWO: TREADING GENTLY ON THE PLANET

SOME time after the middle of the twentieth century, the golden age of the consumer economy arrived. Flush with growing disposable incomes, families in the developed world were encouraged to associate prosperity with buying all kinds of consumer goods. To meet the demand for shiny, new things, companies rolled out waves of the latest televisions and stereos, household appliances, automobiles, clothing, shoes, and a host of other gadgets and gizmos that filled the shelves at department stores and shopping malls. As soon as one product model was rolled out, a newer, faster, shinier model was minted and introduced on the market. Seductive marketing campaigns in TV commercials, magazine ads, and billboards bombarded households. Consumers became accustomed to buying new stuff just because they were tired of the old stuff. When items broke down, it was often cheaper to replace them than have them repaired. Consumer goods were designed to rapidly become obsolete, and it was regarded as the norm to buy and use disposable products from coffee cups to cameras.[1]

This explosion of consumer goods depended on production processes with voracious energy appetites. Our technological capabilities and scientific know-how to extract, process, and make the component parts for all of these consumer goods distracted us from the unintended, but very real, adverse impacts on our planet. The consumer economy was praised as progress, but there were hidden costs. As my paternal grandmother used to say, society had become "blinded by science." Our appetite for goods coupled with our technology and manufacturing advancements created an industrial complex that consumed finite resources, polluted ground water and natural water systems, and created mountains of trash that choked landfills.

Looking back through a cultural lens that now includes a growing public consensus on climate change and the environment, the sting of the recent financial crisis and housing crash, and a shift toward a collaborative, sharing economy (think of companies like AirBnb, Zipcar, Skillshare, Etsy, as well as movements like coworking and crowdfunding) this roaring, consumerist culture feels distant and quaint—the foolhardiness of an era. What's more real and startling today is the aftermath of that consumerist trajectory: abysmal savings rates among families, wasted resources, and environmental problems.

In response to this legacy, business has been surprisingly responsive. Many industries are now making inroads to getting off this unsustainable path. Mainstream corporate giants like SC Johnson and Google are taking active steps to reduce their environmental impact on the planet. For example, SC Johnson has eliminated chlorine-based external packaging and decreased its use of fossil fuels by 10%, and it has also developed a "Greenlist" process for assessing the environmental impact of each raw material it uses. It has even shared its Greenlist with governments, universities and other corporations.[2] Google has focused many of its efforts on reducing fossil fuel consumption by installing thousands of solar panels on the roofs of its buildings, providing a corporate shuttle commuter service for its employees, offering employees cash incentives to purchase hybrid cars, and promoting plug-in hybrid technologies for cars.[3]

Even a company such as Seventh Generation, which has always positioned itself as a "green" corporation right from its start in 1988, strives to make its business operations ever more sustainable. Seventh Generation, a certified B Corporation, has not only continued to improve the eco-friendliness of its cleaning products, but has also actively sought to reduce greenhouse emissions, expand the use of renewable energy, and has made its buildings LEED-certified, among other initiatives.[4]

While much still needs to be done, it's heartening to see how the spendthrift, reckless attitude toward the planet has dramatically shifted in recent years at all levels of business. Now, even smaller businesses are getting in on the action. In writing this book, I talked to several small businesses that have made strides in becoming more "green" and environmentally conscious in their business practices. Some took action only after they had already been in business for several years, or while they were still in the process of designing their products.

It was six years before Toby Barazzuol decided to bring his personal sustainability values to work and transform Eclipse Awards into an environmentally friendly business. The first actions he took included getting energy certifications. When his company moved to a different office space, he also made some green renovations—installing large windows, creating a green roof to create better insulation—that would help to reduce the amount of energy needed to illuminate and cool spaces. The building, which he shares with Saul Brown, another entrepreneur featured in this book, is powered 100% by alternative energy. The green measures didn't stop at the workspace. Toby also works with suppliers who use sustainable materials like recycled glass and reclaimed wood to manufacture his green recognition awards.

British entrepreneur James Castro Edwards wanted to make London inner city areas greener and to replenish the diminishing bee population in Britain. He was inspired to create the "greenstack," a vertical planter for homes and gardens. The planter evolved through several iterations. The first version of the greenstack was made of plastic, but James and his business partners realized a plastic planter didn't square with their vision of creating a product that was eco-friendly through all of the stages of its lifecycle, so they went back to the drawing board. The greenstack was later redesigned using 100% biodegradable materials. James and his partners could have stopped at "good enough," but they decided to take the socially responsible high road and make the best product possible.

> **"**Our whole business is based on socially responsible practices. The business arises from our passion for reducing a disposable lifestyle—reusing or repurposing containers, reducing the amount of plastic goods, specifically, and waste, generally, and recycling whatever can't be reused. The store is an extension of our personal lifestyles.**"**
> - Linh Truong, The Soap Dispensary

There are also microentrepreneurs I talked to who incorporated green and socially responsible practices from day one. For many of them, running an environmentally sustainable business is simply an extension of their personal lifestyle. "Our whole business is based on socially responsible practices," says Linh Truong, the owner of The Soap Dispensary, a Vancouver-based eco-friendly refill store. "The business arises from our passion for reducing a disposable lifestyle: reusing or repurposing containers; reducing the amount of plastic goods, specifically, and waste, generally; and recycling whatever can't be reused. The store is an extension of our personal lifestyles."

Lori Del Genis, the owner of Pennsylvania-based Conscious Elegance, and Jane Faye, the owner of Glasgow-based Gaia Noir, are both proprietors of eco-conscious fashion businesses. They have demonstrated their commitment by choosing used tools or secondhand display equipment instead of buying new tools Lori and Jane also repurpose or "up-cycle" fabrics from existing garments. When they do use new materials, they opt for fabrics made from organic, fair trade material to reduce the ecological footprint of the clothes they make. Both women seek to create as little waste as possible by finding uses for nearly every scrap of fabric.

Other entrepreneurs, such as Eileen Webb of New Hampshire-based webmeadow and Saul Brown of Vancouver-based Saul Good Gift Co., are firmly of the opinion that businesses have a responsibility from the very beginning to be part of the solution and be socially responsible. For Joe Staiano, a travel consultant from Seattle and owner of Meaningful Trips, the triple bottom line is a baseline consideration for all businesses. "The triple bottom line is the minimum bottom line: It's the entry ticket. Every business needs to be paying attention to the social and environmental consequences of their business." The bigger issue for Joe—and for many of the microentrepreneurs interviewed for this book—is the extent of "greenwashing" that occurs. In Joe's opinion, it's crucial that businesses "walk their talk" when it comes to sustainability practices.

In this Chapter...

When sustainable business practices are discussed, most people think of environmental sustainability first. At the broadest level, social responsibility (S-R) initiatives that focus on environmental sustainability are based on reducing, reusing (along with repurposing and repairing), and recycling—in that order. Why is recycling last on the list? Because recycling uses energy and draws on carbon-based resources, it's listed as the third "r" in the trinity of environmentally friendly actions. However, recycling is still preferable to dumping plastics and other materials into landfills.

In this chapter, we'll dive into ways to tread more gently on the planet. We'll focus on practical strategies that reduce not only your carbon footprint, but also your water and ecological footprints. You'll get to meet and learn from several microentrepreneurs practicing planet-friendly strategies. You'll also learn the small steps for the following:

- Evaluating and revising your resource usage patterns and reducing your environmental footprints.

- Reducing, or, better yet, eliminating the number of toxic substances you use (either as cleaning supplies or as inputs to the manufacture of your company's products).

- Checking the environmental sourcing of your suppliers.

- Tracking your progress and assessing the impact of the green measures you take.

Do You and Your Business Have the Same Size Carbon Footprint?

Hearing the term "carbon footprint," I used to imagine people stomping around on piles of coal dust and then leaving tracks of sooty footprints everywhere they went. Ironically, this image isn't as farfetched as you would think. The sooty footprint is a rather apt metaphor considering that a carbon footprint serves as an effective measure of pollution levels, although ironically the specific type of pollutant that it measures—green house gases—is invisible. (The visible haze is the particulate matter produced through burning fossil fuels.)

Mike Berners-Lee and Duncan Clark, in a blog post at *The Guardian*, adroitly define the carbon footprint this way: It's the amount (in tons) of greenhouse gases (including, carbon dioxide, nitrous oxide, and methane) generated by human activities, such as commuting in our cars, to heavy manufacturing or resource extraction processes—and their total impact on climate change.[5] In recent years, the concept of the "footprint" has come to encompass other ways we damage our environment. The concept has been extended to our water usage patterns (as in a "water footprint") and even our overall impact on our environment (an "eco-footprint").

Just as we each have different shoe sizes, the size of your environmental footprints will vary depending on the kind of services or products you offer, on whether you're a home-based, virtual, or "brick and mortar" enterprise, and on any other number of variables. Unlike the size of our feet, which doesn't change much once we reach adulthood, we can shrink the size of our environmental footprints.

Aligning Your Personal Values with Your Business

Whether you started out as an "ecopreneur" with a clear environmental mission from the get-go, or as an entrepreneur who gradually came to see the importance and value of adopting more green practices, your customers or other business stakeholders will probably expect your personal and business approach to environmental concerns to be aligned at some level.[6]

If you didn't start your business with a specific environmental mission in mind, it shouldn't be all that surprising if your customers, employees, and people in your business network ask, "Why now?"

Well, why now? What sparked your recently awakened concern for the environment? And, how do your values span your business and personal life? Perhaps you've always been a closet environmentalist, but your business school training led you to believe you had to park your personal values at the door in order to make a profit. Maybe you read or heard a story that produced an epiphany, or you now believe it makes more sense from a bottom line perspective to reduce waste. Perhaps you're more willing to bow to the wisdom and earnest requests of your employees or customers to "green" your business.

Most of the entrepreneurs I talked to started out with a clear idea that they wanted their products or services—or the associated processes—to reflect their personal commitment to a sustainable lifestyle. Kate Sutherland, a Vancouver-based author and consultant who specializes in helping individuals, organizations, and communities come into better alignment with their purpose, clarify principles, and build capacity, has a deep commitment to living green. In her spare time, she started both a plastics recycling depot and the "Two Block Diet," a project aimed at encouraging people to source and shop for food locally.[7] Lori Del Genis, the eco-conscious seamstress who owns Conscious Elegance, volunteers with an environmental group on the campus of a nearby university, collects food quality plastic bags to give to farmers to reuse at local farmers' markets, and gives leftover scraps of fabric to local schools to be used as supplies for art classes. Lori has also switched from print to digital sources of inspiration for her dress designs thereby reducing her paper use. Reesa Abrams, one of the founding members of Santa Cruz, CA-based TechCycle3, a computer recycling and data cleaning service, is a firm believer in the philosophy that "you can't teach the model if you don't live it."

Does this mean you need to have your own house (literally and figuratively speaking) in eco-friendly order before you start implementing environmentally friendly S-R practices in your business? Do you find yourself preaching one philosophy in your personal life and practicing another one in your business?

While the stakeholders in your business probably don't expect you to do everything perfectly all the time, they do expect to see some consistency, transparency, and accountability. It strengthens your credibility and integrity if you can demonstrate that your personal and work habits and behaviors are guided by the same values. Start by acknowledging and recognizing where you successfully uphold your values in your business (or personal life) and where you fall short. Implementing green business practices is also easier if you do similar practices at home. For example, if you recycle at home, it makes it much easier to launch a recycling program and model the behavior at work.

Measuring the Size of Your Footprints

Before you change anything, you'll need to know what you can or should change. In order to make informed decisions about which of the relevant green practices you can reasonably implement, you'll first need to assess how lightly you and your business already tread on the earth.

Here are several ways to measure your environmental footprints:

1.   **Invest in a professional audit.** The most thorough approach is to have a professional environmental consultant or energy auditor come in and do an audit of your business. Many companies, such as Climate Smart (climatesmartbusiness.com) in Canada, or WSP Environment and Energy (wspenvironmental.com) in the U.S., provide assessments for small businesses. Fees often start at US$1,000 for an initial audit.[8] A professional audit might make sense if you lease your business space and/or you know some aspects of your business are energy or resource intensive. If you're unsure whether you would benefit from the services of a professional consultant, check with your municipal or provincial/state government to see if they offer free or low-cost audits, or get a free consultation from The Green Office (thegreenoffice.com), a B Corporation based in San Francisco that also offers an online, one-stop shopping site for green office products and services.

2.   **Take advantage of D-I-Y tools.** You can also opt for a simple, do-it-yourself audit using the information in three books: David Gershon's *Low Carbon Diet: A 30 Day Program to Lose 5,000 Lbs.* (2006); Alex Shimo-Barry and Christopher Maron's *The Environment Equation: 100 Factors that Can Add to or Subtract from Your Total Carbon Footprint* (2008); and *David Suzuki at Work Toolkit* (2008, davidsuzuki.org).

     Gershon's book not only walks readers through the process of auditing their waste production, energy, and water usage patterns at home, it also offers a variety of suggestions for reducing your carbon footprint, and lists the pounds of CO2 emissions eliminated by taking various actions. *Examples:* Replacing five frequently used incandescent light bulbs with compact fluorescent lamp (CFL) bulbs will reduce your carbon footprint by 500 lbs (or 226.7 kg) per year; adjusting your home's thermostat to between 65°-68°F during the day and 55°-58°F at night during the winter will eliminate 1,400 lbs

(635 kg) from your footprint, not to mention increase savings on your heating bill.[9] *Note:* Although the general principles and practices outlined in Gershon's book can be extrapolated to office space, it's really intended for individual homes rather than businesses.

Shimo-Barry and Maron's book goes one step further and provides information about the amount of carbon emissions associated with various work-related activities and products. (*Hint:* This data serves as useful starting points for tracking the metrics associated with your S-R activities.) The information offered applies equally well to home-based businesses and companies that operate in commercial spaces.[10] *Examples:* Shimo-Barry and Maron point out that substituting one ream of paper with recycled paper saves 5 lbs (2.27 kg) of CO_2, and every pound of paper (2.2 kg) you recycle saves 0.9 lbs (0.4 kg) of carbon emissions.[11]

You can also assess your carbon, ecological, and water footprints at the following websites:

- Carbon Fund (carbonfund.org) - for your carbon footprint[12]

- My Footprint (myfootprint.org) - for your ecological footprint

- H20 Conserve (h2oconserve.org) - for your water footprint

In addition to websites, there are also a series of handy web and mobile apps that provide tools for assessing a variety of environmental impact factors, from energy use of appliances to the best transportation routes that produce the least amount of CO_2 emissions. Here are a few to consider:

- GoodGuide (goodguide.com): Led by a group of chemists, toxicologists, nutritionists, sociologists, and lifecycle analysis experts, GoodGuide provides a way for eco-conscious shoppers to vet the products they buy for their home or business. Just enter the name of the product in their search field and find out the product's health, environmental, and social performance (products are rated on a scale from 0-10 on a variety of criteria).

- iRecyle (earth911.com/irecycle): This app helps you locate the recycling centers nearest to your home (or business) for various stuff that you're unable to reuse, repair, repurpose, or "freecycle" (i.e., give the item away to someone else who can use it).

- iViro (envirolytics.ca/iViro) and Control4 (control4.com): Both apps offer useful tools for helping you to assess how much energy your home is using for heating, cooling, and running various appliances. Control4 also offers remote climate control systems for your home or office. Both apps also provide tips on how to reduce energy use (thereby reducing your carbon footprint).

- Carticipate (carticipate.com): If you don't like the idea of single occupant vehicles, or if you'd like to meet new people who are going your way, check out the iPhone app, Carticipate, which lets you arrange for rideshares and carpools.

- Hootroot (hootroot.com): "Give a hoot, green your route" is the tagline for this app. Plan your commute or cross-country travel with hootroot to get from point A to point B with a route that minimizes your CO2 emissions.

- Greenmeter (hunter.pairsite.com/greenmeter): Greenmeter is an iPhone app that measures your car's fuel and crude oil consumption, as well as power use and carbon emissions while you're driving. *Caution:* Avoid checking the fancy graphics that pop up while you're driving and let a passenger monitor your driving performance.

Small Steps to Environmental Sustainability

Revisit your responses to the "What I Do to Be More Green ("Planet")" section on "Tool 2" at the end of Chapter 1. Let's take a look at what you put down. What are you doing now that's already on track? (Remember to celebrate these successes.) What habits and business practices could you change to be more eco-friendly?

If there are a number of actions that you "should" be doing or would like to do, and you can't decide where to start, the sustainability consultants at The Green Office (thegreenoffice.com) recommend implementing green initiatives in the following order:

1. Take action to conserve more resources.

2. Adopt a sustainable purchasing policy.

3. Offset any remaining carbon emissions by investing in emissions reduction or renewable energy credits.

As a starting point that will give you a few quick, easy wins, pick one or two S-R practices from your "Tool 2: S-R Inventory Form" in Chapter 1 that can be readily implemented with a minimum of expense and fuss. If you can't think of any new green practices to take on, consider taking something you already do to a whole new level. Whether it's committing to a zero-waste policy, installing a living, green roof on your building, driving less or telecommuting more often (if that's an option for your business) or sending containers back to your suppliers for refills—there are plenty of innovative green strategies that you can adopt that can help your business and your clients tread more gently on the planet.

Here are a few more ideas that are easy and, for the most part, relatively cost-effective to implement:[13]

The Green Basics: Within 3 months

- Check the size of your carbon, water, and ecological footprints using one of the D-I-Y tools listed earlier in this chapter. Most of these online calculators and mobile-based apps also provide you with tips on how to reduce your footprint and assess your environmental impact.

- Turn off room lights and appliances when you're not using them. Use a central power strip and switch off appliances and electronics from the strip. (*Note*: If your phone line is through your internet connection, make sure your modem and router are plugged into a separate outlet, or you'll inadvertently disconnect your phone service!)

- Activate the energy-saving settings on your computer.

- Switch to rechargeable batteries, and remember to unplug rechargers when they're not in use.

- Invest in a stainless steel water bottle and a travel mug to replace all of your disposable beverage containers.

- Reduce your paper use; be selective about what you print. If you must print, select the double-sided print setting on your printer/photocopier.

- Choose 100% recycled paper when you must print documents. If you must use mixed source (e.g., 30% recycled content), make sure it's certified by a third-party organization such as the Forest Stewardship Council (FSC).

- Use e-mail and cloud-based tools like Dropbox (dropbox.com) or Google Drive (drive.google.com), rather than faxes or snail mail to share documents.

- Reuse paper. Turn your junk mail into scrap paper. If you printed a rough draft using one-sided printing, use the other side as scrap paper.

- Cancel the junk mail and catalogs. Phone the catalog companies to be removed from their mailing lists, and sign up for the Mail Preference service through Direct Marketing Association (dmachoice.org).

- Refill (first choice) or recycle ink cartridges and toners.

- Encourage employees to bring their lunches in reusable containers or wrappers. Make it easy for your employees to bring their lunch from home: Make sure they have a fully equipped lunch room. Adopt one of Toby's strategies and implement a contest to reward sustainable behavior.

- Replace disposable cups, plates, cutlery, etc., with reusable items. If you must use disposable items, find environmentally friendly options that are biodegradable.

- Fix leaky faucets or problem toilets right away, or notify the building maintenance workers if you're in a leased office space.

- Consider letting your employees telecommute one or two days a week.

- Opt for virtual meetings (e.g., teleconferences or web conferences) over long distance travel.

- Buy carbon credits when you do have to travel by air.

One Step Further: Within 1 year

- Be proactive: Solicit feedback or conduct a customer survey to gauge your customers' environmental values and figure out how you can respond to their concerns through your S-R practices. Better yet, engage your customers when planning your planet friendly S-R actions.[14]

- Include environmental information about your product on the labeling. Alternatively, keep printing and packaging to a minimum: Post environmental information about your product on your website, and provide a link to your website on your packaging.

- Switch to environmentally friendly packaging; work with a labeling vendor that uses recycled paper and vegetable-based inks. Go one or two steps further: Minimize packaging as much as possible, and make it easy for clients to recycle or reuse the packaging materials.

- Switch to reading newspapers, magazines, and other materials in digital formats. Also, instead of printing an article or story you see online, save it using a program like Read It Later (readitlaterlist.com) or Instapaper (instapaper.com) that lets you collect all of your online reading material for review later on the device of your choice, such as a tablet, laptop, smart phone, or e-reader.

- Take paperless notes using apps such as Evernote (evernote.com) or Zotero (zotero.org).

- Repair equipment rather than automatically replacing items when you experience problems. When you absolutely must replace something, find out if the manufacturer takes the product back for disassembly, remanufacturing, or recycling.

- Consider using Freecycle (freecycle.org) or Craigslist (craigslist.org) for letting go of equipment that is still in good condition but that you no longer need. Likewise, you could also use Freecycle or Craigslist to find "gently used" equipment that you need rather than buying the items new.

- When it's time to replace your computer, consider switching to a laptop computer as it uses less energy than a desktop computer.

- Replace incandescent light bulbs with more energy-efficient bulbs such as compact fluorescent light bulbs (CFLs) or light-emitting diodes (LEDs). LEDs are ultimately the biggest energy and money-saver because they're the most efficient and last for ten or more years, but they're an expensive investment upfront. (The average cost for one bulb is about US$35). The next best bet is a CFL bulb at a fraction of the cost (around US$4), though CFLs do pose some environmental concerns due to the small amount of mercury present in the bulb.[15]

- Find low-tech, low-cost ways to conserve water and avoid replacing plumbing equipment unnecessarily.

- Choose cleaning products that are environmentally friendly and free of harsh chemicals. If your office relies on the services of a janitor, ask the janitorial services company to switch to eco-friendly products. Alternatively, ask the janitor to use eco-friendly products that you will supply for your office. (*Tip:* Read labels carefully and make sure you know the difference between an authentic eco-label and an impressive looking but meaningless label. Also, baking soda, distilled white vinegar, water, lemon, and either tea tree or pine essential oils are handy ingredients for making your own inexpensive, yet effective, cleaning products.)

- Set up a program of incentives to encourage your employees to opt for sustainable modes of transportation for their daily commute (assuming your employees live within biking or walking distance from work).

- Look into carbon neutral options for local deliveries (e.g., bicycle couriers, delivery tricycles) and purchase carbon offsets for long-distance shipping, if applicable.

Becoming the Ambassador of Green: Long term

- Develop a sustainable purchasing policy and work with your current suppliers to help them meet your standards. Make a commitment to screen all future suppliers and vendors on their sustainability practices. For some ideas on what types of questions you should be asking, consult the resources at the International Institute for Sustainable Development (iisd.org).[16]

- Establish a policy of transparency regarding your own business, production, and distribution policies. Voluntarily disclose your policies and practices to customers and other key stakeholders in your business.[17] Make your policies available and easy to find on your website, and include the URL for the website on your packaging and other promotional materials.

- Become a certified B Corporation or green business through a recognized and reputable organization, such as B Lab (bcorporation.net) or Green America (greenbusinessnetwork.org). *Note:* This process can often take at least six months, so it's a long-term commitment.

- Re-evaluate the design of your product to see if you can improve its overall environmental footprint, and/or extend its lifecycle from production to disposal. If you need some help with the design process, explore IDEO's Human-centered Design Toolkit (ideo.com/work/human-centered design toolkit). If you're stymied by where to research materials that are more sustainable, visit Cradle to Cradle Products Innovation Institute (c2ccertified.org) as a starting point.

- Ensure that all staff and partners are educated about your sustainability policies. Invest in training, if needed. Better yet, include your employees and major partners in the process of designing those policies or putting together a training program.

- Reduce the number of days you use your car to get around, and encourage any employees to do the same. Make it more fun and doable by offering incentives such as bus passes, bike helmets, and the availability of a company bike.

- Encourage your local business community to learn about and apply some basic industrial ecology principles. Work together to create a business ecosystem in which waste is reduced or repurposed. In Chapter 3, we'll discuss a successful materials exchange program started by Saul Brown, owner of Saul Good Gift Co.

- Save for and invest in a professional energy and environmental audit.

- Consider switching to alternate energy sources to power your business.

Conducting a "Green" Cost-Benefit Analysis

If you're not sure whether some of the longer term strategies are a good fit or the right choice for your business, conduct a simple cost-benefit analysis before committing your valuable resources to going down a particular path.[18] Assess the current state of your enterprise in terms of your finances, resources, mission, and sustainability goals, and ask yourself the following set of questions:

1. Is it affordable given your current assets and cash flow?

2. Does the action move you closer to your sustainability goals or vision?

3. Is it measurable? That is, do you have any way of showing that adopting the strategy produced a result? For example, your decision to switch to LED bulbs reduced your electricity usage by "x" kilowatt-hours per month or year.

If your answer to all of the above questions is "no," then clearly it isn't a strategy you want to pursue for the foreseeable future. If your response to all of the questions is "yes," then consider it a green light to go ahead with the initiative. If your response is mixed, you'll have to determine whether the costs (both financial and in terms of your company's brand, reputation, etc.) outweigh the benefits, or vice-versa.

For each S-R practice you decide to adopt, list the following:

*   Necessary steps and strategies for each of the goals you want to meet.

*   Potential challenges and obstacles to meeting your goals.

*   Any support or cooperation from others required to successfully meet your goals.

*   Environmental impacts of your actions.

Example: Using only 100% recycled paper

Project Scope

How far will you go? Does your decision extend to all paper products—printer and copier paper, note pads, file folders, envelopes, paper towels, etc.—or just paper used for printing or copying? What about documents and business stationery that are sent to a print shop? If you decide to commit to using recycled paper, then you should probably extend the policy to any printing that is done off-site, too.

While there are now more available paper products made from recycled paper, not every product is made from "100% post consumer recycled materials," the greenest option. You may have to choose products that either contain the highest proportion of recycled content available for that product, or buy products made from mixed sources that have earned the Forest Stewardship Council's (FSC) seal of approval. Does your current print shop offer greener options (e.g., recycled paper, vegetable-based inks), or will you have to find a new print shop?

Challenges and Key Considerations

Cost: You'll have to consider the financial costs of switching to recycled paper products. While many recycled paper products are much more affordable than they used to be, they are still a little pricier than their non-recycled counterparts. You'll also have to spend some time assessing how much you currently spend on paper products and how much more you would be spending on recycled paper products. Can you keep paper costs down by saving on expenses elsewhere? Remember, you want to be financially and environmentally sustainable.

Likewise, if you extend your recycled paper policy to print shop jobs, you'll have to determine what the cost difference for "green" printing is and how much more costly it will be on a monthly or yearly basis. If it's significantly more expensive, can you be more selective about your printing needs? For example, do you really need to use a print shop's service for stationery with your letterhead on it? Do you really need to print hundreds of brochures or flyers on glossy paper? Maybe you could save money and trees by rethinking your printing needs and going digital.

Getting others on board: If you lease your office space from someone else, or if you're in a coworking environment, you may not have the final say in the purchasing decisions for the office. If this describes your situation, make a compelling case to the decision-maker for switching to recycled paper products for everything from copier paper to toilet paper.

Faux Green: In your analysis, you may discover that not all eco-brands are as environmentally friendly or ethical as you might think. Forest Ethics (forestethics.org) points out how "greenwashing" takes place in the paper industry. When you're using mixed source paper, you need to be aware of where the wood came from. Was it harvested sustainably? Did it come from an old growth forest or an environmentally sensitive area?

As a consumer, you have to rely on someone else to monitor the logging industry and the pulp and paper mill companies and ensure they're conducting their business in a sustainable, ethical manner. But whom do you trust? Labels can be meaningless, misleading, or biased (e.g., in cases where the monitoring organization gets its funding from the very industry it's supposed to be holding accountable). Make sure that the organization that's approving or certifying a product or process is an independent third-party.

Environmental Savings

Switching to 100% recycled paper will deduct 5 lbs (2.27 kg) per ream of paper (i.e., 500 sheets) from your carbon footprint.[19] If you decide to commit to using only 100% recycled paper that has received the Forest Stewardship Council's seal of approval, you might note that this action will also contribute to the prevention of "x" number of trees being cut down.

Using recycled paper also requires less energy and water to produce paper from recycled materials than from virgin forest, so you'll be shrinking your carbon footprint in addition to conserving natural resources. According to the Environmental Protection Agency, saving one ton of paper amounts to a savings of 7,000 gallons of water and 3.3 cubic yards of landfill space.[20]

Example: Eliminating bottled water from the office

Project Scope

Does your decision to eliminate bottled water from the office include removing the water cooler? Do you have a potable water supply from a kitchen faucet? If so, how is the quality of the water? Do you need to install a filter on the faucet or invest in a pitcher with a filter? Does your decision extend to strongly discouraging employees from bringing disposable bottles of water into the office? Do you have reusable glasses or cups, or do your employees need to bring their own cups or water bottles? Do you have facilities and supplies to wash cups and glasses? What happens if employees forget their water bottle or cup? Do they have to then spend their break or lunchtime dashing to the nearest store to buy another cup or glass?

Challenges and Key Considerations

Cost: In the short and long run, a switch to filtered tap water and reusable cups, glasses, or bottles will be considerably less expensive than continuing to purchase bottled water on a weekly or monthly basis. According to The Water Project (thewaterproject.org), Americans spend more than US$100 per person, per year on bottled water.[21] Again, do the math to calculate your projected financial savings.

People's tastes and preferences: If you don't have any potable water at all, you might have to invest in a water cooler that uses and reuses larger, but fewer, plastic bottles. If you have potable water, but it isn't at all palatable, do you opt for the water cooler or strongly encourage your employees to bring their water from home in a reusable container? Keep in mind that you need to balance being planet friendly with being people friendly—especially when the people in question are your employees who help keep your business going.

Measuring up: How are you going to measure the environmental impact of your strategy? What's your baseline measure? That is, how many bottles of water are you and your staff currently buying or consuming each week or month? Are you going to focus on the number of plastic bottles that won't be going to a recycling center or the landfill? Are you going to measure the reduction in greenhouse gases that result from the energy used to recycle the bottles?

As you saw in Chapter 1, indicators that depend on tracking down and assessing the accuracy of data compiled by external sources can often be a time-consuming endeavor. You'll need to decide whether the importance of the indicator justifies the amount of time required to find the information (a one-time event), and then perform any calculations required to demonstrate the impact of your strategy (a periodically recurring event). The good news is that there appears to be much more research and data available on the environmental impact of bottled water.

Getting others on board: What if you have one or two employees who insist that bottled water is safer or better tasting than filtered tap water? How will you foster their engagement and get them on board with your strategy? If they insist on bringing bottled water with them, how will you respond to such behavior?

Consider adopting the following strategy proposed by The Water Project:[22] Implement a "water offset" fund and donate the money saved by opting out of bottled water at the office to a charity. Knowing that the savings from not using bottled water is going to a good cause may encourage buy-in from workers.

Environmental Savings

For each 1-liter bottle of water you're not consuming, you're conserving five liters of water, 160 grams (5.6 oz) of fossil fuel (the amount used to make the bottle), and you're cutting your carbon footprint by 153 grams (5.4 oz).[23] In addition to saving money and resources (water, fossil fuels), reducing the demand for plastics also helps to improve the health of people who live near plastic processing plants.

Tracking and Reporting Your "Greening" Progress

Tracking your progress and impact is vitally important. Knowing the impact you're having will keep you motivated. It's easier to stay motivated and know you're making a difference if you see how much of a difference your actions have. Says Toby of Eclipse Awards, "When you're measuring what you're actually doing you can see the changes you're making and it's inspiring."

As you learned in the previous chapter, tracking your progress doesn't have to be a complicated or costly endeavor. It does, however, require consistency and accuracy if you're serious about tracking your environmental impact and reducing the impact thereof. Whether your approach to auditing your energy use and carbon footprint is professional or D-I-Y, draw on the resources available to you that will help you correctly define, measure, and calculate the results.

> **"**We're currently using a set of benchmarks to formally track electricity use, water use, and our carbon footprint. When you're measuring what you're actually doing you can see the changes you're making and it's inspiring.**"**
> - Toby Barazzuol, Eclipse Awards

So, how widespread is the practice of measuring environmental footprints among small and microbusinesses? Just under a third of the companies I interviewed tracked environmental impact and/or other indicators related to socially responsible business practices. Even fewer companies submitted reports on their environmental performance to external reporting agencies on an annual basis.

Third-Party Green Certification and Tracking

Two of the Vancouver-based companies I interviewed—Eclipse Awards and Saul Good Gift Co.—have completed Climate Smart audits (climatesmartbusiness.com) and regularly track their carbon footprint using a set of benchmarks provided by Climate Smart. Several American businesses I interviewed participated in Green America's Green Business certification process (greenamerica.org), a six-month certification process at three levels—Bronze, Silver, and Gold. A Gold level certification involves an evaluation of data provided by the company, as well as several independent assessments to ensure that the company's commitments go beyond general sustainability practices.

Soon after loyal customers nominated Conscious Elegance as a green business for Green America, owner Lori Del Genis completed the certification process and has been a Green America approved business since 2009. VOS Flips and LittleFootprint Lighting are also Green America certified green businesses. In addition, Nancy Wahl-Scheurich also tracks the carbon footprint for LittleFootprint Lighting through CleanMetrics (cleanmetrics.com).

Green Self-Tracking and Monitoring

While outside certification and monitoring is best, you don't need to use an outside agency to track your impact. Many entrepreneurs use a variety of self-monitoring methods to track their progress and impact. Aside from using CleanMetrics, LittleFootprint Lighting tracks their impact directly through their manufacturing process. Nancy realized that while using LED bulbs in the task lamps they produce was a great start to reducing energy use (Imagine having a lamp where the light bulb alone would last for over ten years!), she knew that even more could be done to reduce their energy footprint. Nancy and her co-founders decided to focus on the entire production process using recycled materials for the other lamp components, sourcing materials locally, and manufacturing the lamps locally, too—all elements they track.

José Alejandro Flores of VOS Flips partnered with the UN Global Compact (unglobalcompact.org), which means his company volunteers to abide by the ten principles set out in the Compact and submits reports that document their performance on those ten principles. Although they don't report externally on their S-R performance, Plantagon, an innovative Swedish company that designs urban, vertical greenhouses and other green products, does have to answer to its green-minded board. Plantagon's board has set down guidelines in its in-house "Articles of Association," which are based on the principles of the UN Global Compact and the Earth Charter (earthcharterinaction.org). Eileen Webb, along with her partner at web development firm webmeadow, self-track how much energy they generate through their solar panels. The Soap Dispensary's Linh Truong tracks how many plastic containers her customers bring back to the store for product refills.

Reminder: If you want to become either a certified B Corporation or a certified Green Business, you'll have to track certain key metrics and submit them to the certifying organizations as part of the certification process. Once certified you'll probably be expected to keep some records on these key metrics on your own, even if you don't have to submit them every year.

Engaging Others in Your Green Vision

As the proprietor of your business, you get to make the strategic, operational, and financial decisions for your business—especially if your business is structured as a sole proprietorship and you are a one-person operation. But, depending on the nature of your business and how many other people are involved directly or indirectly, you'll most likely want to collaborate with or get buy-in from your company's significant others; namely, your employees, customers, suppliers, vendors, delivery service providers, and other key business associates.

Employees and Other Workers

Start with having your workers (employees, interns, other workers) identify a few environmental goals with you. Many times, your workers will have ideas and strategies for implementing sustainable practices that hadn't occurred to you. Don't forget that increased responsibility is also a great way to empower others. Over time, you might want to give them the freedom to generate and even oversee some of their own initiatives. Giving over the reins on a few key initiatives gives your people a sense of ownership. Entrusted with an appropriate amount of autonomy, they'll feel more engaged with their work in general and with the process of "greening" your workplace, specifically.

Greening the Workplace

Recognizing employees and other workers for their green contributions and finding ways to make the "greening" process fun for them works wonders for sustaining engagement and enthusiasm for a project. When Toby Barazzuol noticed that his employees seemed to be spending most of their lunch hours driving around to find a place to eat and coming back from lunch more stressed than refreshed, he decided to launch the "Brown Bag Award." Toby sees the award as "…a way of being mindful of our values, reducing our carbon footprint, and reducing stress." The award, a CAD$300 bonus, is given out every two months to the person who brings his or her lunch to work most often during that time period. Toby has made it easy for his employees to bring their lunch to work: The workplace not only has a kitchen area equipped with reusable plates, glasses, cutlery, etc., it also has a green, living roof where employees can sit and mindfully enjoy their lunch or even do a little gardening during a break. Toby also discovered that including his employees in the energy audit and certification process had profound effects on the level of employee engagement. For employees, helping the business follow through on its commitment to being socially responsible increased their sense of loyalty, pride, and passion for the company.

Remember to include your interns, contract workers, or volunteers in your S-R initiatives at both the planning and implementation stages. Invite them to offer their feedback, suggestions, and strategies for assisting you in greening your business. Let them know about your company culture—whether it's a contest that encourages staff to bring their lunch to work or reminds them to switch off their computers at the end of the day—and encourage them to share their ideas, knowledge, experience, and resources when you're planning new initiatives. Work with all of your workers to create meaningful S-R related office projects that play to their strengths and give them a sense of ownership for the projects and their positive results. Even if you hire contract workers or consultants who work off-site, invite them to contribute to and participate in your S-R plans remotely. They may not be able to participate in an office-based contest or project, but if they live in the same city, they may appreciate being included in training opportunities or activities related to reducing your and their ecological footprints.

Team Projects and Volunteer Opportunities

Aside from engaging in company-wide, planet-friendly actions in the office, encourage your people to participate in individual or small-team projects off-site. Admittedly, it can get a bit tricky trying to find an outside activity or project that excites everyone to the same extent—but with a bit of open discussion, you may be able to generate a few projects that appeal to everyone. Consider taking on a greening project, such as working in a community garden, cleaning up a local park, and combining it with a zero-waste picnic; organize a local materials exchange program or a recycling drive with a local organization; or volunteer with a local ecology or environmental organization on an event.

Let your staff participate in projects in a way that speaks to their strengths and interests. Additionally, if you have interns, volunteers, or consultants working for you, invite them to the table to discuss potential volunteer and team projects alongside your staff. Be generous about recognizing everyone's participation and find ways to make it fun for them.

Vendors and Suppliers

Your level of social responsibility extends to and is influenced by the S-R policies of other businesses in your value chain. Speak to your manufacturers or suppliers and find out about their in-house environmental policies and practices. Taking the time to find out more about your suppliers' and vendors' policies not only keeps you mindful of your own sustainability practices, but also encourages others to explore greener options. If your suppliers know you value greener production processes, it may encourage them to change their ways to avoid you cutting ties or exiting the business relationship.

Materials and Product Sourcing

Make it a point to learn more about the materials used in the components you source for your own products and the manufacturing processes. If you're a certified B Corporation or a certified green business, not only will you be expected to know for sure whether the materials for your products are from sustainable sources and manufactured under fair labor conditions, you'll also be expected to have a written policy in place for the minimum standards your suppliers and vendors must meet in order for you to do business with them.

As a certified B Corporation, Saul Good Gift Co. has a formal "Suppliers Code of Conduct" that sets out the principles related to fair labor and basic level of environmentally sustainable practices and standards that suppliers must be willing to uphold and comply with to partner with the company. However, for owner Saul Brown, the code of conduct "serves as a starting point for discussion with new suppliers, rather than as an audit." Saul's code of conduct and guiding principles, published on his company's website, are a great source of inspiration on how to communicate your standards and values to suppliers and how to make better purchasing decisions.

Once you've crafted your policy for an ethical and sustainable supply chain, you may find that you have to seek new suppliers that are better equipped to work with your new practices. Finding the right suppliers can be a time-consuming process and requires patience, but keep in mind that changing vendors or suppliers may also have other benefits that translate to better customer service and streamlined business operations for your company.

Shipping and Delivery Services

Do you regularly use the services of a delivery truck or courier service? If so, then inquire about their environmental policies and the fuel efficiency of their vehicles. Are there other modes of delivery services (e.g., bicycle couriers or delivery tricycles) with a smaller carbon footprint that could still effectively and efficiently meet your needs? If you're shipping your products over long distances (but on the same continent), investigate which mode of transport— rail or road—produces the least amount of CO_2 emissions.

If green delivery services aren't available, consider buying carbon credits to offset the CO_2 emissions produced by your current vendors and their modes of transport. You might also consider adopting Nancy Wahl-Scheurich's strategy for reducing the environmental impact of long distance shipping: partnering with a company like UPS that offers carbon-neutral shipping.[24] Although Lori Del Genis, the owner of Conscious Elegance, strongly encourages potential clients who live cross-continent or overseas to seek locally based wedding dress designers as their first and most environmentally friendly option, Lori also realizes that some of her potential clients don't have that option and prefer her services. For these clients, Lori provides the option of carbon-neutral shipping.

What is Carbon-Neutral Shipping?

Carbon-neutral shipping is a form of carbon off-setting to account for the unavoidable CO_2 emissions that are generated by various modes of transport. For example, to be carbon-neutral, a shipping company purchases carbon credits equivalent to the amount of carbon emissions produced in its shipping operations. The amount paid for the carbon credits then goes to a project or program that reduces an equivalent, future amount of carbon emissions.[25]

Generally speaking, carbon credits are best considered as a last resort after all other efforts have been taken to reduce one's carbon footprint. As with other green products, the buyer should do careful research to assess the credibility of the organization offering the credits and the long-term value of its carbon off-setting projects. For example, it's better to purchase carbon credits for projects that support the development of clean energy sources, rather than tree planting projects, unless there is a guarantee that the trees will be left in place for several decades.

Janitorial Services and Cleaning Supplies

If your business employs a janitorial service, speak to the owner of that business and request that the company considers switching to eco–friendly products. The question then becomes, are you willing to pay a higher cost for cleaning services so the janitor can recoup the additional expense of buying environmentally friendly cleaning products?

If you don't rely on a janitorial service, you might still want to review your own cleaning products and what you plan to do with all those leftover, empty plastic containers. If you live in a city with an eco-friendly refill store like The Soap Dispensary that encourages you to reuse your plastic containers, give yourself some "brownie points" for using nontoxic cleaners *and* keeping those plastic bottles out of the landfill.[26] If you don't have a local equivalent of The Soap Dispensary in your city, you can still make your own eco-friendly cleaning products. There are plenty of "recipes" for D-I-Y cleaners on the Web, and most of the ingredients are readily available even in mainstream stores.

Customers

All of the entrepreneurs interviewed for this book recognize the importance of engaging with customers around their S-R values and practices and inspiring them to give more thought to environmental issues. Although, as Toby points out, as much as we might wish it were otherwise, sometimes our community engagement and sustainability practices don't mean as much to our customers as they do to us. If you find yourself in a position where your customers don't care as much about environmental and social sustainability as you do, don't despair. We'll return to the subject of your customers and their responses to your decision to become (or start) a socially responsible business in Chapter 5. In the meantime, there are several initiatives you can try out that may help to raise awareness among your customers and patrons:

Educational Tours and Workshops

Melissa Cartwright, an urban beekeeper in Vancouver, often attracts the attention of passersby when she's working with her bees. When this happens, she offers impromptu tours of the hives and uses the opportunity to raise awareness about bees. As a result of these experiences, she plans to start offering educational tours of her bee hives to educate more people about declining bee populations and why that's a problem for everyone. As she teaches her customers (or potential customers) about the importance of bee-friendly hive management strategies, she offers them a better understanding of why thriving, healthy bee populations are important.

If you knew how much of a positive impact you were making on the environment through choosing to reuse and refill plastic containers instead of throwing them in the recycling or trash bin, would you feel encouraged to keep up the good behavior? Linh Truong of The Soap Dispensary engages her customers' interest in and concern for environmental issues in a couple of ways: First, she tracks the number of plastic bottles each customer brings in for refills of the various products her store stocks. Second, she educates and empowers customers to shift from a disposable lifestyle to a more sustainable one by offering workshops on everything from creating non-toxic cleaning and personal care products at home, to repurposing various items that aren't easy to recycle. Reflecting on their business' mission, Linh says, "We are generally changing people's shopping habits by getting them to pause and think before automatically buying a plastic product."

Linh and her husband (he also helps out with the store) have been long-time advocates for and practitioners of leading a less disposable lifestyle. Their values are echoed in the principles behind The Story of Stuff (storyofstuff.org), a popular, global initiative to promote sustainable living. Running The Soap Dispensary, Linh and her husband take the time to engage with, educate, and empower their customers to create and maintain more sustainable purchasing practices. Sharing their values with others affirms their own S-R commitments as a business and signals to customers their steadfast ideals about sustainable, green living.

Media Outreach

Saul Brown shares his environmental values with his customers both in-person and through social media, engaging them with announcements on Twitter and with stories of sustainability on his blog, *Stories from the Gift Box*. Lori Del Genis of Conscious Elegance, Joseph Hodgkinson of northern California-based Foda Catering, and Jane Faye of Gaia Noir all engage with their customers through their websites.

Both Lori and Joseph feature information and links to other resources (e.g., reading material and organizations) pertaining to sustainability issues in their respective business sectors. For example, Joseph, a chef and local food advocate, provides links to websites on food security, local food movements, farmers markets, and food costs. Lori, a dressmaker, features short summaries of articles and links to stories on sweatshop labor, pesticides and their effects on both the farmers and the soil, and sustainable fabrics. Lori also sells eco-friendly fabrics to individuals who want to make their own wedding dresses.

Jane embedded *The Story of Change* video (thestoryofstuff.org) on her blog to remind her customers and blog followers that eco-consumerism is just one of the many actions we need to ensure we have a sustainable planet in the future. Jane has also used her blog to invite readers to send her their postal packaging (rather than dispose of it), which she reuses or repurposes.

Other ways to engage with your customers and to inspire them to support planet friendly actions might include: encouraging them to sign petitions for causes you care about; motivating them to write letters to their local, provincial (state), and federal representatives to lobby for the kinds of changes they (and you) want to see in the world; and pointing them to resources and projects that raise awareness about environmental issues.

Think of the suggestions listed here as a starting point. Connect with your networks and communities of like-minded individuals and ask the other entrepreneurs in your circles how they engage with their own customers.

Generate a list of suggestions that you can share with each other. And of course, don't forget to ask your customers for their suggestions, too; after all, they're the experts on what they like and what would work best for them.

WE'LL RETURN TO a discussion about how you can better connect with your customers in Chapter 5. In the next chapter, we'll narrow our focus from the planet to our local communities.

CHAPTER CHECKLIST:

✔ Assess your current S-R practices using the S-R Inventory Form in Chapter 1 if you haven't already done so.

✔ Do an audit of your carbon footprint. If you opt for the D-I-Y approach, resources such as Alex Shimo-Barry and Christopher Maron's *The Environment Equation: 100 Factors that Can Add to or Subtract from Your Total Carbon Footprint* (2008) and Kim McKay and Jenny Bonnin's *True Green at Work: 100 Ways You Can Make the Environment Your Business* (2008) not only give you specific details about the carbon footprint and costs associated with various workplace equipment and practices, they also explain how to change those practices and behaviors to reduce the costs.

Likewise, David Gershon's book, *Low Carbon Diet: A 30 Day Program to Lose 5,000 Lbs.* (2006) and David Boyd and David Suzuki's *David Suzuki's Green Guide* (2008), provide some useful figures to help you estimate potential savings in both carbon emissions and money when you implement certain practices at home, as well as some useful strategies that can be applied at home.

✔ Get started with environmentally sustainable practices at home and in the office and focus on implementing a few key initiatives over the short, medium, and long term. Consider it a bonus if you work from home—you can make your home and business greener at the same time. (*Reminder:* Just be sure to meticulously keep your record-keeping for business expenses, taxes, and S-R tracking separate from your home-improvement projects.)

✔ Introduce new practices with the buy-in, feedback, and contributions of your employees, suppliers, and customers.

✔ Ask relevant vendors about their green policies.

✔ Establish a policy of transparency regarding your own green policies. Voluntarily provide information about your environmental policies and practices to insurers, financial institutions, investors, suppliers, vendors, and customers.

✔ Become a certified green business through a recognized and reputable organization.

✔ Become a certified B Corporation.

Lori Del Genis, Conscious Elegance

Location: State College, Pennsylvania, U.S.

Product/Service: Custom-made wedding gowns hand-made exclusively from sustainable, eco-friendly materials.

Company start date: 2006

Company website: consciouselegance.com

Bio: Lori Del Genis is a self-taught, third generation dressmaker and has been a seamstress for over twenty-four years. Lori supported herself through grad school sewing for a local theater group. Before she started Conscious Elegance, Lori earned a Master's degree in the medical field and worked as a specialist in swallowing disorders (dysphagia).

Inspiration: Lori's business started out as a dressmaking service for hard-to-fit brides. She was inspired after she'd had one too many plus-size friends cry on her shoulder about how shabbily they'd been treated at conventional bridal salons. When Lori started doing the research for suppliers for her materials, she was horrified at what she learned. She decided that she couldn't in all good conscience profit from what the clothing industry was doing to the earth and farmers—poisoning both with toxic pesticides and synthetic fertilizers and using sweatshop labor. She decided her business was going to be based exclusively on sustainable materials and business practices, and she would only work with similarly minded people as suppliers.

Business philosophy: At a personal level, Lori believes that every choice we make has social ramifications: the food we buy (or grow), the clothes we wear (and where we get them), the hobbies we enjoy, and our use of fossil fuels to run our cars and heat our homes. She questions where each item that crosses her hands comes from, and asks herself whether there are better alternatives. Lori buys used goods whenever possible rather than taking up new resources, with the exception of when she wishes to support small businesses and artisans. For Lori, garbage doesn't simply disappear when she's done with it; almost anything non-edible can be gotten used or re-used.

Lori's business philosophy is a seamless extension of her personal philosophy and practice. This translates to avoiding cheap, petroleum-based fabrics; using reclaimed silk rather than new silk to avoid harming more silk worms; making her dresses affordable and accessible to less wealthy clients by charging a fair price based on materials and labor; using her own printer and recycled paper for business stationery and communications; reusing packing materials; and replacing fabrics with more eco-friendly options if she discovers that her first choice isn't as planet or people friendly as she believed.

Social Responsibility in Action

Overall: Lori's S-R practices are designed to support both people and planet by minimizing waste and using reclaimed dresses or eco-friendly materials produced by fair labor. She also provides excellent service and reasonable prices, holding both herself and her suppliers to a high standard of ecological and humanitarian standards. She also volunteers with a local eco-action student group.

People: Where suppliers are concerned, Lori holds them to the standards to which she holds herself. She evaluates whether suppliers are a good fit with her business based on the transparency of their business processes; whether they're available and accessible to answer clients' questions and e-mails; whether they deliver on their promises; whether they use non-reactive dyes or bleach in their products; and how much thought they give to the afterlife of their products and packaging.

In terms of clients, Lori often starts with finding out why they chose to work with her. While Lori's clients can learn all they need to know about her company from her website, she also makes it clear that she's happy to answer any questions that they might have.

Although the driving motto for her customer service approach is to "always go the extra mile," she also likes to find out how willing clients are to discuss issues and make compromises or accommodations if they ask for something that might take longer or cost more than they expected. While Lori understands how important the dress is to brides, she has "no patience for divas or Bridezillae" and will turn away customers that become angry, abusive, make unreasonable demands, or are otherwise disrespectful of her time and labor costs. Her policy of not working with "disrespectful divas" or allowing a hostile work environment demonstrates Lori's commitment to honoring herself and her assistants. "By rewarding kind practices and considerate behavior, I help to promote the sort of interaction that helps the world to be a better place," says Lori.

Community: According to Lori, there isn't a strong socially responsible or green local business community in Central Pennsylvania. "The values are much more conservative than progressive, and the wedding-industry SMEs here don't seem to really care so much about social justice," she explains. "There's a lot of potential for education but change comes slowly."

However, the lack of a well-developed, socially progressive local business community has not stopped Lori from becoming involved in planet-friendly activities at a personal level. She's involved primarily with an eco-action student group at the local university campus that has been active in trying to get legislation passed to protect the environment (banning fracking), reduce the use of plastic cutlery on campus, and initiate community-wide composting collection. In addition to her environmental activism, she donates 5% of her annual gross income to charities with an environmental or humanitarian focus.

Planet: Lori's planet friendly actions embody the "Reduce, Reuse, Recycle" mantra. She keeps waste to a minimum (and therefore out of landfills) by using every scrap of fabric and giving away what she doesn't need either to people she knows or through the Freecycle Network (freecycle.org). For example, before she switched to collecting and storing inspirations digitally, Lori gave her old magazines to schools for art projects. Food quality bags are given to vendors at farmers' markets to reuse or repurpose. She also uses Freecycle to acquire items she may need.

Lori tries to create every dress using as little new fabric as possible. She won't use synthetic materials (e.g., petroleum-based fabrics like polyester or rayon) or new silk. In the recent past, she has used hemp silk, which is a blend of hemp and deserted silk worm cocoons (i.e., the silk worm had already left the cocoon under its own volition), but she's now moving away from this choice of fabric due to the carbon footprint attached to importing the fabric from China and her concerns about questionable labor and business practices. She's now transitioning to using either reclaimed natural fabrics or U.S.-grown, organic, Fair Trade cotton.

Lori reuses all packing material and reuses old sheets as pattern pieces. She also uses her own printer, recycled paper, and recycled ink cartridges to create her business stationery and marketing materials. (For a complete list of Lori's planet-friendly S-R practices, check out her website.)

S-R advantage: S-R practices such as using reclaimed fabric and finding ways to reuse, repurpose, or recycle waste means that there's less material going to landfills which, in turn, is better for the planet. Lori's S-R practices also cut down on clutter and garbage in her studio and work environment. Furthermore, reducing waste and making dresses from reclaimed fabric and only minimal amounts of new fabric reduces supply costs and saves her business money.

Lori also finds that working with natural fabrics and threads is much easier on her eyes and skin than working with synthetics. In addition to the environmental and health benefits, Lori has also gained the trust of her clients and colleagues through her ethics and practices. She has found a very supportive, worldwide community of businesses and entrepreneurs who think as she does. Says Lori, "We're all together and united by a common purpose."

At a personal level, Lori also gets enormous satisfaction from the knowledge that she's doing right. Believing in what she's doing because it matters makes her more productive in that she feels like what she's doing contributes to making a better world.

Transformative power of an S-R business: Her philosophy, which she shares on her website, and her practices serve as both a model and inspiration for clients and other entrepreneurs alike.

Words of wisdom: Lori is a big proponent of practicing what you preach and putting your personal values into your products and services. "If you don't believe in your product, prospective clients will go elsewhere and the greenwashing will reflect badly on S-R enterprises in general." Beware of greenwashing and happy-talk, warns Lori. "Walk your talk and be honest. Keeping one's integrity is the only way to truly be successful in business. Do what you truly love—not merely what will sell. You will feel better about your business and thus be willing to work as hard as you need to [in order to succeed]."

Lori recommends reading the book *The E-Myth* (1995, e-myth.com) by Michael E. Gerber, as it provides timeless advice for running a business.

Service is the golden rule of running an S-R business. "Always, always, always go the extra mile for a client," Lori advises. "And always say 'thank you' in every business interaction possible. Give honest but constructive feedback and ask for the same. Praise others' excellent work lavishly; put your praise in writing and make sure it's sent to where it would do the most good."

Changing the world starts with you. "You as the business owner are every bit as important and worthy of care as your employees and colleagues, so be gentle to yourself and give yourself the best work environment you can," says Lori. "It will reflect not only in your products but in your quality of life."

Linh Truong, The Soap Dispensary

Location: Vancouver, British Columbia, Canada

Product/Service: Refill stations for a variety of premium quality, eco-friendly cleaning and personal care products; other lines of personal care and household products made from natural, biodegradable materials.

Company start date: October 2011

Company website: thesoapdispensary.com

Bio: The Soap Dispensary is Linh's first business. Before opening shop, Linh worked primarily as a painter and gained invaluable experience through her side jobs in a diverse array of sectors, ranging from retail and office administration to teaching English abroad and professional cat-sitting. Linh's eclectic experiences and her arts training have all informed her business philosophy and practices, from customer service, operations, and administration, to the aesthetic and design choices for the shop.

Inspiration: Both Linh and her life partner are passionate about living a sustainable lifestyle, which includes keeping the amount of disposable goods and other waste to a minimum. When they moved to Vancouver from Victoria, they missed the refill store that they frequented in that city and couldn't find a similar store in Vancouver. Fortunately for the Vancouverites who care about reducing the amount of plastics and disposable packaging in their own lives, Linh and her partner turned their unmet need into an opportunity to create a niche business: a refill store that allowed customers to use their own containers to stock up on many of their favorite brands of detergents, cleaners, and personal care products.

Business philosophy: The Soap Dispensary has three main purposes: Sell soaps, cleaning products, and personal care products in a sustainable format (i.e. refillable and with as little packaging as possible); carry good quality, eco-friendly cleaning products that are gentle on the body and planet; and bring in products that help customers shift to a less disposable lifestyle by encouraging them to reuse their plastic or glass containers, use renewable resources (or use existing resources), and reduce the amount of packaging in their lives.

Social Responsibility in Action

Overall: Linh's personal values and practices have shaped her core business practices. Her overarching goal is to help others choose reducing and reusing over recycling, and to offer sustainable, eco-friendly products. As much as possible, Linh chooses suppliers who are willing to let her reuse the containers in which products are shipped to the store. While not all of her suppliers are local, many of them are because Linh finds that smaller, local suppliers sometimes have more flexibility in how they work. She also asks that suppliers disclose the ingredients in their products, so she can be sure that the products are, in fact, gentle on both people and the planet.

On the social dimension of social responsibility, Linh coordinates workshops on self-sufficiency skills—often in partnership with value-aligned organizations, such as the David Suzuki Foundation or other local small businesses. The topics for her workshops range from how to make soaps and cleaning products, to how to reuse or repurpose various items.

People: While many of Linh's customers are sustainability-savvy, some first-time customers off the street may not always be aware that while recycling does ultimately reuse the materials, it still requires considerable resources (energy and water) and that it's better to reuse existing containers.

Linh and her partner educate customers and offer them a new way to think about the value of purchasing sustainable, reusable products, rather than disposable goods. "We educate our customers and we build relationships with them. We learn from them, and in the course of general discussions and conversations with them, we find out about experts in all kinds of fields," Linh explains. "We also engage with our customers by tracking the number of bottles they are getting refilled and are keeping out of landfills or recycling depots by reusing the containers."

Learning and listening to customers extends to Linh and her partner taking their clients' concerns and recommendations seriously. "We bring in recommended products and will research products for clients," she says. "For example, we had a few customers asking for toothpaste alternatives, so we did some research and eventually found a local company (Royal Herbs) that agreed to let us bring in the product in a refillable format."

Community: While practicing the "3 Rs" is a major component of a sustainable life, learning new skills that enhance one's ability to be self-sufficient is also a key part of the process. What better way to empower others with useful new skills and reach out to the community than by attending community events and inviting community members to participate in fun yet educational workshops at the store? Linh has partnered with value-aligned nonprofits to present workshops and has donated workshop fees to the organizations. For example, The Soap Dispensary partnered with "the Queen of Green" from the David Suzuki Foundation to give a workshop and talk on homemade, green cleaning products. On other occasions, Linh has collaborated with other like-minded, small, local businesses to present workshops and talks. It's a strategy that not only provides some publicity for the other companies, but also indirectly contributes to the increased wealth of other local businesses by expanding those companies' networks and customer base through referrals.

Planet: The Soap Dispensary doesn't just provide a place for customers to reuse their plastic containers—the company also engages in the same practice with its suppliers. Linh has agreements with her suppliers that allow her to use refillable containers for the various products stocked by The Soap Dispensary. Containers that can't be reused often get repurposed in some creative way that further help to reduce waste. In one such case, Linh used the plastic containers from a supplier to make indoor bokashi composting containers that rely on a certain type of microbacteria rather than worms to break down organic waste material. (For more information about bokashi composting, visit http://www.bokashicompostinghq.com/what-is-bokashi-composting/.)

In order to support customers in moving to a less disposable, plastic-ridden lifestyle, Linh stocks cleaning supplies made from natural, sustainable resources, such as bamboo, wool, and other natural fibers. The business is also committed to stocking eco-friendly products.

In keeping with their policy of minimal waste, The Soap Dispensary aims for as little packaging as possible; what can't be reused then gets recycled so the burden isn't passed along to customers.

S-R advantage: With its commitment to reducing the amount of materials that end up in either the waste or recycling systems through reusing and repurposing items, The Soap Dispensary produces very little garbage. Not only is the zero or minimal waste policy a good business model, it also translates into savings for the business since commercial properties in Vancouver have to arrange and pay for a private waste disposal service to remove their garbage. Although the commitment to reusing containers from suppliers and offering full service refills to customers often seems to create more work (e.g., washing and cleaning containers) and takes more time in the short run, in the long run these practices yield more savings for both the planet and the business and better quality control.

Transformative power of an S-R business: Driven by the same principles that inspired *The Story of Stuff* (storyofstuff.org), the owners of The Soap Dispensary engage with, educate, and empower their customers to practice more sustainable consumer habits. "We are generally changing people's shopping habits by getting them to pause and think before automatically buying a plastic product." In the eight months since the store opened, Linh has noticed that customers take several business cards so that they can refer other people to the store. She also observed that in the hopes of shifting others' shopping habits, regular clients buy presents for family members and friends as a way of introducing them to the shop's cleaning products or tools. She's also seen the emergence of buying groups from communities outside Vancouver. Linh explained that members of the buying groups take turns coming into the store to refill products for other group members.

Words of wisdom: Never scrimp on your market research. According to Linh, "What helped us was to do lots of market research and engage with the community. We did a survey before we completed our business plan."

Social media has also had a huge impact. "We've found that using social media is very effective for finding out what people want and for promoting the company." The Soap Dispensary has a blog, a Facebook page, and a Twitter account.

Finally, Linh advises others to commit to transforming their business. You may face innumerable challenges at first, but the payoffs are enormous in the long run. "You have to really believe in the enterprise. You can't just do it because being green is the latest trend—you have to actually live it and believe in it," she says. "Our business practices are an extension of, and inherent to, our personal practices. It's a lot of work, but it has also been a long time since I've found something that's so energizing, so I find the extra energy."

Nancy Wahl-Scheurich, LittleFootprint Lighting

Location: Santa Cruz, California, U.S.

Product/Service: Littlefootprint Lighting is a lighting manufacturer dedicated to reducing the carbon footprint of lighting. They do this by producing an LED desk lamp that uses only a fraction of the energy used by conventional lamps. The lamp is made in the U.S. from recycled e-waste and steel.

Company start date: February 2009

Company website: littlefootprintlighting.com

Bio: Nancy Wahl-Scheurich draws on more than twenty-five years of sales and marketing experience, having held key roles in international product management, international sales, and international marketing in the software industry. Prior to founding her company, Nancy served as vice-president of International Sales at General LED. Nancy is a LEED Accredited Professional and a member of the U.S. Green Building Council. She earned a BA in Inter-American studies and French and a BS in business administration at the University of the Pacific. She has an MS in Marketing from California State University Long Beach. Nancy is fluent in Spanish, French, and German.

Inspiration: Nancy fell in love with light-emitting diode (LED) lighting and the energy efficient technology behind them when she worked at General LED in a marketing position. What Nancy loves about LED lighting is that it can be aimed carefully, so light and energy doesn't dissipate everywhere. Other benefits of LED lighting are that it's directional, it doesn't create heat, and one bulb that's used eight hours per day can last up to fifteen years.

One thing that she noticed while working at General LED was that while the LED technology was green, it didn't pay attention to the sustainability of the entire product cycle. While taking a course to find out how LED lighting fit into LEED, Nancy discovered that companies could get LEED points for using recycled materials and for energy savings by using energy efficient task lighting indoors.

After Nancy left General LED, she had a "light bulb" moment, and she decided to start a company that manufactured task lighting from recycled materials (e.g., e-waste and scrap metal) and used LED light bulbs.

Business philosophy: The company's philosophy is to have as little impact on the environment as possible in terms of the materials, processes, and suppliers it uses. Nancy works on the premise that if the greenest option is too expensive, then they'll opt for the next best choice. As Nancy points out, "it doesn't make any difference [being green] if no one can afford the product." Her company wants to make the greenest product possible and still keep it affordable.

Nancy also feels very strongly about supporting green jobs in the U.S. and doesn't buy the myth that the U.S. has to send manufacturing overseas. Her company's approach is to build the cost of manufacturing in the U.S. into her business process and price.

Social Responsibility in Action

Overall: In the near future, LittleFootprint Lighting intends to change its structure from a C Corporation to a B Corporation, which will enable Nancy and her partners to make decisions without maximization of profits being the major consideration. LittleFootprint Lighting is currently certified as a Bronze Level Green America Green Business. Their S-R strategies focus primarily on various people, community (local business), and planet friendly activities.

People: LittleFootprint Lighting offers its employees health insurance and telecommuting options. The company is supportive of families and offers both family time and flexible work arrangements. Because shared values are important to Nancy and her partners, they invest a lot of time and energy into personally finding and cultivating relationships with their suppliers. For example, "finding an injection molding company for the lamp bases took a while because some of them didn't 'get it' when it came to sustainability," says Nancy. Nancy observes that often companies don't follow best practices because they don't have the knowledge, so while she won't work with suppliers who don't get it (and don't want to understand), she'll consider working with suppliers who get what her company is about and are open to incorporating sustainable business processes.

When Nancy was interviewed for this book in February 2012, LittleFootprint Lighting had not yet sent out its first shipment of task lamps, but customers were already contacting them to place orders. According to Nancy, "[Customers] like us because we practice what we preach, and because we educate them about sustainable lighting." Since starting, Nancy and her business partner have reached out to government, the hospitality industry, and green builders for sales. The product appeals both to individuals who care about the environment and to companies who recognize the positive value of incorporating sustainable practices and products into their organizations.

Community: LittleFootprint Lighting is a member of the Think Local First organization in Santa Cruz, California. As with other BALLE networks and affiliated networks, the organization strives to build the local economy by supporting local businesses. Although LittleFootprint Lighting does have to go a bit outside of the local area for some of the product's components, Nancy and her partner bank with a local credit union and choose local companies in the Santa Cruz area for their printing and PR needs.

Nancy also currently volunteers her time on a weekly basis with an organization that mentors youths at risk and young former inmates—males between eighteen and twenty-five years of age—and helps them find better alternatives than returning to criminal activity. Nancy indicated that when they have more employees, the company will create a program that lets employees donate time for volunteer or community engagement activities. In addition to donating money to causes once the company starts to earn revenue, Nancy has a vision for how she'd like the company to give back to the community. She'd like to start a nonprofit organization that creates meaningful work for former inmates and at-risk youth, giving them work to manufacture electrical products that are currently made overseas.

Planet: In keeping with their company's name and their desire to minimize their carbon footprint as much as possible, Nancy and her business partner were determined to manufacture the task lamps in California and to source as many raw materials and components from as close to home as possible. Manufacturing closer to the company's key markets means less fuel is used to get the products made and into the hands of customers. Not only is most of the production either local (i.e., in California) or within the U.S., most of the materials (recycled e-waste and reclaimed steel scraps) and components are also sourced from within the state. About 80% of the materials used for making the desk lamps are sourced from within the U.S.

In addition to finding ways to minimize the footprint of their manufacturing process, Nancy and her partner also keep the company's footprint small through the following practices: choosing to work as a virtual team and thereby avoid using energy to power a separate office; working with the shipping firm UPS to attain carbon-neutral shipping; paying attention to the entire product lifecycle (cradle to cradle); responsibly disposing of their e-waste by ensuring that it doesn't go to a recycling company that then dumps the waste in a developing country; and measuring their carbon footprint through CleanMetrics; and setting up a process for purchasing carbon offsets to ensure that their manufacturing and sales activities are carbon-neutral.

S-R advantage: Nancy noted that choosing to do the right thing and refusing to take shortcuts has often made the process of setting up and running LittleFootprint Lighting a little difficult. Initially, there were challenges when it came to finding the right suppliers. But, as she's also quick to point out, "We started out as a company with a passion for the environment, so we wouldn't do it if we didn't believe in it."

Transformative power of an S-R business: LittleFootprint Lighting transforms its customers both through education and by giving them the option to make a difference by purchasing a product that's sustainably made, energy efficient, and lasts for a long time. The company has also positively affected other companies through its willingness to work with and educate some of its suppliers about environmental best practices. The business has also provided its founders and employees with an opportunity to do something that has a positive impact on both the planet and local economy.

Words of wisdom: Walk your walk. "Don't greenwash; don't take shortcuts," says Nancy.

THREE: Social Capital and Social Impact on Your Community

ANOTHER significant way your small business can become more socially responsible is in the way you contribute to or give back to your community. "Community engagement" has long been a popular corporate social responsibility (CSR) strategy for big businesses. For example, Campbell Soup earmarked around US$10 million for a five-year community revitalization effort to clean up local parks, restore aging buildings, and fund community programs in neighborhoods around its headquarters in Camden, New Jersey.[1] The Ford Foundation, which provides fellowships to graduate students in twenty-two countries owes its funding to the millions of dollars provided by the Ford Motor Company.[2] As one of the largest credit unions in Canada (it has nearly half a million members), BC-based Vancity Savings Credit Union (vancity.com) contributes to the well-being of local communities through grants and community investment initiatives as well as through its powerful advocacy for social justice and environmental issues. For example, earlier this year, Vancity Credit Union contributed CAD$1.2 million to support a local nonprofit foundation's capital campaign to break the cycle of homelessness in Vancouver.[3] Most recently, the financial institution issued a press release stating its support for the World Wildlife Fund's campaign to protect the Great Bear region in northern BC.[4]

For microentrepreneurs, community engagement must take a much more subtle form. Microentrepreneurs, who face a different set of challenges, must sometimes be creative in how they become more involved and give back to their communities. In this chapter, you'll meet several microentrepreneurs who wield an influence beyond their neighborhoods and borders. Take José Alejandro Flores, the proprietor of VOS Flips. For José, community engagement means giving back to the communities that work on Guatemala's rubber tree plantations where he sources the raw material for his company's flip-flops and sandals. A large share of the company's humanitarian and philanthropic giving is directed toward improving the living conditions of the rubber tree plantation workers. Working with two local NGOs, Gremial de Huleros (gremialdehuleros.org) and AgroSalud (agrosaludguate.org), VOS provides health care, including vaccinations and on-site health advocates; education, such as hygiene and family life lectures; and empowerment initiatives. Back in the U.S., VOS works with partner organization Soles4Souls (soles4souls.org), a charity that collects new and used shoes from footwear companies and through donations, and then distributes these shoes to people in need around the world.

Joe Staiano, who runs Seattle-based Meaningful Trips, also works with communities at home and abroad. Joe leads travel groups on tours around the world, often to exotic destinations in developing nations. Unlike other commercial tour operators who shield travelers from the poverty and social ills found in many travel destinations, Joe encourages his group to become more engaged with local communities. Whether he has his tour group working on hands-on volunteer projects, or raises their awareness of the links between social ills, like illiteracy and poverty, Joe's mission is to forge an unforgettable and one-of-a-kind travel experience that changes the lives of both visitors and local communities.

An example of a Meaningful Trips itinerary is the Annapurna Sanctuary trip, which includes trekking in the Annapurna section of the Himalayas in north-central Nepal and a visit to a local NGO that trains women trekking guides. Travelers learn how the NGO provides livelihood and employment opportunities for Nepalese women and their families. Inspired by their experiences, people in Joe's travel group have often returned home from trips to organize fundraisers for the organizations they were exposed to on their tours. Joe connects travelers through their shared experiences abroad, and he actively encourages his clients to stay in touch with each other and to follow global development issues. Joe also participates in various LinkedIn discussion groups on global development and women's issues.

From his home base, Joe regularly makes connections with community organizations and fellow tour operators through his consulting work on participatory and community-based tourism. Joe provides consulting services that include exploring the links between travel and global development issues, helping tourism businesses plan their strategy and assess their social, environmental, and economic impacts, and developing training programs in customer service and hospitality.

He also volunteers and speaks at conferences organized by regional tourism associations, such as Sustainable Travel International and Adventure Trade Travel Association, and works with local tourist boards and NGOs to assess economical, social, and environmental impacts of tourism initiatives. He's a signatory of the ECPAT (Ending Child Prostitution, Pornography and Trafficking of Children for Sexual Purposes) Network's Code of Conduct intended to put a stop to the sexual exploitation of children in travel and tourism and the associated crimes of trafficking, child prostitution, and child pornography. Joe recognizes that "charity begins at home," and he makes a point of volunteering locally and donating to global giving projects that target poverty and hunger in the U.S.

You'll also learn about a few entrepreneurs who stay closer to home, choosing to focus their social giving on local projects and causes. For example, James Castro-Edwards of Greenstack Ltd. initially decided to get his company's vertical plant hangers manufactured by a locally established social enterprise. The organization that Greenstack Ltd. worked with provided employment opportunities for individuals who are unemployed and not in school. When James and his partners realized the scale of production was going to exceed the capacity of the social enterprise, he and his partners searched for another local, ethical manufacturer with a good record for giving back to its employees and community. James and his company also engage with the local community through various educational programs, such as the Conserve B campaign (conserveme.org), an environmental initiative that raises public awareness of the decline in the bumblebee population in the U.K. and its impact on local ecosystems.

In this Chapter...

As a socially responsible business, you'll want to ensure that your business adds to, rather than detracts from, the economic and social well-being of your community. Whether you're a storefront operation such as a retail business or local café, a service-based business operating from commercial property, or a solopreneur with a home-based enterprise, your company, for better or worse, will have a social and economic impact on those around you. Even if you conduct 99% of your business online from your home office, your company is still a part of the wider community and your choices as to where you buy your supplies or go for coffee may have a bigger impact than you might expect.

In this chapter, we'll address questions about your potential social and economic impact, such as:

- Does your business add to the overall vibrancy and quality of life in the area?

- Does it contribute to local economic growth by providing jobs, generating—and sharing—wealth, and supporting other local businesses?

- Do you give back to the community through donations of time or money?

- Does your business participate in community engagement activities that help to strengthen the social and environmental fabric, as well as the economic well-being of the community?

We'll consider the social and economic impact of your business and how your business can engage its communities in financial and nonfinancial ways.

Your Money as a Vehicle for Change: Financial Ways to Support Your Community

We're often told that one of the most powerful ways to bring about economic and social change is to vote with our wallets. There are a number of ways you can put your money to good use as a vehicle for social change, both locally and globally. One way of sending a clear message to the finance and investment sectors, for example, is to support and patronize ethical investment funds, sustainable banks, and local organizations.

Admittedly, it's often easier just to keep going along with what works. For example, you may feel wary about devoting some portion of your retirement account to socially responsible funds that only have a few years of performance data, or you may like using your commercial bank for the interest rates they give you. But in the long run, if you've worked hard to build a socially responsible business, it would make more sense to keep that money circulating in a business network that shares your values.

Here are a few suggestions that you can begin exploring for the long term:

- **Investments:** Use a portion of your income from your business to invest in ethical mutual funds or other socially responsible investments (SRIs). Alternatively, buy stocks in publicly traded companies with a solid reputation for social responsibility.

- **Banks:** Choose a local, regional bank or one that supports sustainability issues. Yes, there are financial institutions committed to investing in sustainable development projects for underserved people and communities. Check Global Alliance for Banking Values (gabv.org) for a list of sustainable banks.

- **Donations:** Donate to local or international organizations that make a positive difference in the world through their programs and whose mandates align with your company's vision and mission. Donations through your business can be either financial or "in-kind."

- **Contributions to Community Foundations:** Consider making contributions to regional community foundations that provide grants for various social programs or social enterprises. In Vancouver, one example is the SE Portfolio grant program, administered through the Vancity Community Foundation (vancitycommunityfoundation.ca).

- **Grant Partnerships:** Work with a community foundation and/or a local credit union to create either a small grant or partnership program that supports other socially responsible businesses or "enterprising nonprofits," which are for-profit enterprises connected to a nonprofit organization.

Giving Back

Roughly one-third of the microentrepreneurs I spoke to have contributed cash or in-kind donations to organizations and causes they support. The Soap Dispensary's Linh Truong has donated to several local environmental organizations since she started her business in October 2011. If she partners with an organization, such as the David Suzuki Foundation's "Queen of Green," to offer a workshop or event at her store, Linh will usually donate the workshop fees to the organization. Julie Beyer, owner of For the Love of Food, employs a similar strategy. She donates the proceeds from her open houses (admission by donation)—an event where people can sample the various goodies from her GLOW collection and learn about their nutritional benefits—to various local organizations.

Other microentrepreneurs decide to donate a percent of their revenues, or a percent of the cost of their products to values-aligned community organizations. Joanne Chang, the owner of Vancouver-based Nice Shoes, a vegan shoe store, plans "giveaway weekends" where she gives 10% of her sales revenue from that weekend to a local, values-aligned organization. Saul Brown of Saul Good Gift Co. has implemented a "Gifts that Give Back" program where a 1% donation is integrated into the gift: The recipient of the gift basket can choose to make the donation to either SOLEfood Farm (1sole.wordpress.com), an inner city urban farming organization; Canopy (canopyplanet.org), an environmental organization that saves old growth forests; or Engineers Without Borders (ewb.ca), the Canadian chapter of the international organization that designs and implements sustainable engineering projects.

Joe Staiano has pledged 1% of his year-end net profits to a Meaningful Trips Trust, which then goes to one or more of the several nonprofits that Joe's company supports.[5] Lori Del Genis, owner of Conscious Elegance, has pledged to donate 5% of her gross annual income to charities with an environmental or humanitarian focus.

If you're experiencing some lean financial times, it's admittedly difficult to make contributions to any kind of fund that requires regular contributions. Likewise, unless your microbusiness is well established and consistently generating a healthy net revenue, it won't be feasible to make a sizable donation or contribution to a community foundation or grant program that supports social programs or social enterprises. With a little bit of planning and budgeting, however, it's probably feasible to set aside a small fund to donate to a local or international organization whose mandate and projects either align with your vision and mission or inspire you.

We'll learn how to deal with the unsettling disconnect between what you would like to do and what your resources allow you to do in Chapter 6. For now, you might want to consider another way you can put your money to work: supporting your local economy by buying and sourcing from local businesses.

Supporting the Local Economy

While it's true that it's sometimes much more convenient, or less expensive, to purchase supplies online or through a large chain store, in the long run, the economic costs to your local community are significant. You may have clients that are scattered all over the globe, but that doesn't mean you have to automatically follow suit when it comes to selecting suppliers, vendors, contract workers, or even your favorite coffee bar hang-out.

It matters where you shop. Recent studies analyzing the recirculation of revenue into local economies consistently show that when you buy local, anywhere from 30% to upward of 50% of those revenues are circulated back into the local economy. How? Money recirculates in the form of wages, purchases of local goods and services, and charitable donations to local nonprofit organizations. In contrast, only 15%-17% of revenue from purchases made at national (or multinational) chain stores is circulated back into the community—mostly through wages paid to local employees.[6]

The Power of the Multiplier Effect

The multiplier effect works this way: If you support other independent, local businesses, this may encourage them to hire employees, which they usually do from the community. They also end up buying local goods and services, which in turn supports local businesses. The employees who work at these local businesses patronize other local businesses when they go out for coffee, eat lunch, do their banking, pick up their laundry, hire contractors for their homes, and so on. The effect can be exponential—and regenerative.

Saul Brown likens communities to complex ecosystems, with economic decisions having wide-ranging impacts on everyone in that community. Supporting local businesses or spending at big box stores affects the delicate balance of that community. Local economic support is like providing an abundant supply of water and nourishing resources to a rainforest where the nutrients and water stay in the soil (the community) and benefit the plants and animals within the ecosystem. Conversely, business that takes place mostly with larger companies that aren't locally owned dissipates that nutrient supply in much the same way that moisture dissipates out of an arid landscape where there is little plant life to trap and circulate the water. The difference in outcomes is stark. It's like comparing a rainforest to a desert: One ends up vibrant and diverse, while the other is parched and dry.[7]

It's difficult to appreciate how the multiplier effect works in the abstract, so here's how it played out in Portland, Maine. The Maine Center for Economic Policy (MECEP) recently conducted a survey of twenty-eight local businesses that generated approximately US$57 million in revenues.[8] MECEP researchers found that for every US$100 spent at a locally owned business, an additional US$58 went back into the local economy; furthermore, 65% of the expenses for those businesses were paid out to other local businesses for goods and services.

A 10% Projected Impact

If you're wondering how the 10% plays into this discussion, here's the answer: When organizations such as MECEP and Urban Conservancy and Civic Economics conduct studies on the economic impact of local businesses, they don't stop at reporting the descriptive data (real impacts in the present); they also calculate projections of how much more in the way of revenues and jobs could be generated if consumers shifted just 10% more of their spending to local businesses instead of spending their money at national chains. When MECEP ran the calculations for Cumberland County, they found that a 10%

shift in retail spending would generate 874 jobs and US$35.5 million in wages, not to mention an additional US$127 million of economic activity.[9]

Are there other benefits besides the economic? Definitely. By working with local suppliers or vendors, you can be a doubly good, socially responsible business citizen. Not only do you strengthen the local economy by choosing local suppliers, you also shrink the size of your company's carbon footprint (see Chapter 2) by reducing the energy waste that comes with transporting supplies across state or provincial lines and international borders.

Buying and Sourcing Locally

Getting involved in a "buy local" initiative is one of the best things you can do to support both the local economy and other local, independent businesses. The results of a 2011 annual survey of independent businesses showed that in areas with an active "buy local" or "local first" campaign, independent businesses saw a 5.6% increase in revenue compared to just 2.1% for businesses in areas that didn't actively promote buying from local businesses.[10]

> Getting involved in a "buy local" initiative is one of the best things you can do to support both the local economy and other local, independent businesses.

Economic benefits are only one of the benefits of "buy local" initiatives. Businesses and residents also reaped "intangible" social benefits (for lack of a better term), such as stronger connections among businesses, customers, and municipal governments, and bolstered community links and civic pride. From the same 2011 survey, 55% of respondents reported improved loyalty among existing customers, 51% observed that city officials became more aware and supportive of independent businesses, and 49% noticed increased levels of collaboration, purchasing, and mutual support among local businesses.[11] These are far-reaching impacts with even greater multiplier effects, and it's not hard to imagine how it can happen. For example, the stronger sense of community fostered through "buy local" initiatives may lead to other investment and revitalization projects in a city. The outpouring of collaborative energy and support across different stakeholder groups can have a profound impact on the community as a whole.

As one of the founding members of LOCO BC (locobc.com), a Vancouver-based alliance of small businesses committed to supporting the local economy, Saul Brown of Saul Good Gift Co. is well aware of the benefits of buying from local businesses. When it comes to his suppliers, he has a marked preference for suppliers that are social enterprises and/or located within British Columbia. Ten percent of the products he procures for his gift baskets come from companies, mostly social enterprises, located in impoverished neighborhoods such as Vancouver's Downtown East Side.

Vancouver-based Melissa Cartwright of Mellifera Bees tries to support local businesses and other vendors as much as possible. "When I need something, I always think of people I know whose values are aligned with mine and how we can help each other out," she says. For example, she purchases the spices she uses for her infused honey from a supplier she knows on Cortes Island. She knows she can trust that the spices from this supplier are organic, fair trade, and sustainable.

For Joseph Hodgkinson, the owner of Foda Catering, shopping locally for his supplies and equipment is a core driver of his S-R philosophy. In addition to the regenerative benefits of buying goods from local businesses and farms, Joseph has found that "the quality of the products he purchases is almost always far superior" to those that have been shipped across great distances. Not only is the produce from local farms fresher, tastier, and more nutritious, but the money spent on the food also supports local economic growth.

How to Find Like-minded Businesses to Support

These days, I sometimes think the bigger challenge is *finding* a local business where I can spend some of my money back into the local economy. To find local businesses to support, start by getting a list of all of the local businesses in your area from your Chamber of Commerce, City Hall, or from your public library. (Ask your librarian!)

If you specifically want to find other socially responsible businesses in your area to network with, check to see if there's a BALLE network (livingeconomies.org) or some other association for local, independently owned businesses. Also, consult B Lab's community page (bcorporation.net/community) for a list of certified B Corporations in your area, or browse through Green America's National Green Pages (coopamerica.org/pubs/greenpages) for a directory listing of green products and services.

Earning Your Social Capital: Nonfinancial Ways to Support Your Community

Don't fall into the trap of thinking that financial transactions are the only way of supporting other business owners in your community. There are powerful ways to create change and support the local economy without spending money, mainly through building up social capital.

One way to build social capital is to find ways to reach out and forge relationships not just with other colleagues in your field, but also with other business owners in your community. According to Vancouver-based holistic health practitioner Mia Kalef the owner of Emerging Families, social capital isn't just nice to have—it's a must-have for S-R-focused businesses.

> **"**Social capital is not just a great asset; it's essential for survival. It's important to find a community of people where everyone matters and has each other's back.**"**
> — Mia Kalef, Emerging Families

"Social capital is not just a great asset; it's essential for survival," says Mia. "It's important to find a community of people where everyone matters and has each other's back. It's important to find that within one's self as well." Mia believes, along with many others, that business is about building relationships—social capital. So, start reaching out, expanding your network, and finding out how you can support others. Not only will you reap the inherent benefits of operating from a place of generosity, you'll also bolster your social capital, an invaluable asset for any socially responsible business.

In this section, we'll discuss the following strategies both for finding or expanding your "tribe" and for giving back to your community:

- Collaborating with other entrepreneurs.

- Referring or recommending other businesses to your customers and other people in your business and personal networks.

- Sharing valuable business information with others.

- Volunteering your time and expertise (mentoring) to help other businesses and organizations.

Collaborating with Other Entrepreneurs and Other Organizations

Another way to give back to other local businesses is through collaborative efforts and community projects. Large corporations have often partnered with smaller social enterprises and nonprofits to the benefit of everyone involved. Microentrepreneurs can do the same, albeit on a much smaller scale.

Vancouver-based Toby Barazzuol of Eclipse Awards and Saul Brown of Saul Good Gift Co. both derive much satisfaction from volunteering with the Strathcona Business Improvement Association (SBIA) and collaborating on projects that promote social and economic development in the inner city community where they are located. In fact, Toby and Saul first met after attending a sustainability expo organized by their local Business Improvement Association. They started talking about their visions for creating a more sustainable business community, and soon their collaborations led to a number of projects. They organized another sustainability expo that emphasized the power of collaboration. They launched a business community materials exchange program to help business owners in their area figure out how to make use of each other's waste streams.[12] Eventually, they established the Strathcona Green Zone that helps local businesses maximize their value through sustainability practices. Toby and Saul also support local urban farms and a community supported agriculture (CSA) program run by a social enterprise SOLEfood Farm (sole.wordpress.com).

The Strathcona Neighborhood: Urban Revival through Business Collaboration

Cooperation and collaboration among businesses in the historical Strathcona neighborhood of Vancouver has become a catalyst for revitalization in the area, attracting the interest and investment of like-minded entrepreneurs. This tradition of investment by socially responsible businesses and social enterprises has powerful social and economic implications for a community with the dubious distinction of being part of Canada's poorest neighborhood—the Downtown East Side.[13]

The neighborhood has struggled with extreme poverty, high unemployment, and rampant crime, which transformed the traditionally working class neighborhood into an inner city "landscape of despair."[14] Under-funded shelters and social services struggle to meet the needs of marginalized residents. Businesses and families have fled.

This is gradually changing. As more innovative and socially minded businesses move into the area, drawn by economic incentives and a higher purpose, the neighborhood and the local economy is making a comeback. Programs started by social enterprises and forward-thinking businesses like Eclipse Awards and Saul Good Gift Co. have provided opportunities for many residents to regain a sense of dignity. More and more people are gradually re-entering the labor market and finding jobs to support themselves. The programs have also helped to restore a sense of civic pride and conscientiousness among residents. Programs like the SBIA's Green Zone and Materials Exchange, for example, are teaching individuals and businesses throughout the city to save money, minimize waste, and create green spaces such as community gardens and urban farms. The Strathcona area continues to transform and improve with the collaboration and cooperation of local businesses and organizations.

If you're not quite up to taking on large-scale or ongoing collaborative projects like the kind Toby and Saul have committed themselves to, you can always take on smaller projects with other, value-aligned local businesses. Linh Truong of The Soap Dispensary doesn't just partner with nonprofit organizations for the workshops she offers through her stores; she has also partnered with other local businesses to create win-win outcomes. She invites other like-minded entrepreneurs to come and teach workshops at her store, giving talks and seminars on promoting self-sufficiency skills and tips for reducing consumption and waste. It's a win-win-win for everyone involved.

Sharing the Love: Referrals and Recommendations

One of the simplest strategies you can adopt to support other businesses is to refer or recommend them to your customers and the people in your networks. If you blog or use Facebook and Twitter, it couldn't get any easier to give other businesses a free publicity boost. Of course, you don't have to use social media as your medium of choice: You can also do this in person.

When Kate Sutherland likes a business that resonates with her own values, she's enthusiastic and generous about referring people to that company, as Linh, owner of The Soap Dispensary, discovered. Kate lives in the same community in Vancouver where Linh's store is located. Given their shared commitment to leading a sustainable lifestyle, Kate and Linh easily found a rapport. Kate heard about the store and was soon shopping there. She became a fan of the soapnuts—a reusable, plant-based cleaning product that can be used to wash dishes or clothes—sold at The Soap Dispensary. Kate was so impressed with the soapnuts that she bought more to give out last Christmas.

I already had a personal connection with Kate prior to writing this book, so, of course, I was gifted a small bag of soapnuts and introduced to Linh's store. Kate had also suggested that Linh would be a good choice to include in this book. Since becoming a customer at Linh's store, I've mentioned The Soap Dispensary to several of my friends and business colleagues, too.

Sharing the Love: Valuable Information or Tips

Community-based, pro-local S-R initiatives are also about nurturing and expanding relationships through the sharing of information and skills. Helping fellow entrepreneurs learn a skill that will ultimately save them time and money or expand their business opportunities and prosperity is probably one of the best things you could do to support others in your community—and yes, that includes your competitors.

Julie Beyer of For the Love of Food happily offers helpful tips and advice to value-aligned competitors. As she sees it, her competitors "are also making life-giving products that help others," she explains. In the larger context, they're both working toward the same goal: helping to spread their ideas and values about living a sustainable life. Julie sees more benefit to businesses being collaborative rather than competitive. "We could see a lot of change in the world if business leaders really thought about where they make decisions from: love and trust or fear and competitiveness," she points out.

Finding opportunities to connect with socially responsible professionals is at the heart of Joseph Hodgkinson's sustainable business practices at Foda Catering. "I work with local chefs who share the same mentality; this further connects our network of like-minded people," he says. "This is a constant process of me learning and teaching, but also learning from my customers. Other times, forging those connections appears in the guise of mentoring young people with an interest in cooking."

Getting Together: How to Build Your Social Capital

If you're just starting out in your business, or if you've just moved to a new location, you may want to start with finding and joining an existing local business group, or attending a local business networking event. Groups and group events are a great way to reach out (and give back) to your community because they connect you with other local businesses and let you work collaboratively on projects that impact the wider community. Do some research and see if there are like-minded groups of people you could connect with, or start by asking friends and acquaintances if they have other contacts who share your passion for socially responsible and sustainable business practices.

Here are a few ideas for groups:

Recruit like-minded business and social change professionals in your business network to join a **coworking space** (wiki.coworking.com) or to start a **Jelly** (workatjelly.com) for the express purpose of fostering collaboration and modeling S-R business practices through sharing costs and resources (e.g., knowledge, experience, and contacts).

Both coworking spaces and Jellies are open-plan, collaborative, shared work arrangements where different businesses and independent professionals work alongside each other. Coworking spaces generally charge membership fees and offer amenities like conference rooms and event spaces, office equipment, and shared kitchens, while Jellies are informal get-togethers, usually in someone's living room or in a coffee shop.

Meetup (meetup.com) groups are becoming increasingly popular. Independent travel consultant Joe Staiano (meaningfultrip.com), whom we met earlier, specializes in organizing meaningful, socially responsible travel trips for travelers, but for Joe, it isn't just about organizing and leading socially responsible tour groups; it's also about raising awareness that we each have the power to give back to our communities, whether at home or overseas. As Joe points out, there are social injustices and environmental challenges at home and abroad, and people are looking for ways to make a difference in their everyday lives—not just when they're traveling. To discuss these issues with his community, Joe runs Meaningful and Responsible Travel Club (meetup.com/Meaningful Trips), a Meetup group in Seattle.

Another type of group I personally recommend is a **"Be the Change" Action Circle** (bethechangeearthalliance.org/circles/about). An Action Circle consists of eight to twelve individuals who meet for six to eight 2-hour sessions to explore their values and/or responses to a specific set of readings (depending on the circle's theme) and establish new habits that contribute to a more sustainable, socially just, and spiritually fulfilling world.

Participants use the *Action Guide* at each session to select and track one or two achievable objectives related to the following clusters of values: health and well-being; reducing material consumption; conserving energy and natural resources; reconnecting to oneself, others, and the Earth; supporting a green and just society; and, greening one's community or workplace.

For microentrepreneurs, like Vancouver-based Kate Sutherland (katersutherland.com), who see their personal and professional S-R values and practices as a seamless whole, convening or hosting an Action Circle is a great community-focused activity. "Connecting is part of my work," says Kate. "It's not hard—there is integrity to it. How can I talk about community to my clients if I'm not in connection or community with others in a way that is co-creative?"

A word of caution: With any group you join or create, you'll get to know others who also want to become change agents. However you choose to make connections and grow your community of kindred spirits, remember that you want to allow for diversity. Welcome individuals who are at different stages of exploring social responsibility in their business practices. Try widening your circle and avoid promoting an exclusive, too tightly knit group.

Mentoring and Volunteering Your Time and Expertise

Another approach to finding ways to give back to the community is through volunteering your time and expertise to groups or organizations that fit with your vision or passions. Jane Faye, the owner of the fashion business Gaia Noir, helps out at fundraising events for one of the oldest surviving music halls in Glasgow, Scotland. She runs stalls for merchandise, donates items as prizes, and performs in some of the shows produced by the venue, which she describes as "part renovation project, part re-enactment venue."

Mia Kalef of Emerging Families gives free talks for post-natal groups in Vancouver. In addition to giving his services for various fundraisers, Joseph Hodgkinson of Foda Catering also talks to high school students about his career as a chef. Toby Barazzuol of Eclipse Awards chooses to spend 20% of his time on volunteer work within his community, mostly through the Strathcona Business Improvement Association. Eileen Webb of webmeadow volunteers at her local library to help people figure out how to download library books onto their tablets and e-readers.

In addition to giving cash and in-kind donations to various registered nonprofits such as the Grey Bears, which provides food for homeless and indigent persons, and Hope Services, an organization that provides services and job training programs for developmentally disabled adults, Reesa Abrams of TechCycle3 also gives back to her community through mentoring. To Reesa, serving as a mentor is a wonderful way to "pay it forward," as her grandmother once taught her. She shares her wisdom and experience with young entrepreneurs and business professionals and continues to serve as a mentor on Mentor.net, mentoring a new person every year while maintaining contact with her previous mentees. In the future, Reesa plans to work with her community partners to develop a job-training program in computer disassembly for people with autism. The program would help reduce employment barriers for this group.

Nancy Wahl-Scheurich of LittleFootprint Lighting currently does some volunteer work with former inmates. Her long-term vision is to "… start a nonprofit that would provide meaningful work for former inmates and at at-risk youth manufacturing electrical products that are currently [produced] overseas."

Other ways of volunteering your time and expertise might include providing some publicity for an upcoming community event if writing and marketing happen to be your specialties. If, instead, your passions and professional expertise coalesce around public speaking or education, offer to give a presentation to help raise awareness about a local community (or global) issue, or advocate for a nonprofit working on issues you care about.

Finally, to become a socially responsible business that makes a big difference in your community, it sometimes means having the courage to step up and find new ways to meet a social need, or having the integrity to say "no" to a project that would potentially lead to negative economic impacts. Plantagon's Hans Hassle discovered that doing what's best for a community sometimes means making hard decisions such as turning down client requests if the resulting project would bring more economic harm than good. However, Plantagon doesn't just leave it there. Rather than simply turning clients away, the staff at Plantagon offers to help revise project requirements and specifications to promote socially responsible and financially sound outcomes, thereby generating a win-win-win situation for their clients, the community, and the company.

Extending Your Social Responsibility to the Second or Third Degree of Influence

Social responsibility also applies to finding out about the social impact our vendors and suppliers have on their own communities through their business practices and operations. I touched on this subject in Chapter 2 when I discussed how social responsibility also extends to finding out about the environmental policies and practices of your suppliers and vendors. In this section, we'll look at the broader social considerations (labor conditions, economic impact) you need to consider when assessing your suppliers and vendors' policies and practices.

To start, make sure that you know the fair labor, ethical, and S-R track records and practices of the following groups in your business network:[15]

- Vendors and suppliers both at home and abroad. (*Do they engage in any unfair or illegal labor practices in their operations?*)

- Banking institutions. (*Do you deal with a credit union or bank that has a good record for supporting small business and community economic development initiatives?*)

- Accountants or business lawyer or legal team. (*Are they on board with your vision of becoming a socially responsible business?*)

My philosophy of yoga teacher, Jeffrey Armstrong, occasionally likes to remind his students that over time "we become like those we associate with."[16] The other side of the equation is that over time, our various business colleagues are also likely to become like us through their association with us. This is another way of saying that we both influence and are influenced by others in our social and business networks.[17] At its best, this dynamic will guide us to associate with and learn from other socially responsible entrepreneurs and, in turn, inspire other business associates to start adopting (more) socially responsible business practices.

While you may not be able to change the practices and policies of all the people you do business with, the rest of the world (or, at the very least, your customers and other important stakeholders) will evaluate your commitment to social responsibility by the companies you choose do business with. If those companies don't have a good record for upholding sustainable, socially responsible practices, you risk tarnishing your reputation and credibility.

Businesses often lose credibility and customers just by aligning themselves with corporations or companies that aren't perceived as being particularly people, animal, or planet friendly in their operations. In 2009 and

2010, Nestlé, Unilever, and several other corporations received widespread criticism for purchasing palm oil from agricultural firms that cleared fragile rainforests in Southeast Asia to make way for its palm tree plantations. Both Unilever and Nestlé, along with two other multinational corporations, eventually agreed to cancel their contracts with the suppliers and seek a more environmentally responsible source of palm oil.[18] While neither of the corporations in this instance specifically branded themselves as socially responsible companies, widespread consumer criticism for relying on suppliers with poor environmental records affected their business operations.

Consider how some customers reacted to the news that Burt's Bees, a natural cosmetics company, had been sold to Clorox. Many viewed it as an unusual acquisition (Clorox is a company known primarily for its household and industrial cleaning products)—and possibly a way for Clorox to burnish its green credentials. Even though it seems that Burt's Bees is still committed to its S-R values, it lost credibility in the eyes of some deeply green consumers.

Of course, your commitment to S-R practices will also be evaluated on how well you treat people individually: your employees, contractors, customers, suppliers, vendors, accountants, lawyers, and others. We'll explore those S-R practices as they apply to your interactions with individuals in Chapters 4 and 5.

Small Steps to Giving Back to Your Community

Here are some quick-fire and long-term suggestions to get you started on giving back to your community through your business. They don't necessarily require large sums of money (or any money at all, in some cases), but they do contribute to fostering lasting social change in your community. I've adapted some of the following strategies from what I learned in the interviews for this book, as well as from the existing literature on designing and implementing S-R strategies.[19]

Community Basics: Within 3 months

- Research and implement any financial or legal processes that need to be in place to allow your company to make a donation to a registered local or international nonprofit organization.[20]

- Consider switching to a credit union or financial institution with a good reputation for supporting micro and small businesses and supporting economic development projects that yield positive social change. Alternatively, chat with your current bank's small business department and find ways to educate/encourage them to offer more community support.

- Join a business association that advocates for local, independently owned businesses and building local economies. If there's no such organization in your area, contact an organization like BALLE (livingeconomies.org) and research the feasibility of setting up a chapter in your area.

- Get involved with launching or supporting a "buy local" initiative in your community. Evaluate where you can shift up to 10% of your retail dollars to local businesses and suppliers.

- Invite staff or volunteers from a local nonprofit to set up at your business (if you operate out of commercial space) to raise awareness about any new campaigns they've just launched.[21] Depending on the type of business you run, you could donate a portion of each sale to the organization, or you could invite the organization to a staff meeting and give your employees the option of donating time (volunteering) or money.

- Sponsor a charitable event in your local community. If you don't have the resources to actually sponsor events, find some other way of making a significant contribution to events.

Strengthening Your Community Ties: Within 1 year

- Convene or sponsor an Action Circle (bethechangeearthalliance.org/circles), Jelly (workatjelly.com), or Meetup (meetup.com) group to explore how individuals and companies can adopt sustainable behaviors, or to make a tangible difference in solving a social or environmental problem at the community level.

- Collaborate with fellow socially responsible businesses to raise awareness of values-driven businesses and encourage other businesses to become values-driven. *Tip:* If you're a home-based business that provides an information-based product or service (e.g., editing, writing, web design, etc.), look into joining a coworking space (wiki.coworking.com) to expand both your network of like-minded individuals and your opportunities for collaborative projects.

- Offer to provide meeting space for an advocacy group that's aligned with your company's mission and vision.[22]

- Set up a company-wide volunteer program (let your employees choose volunteer opportunities that are meaningful to them), or contribute your own time and skills to an organization.

- If your professional skills and personal passions include public speaking, teaching, motivating or inspiring action, or writing, offer to give a presentation or produce an engaging, reader-friendly document to raise awareness about a local issue.

- Support high school career exploration programs; be willing to give talks about your profession or socially responsible business practices, or provide information interviews.

Community Advocate: Long term

- Inspire and encourage youth to step up to the S-R plate. Consider partnering with a community organization (e.g., Be the Change Earth Alliance) and the local school district to introduce (or support) a high school program on sustainable leadership skills.

- Be a diplomat and an advocate: Facilitate win-win connections between the various members of your networks.

- Support job-training programs for individuals with barriers to employment.

- Offer to mentor other micro or small business owners who are experiencing difficulties with trying to grow their businesses.

- Make a point of referring people in your network to other microentrepreneurs who are struggling to grow their business and might be facing additional barriers.

- Find out from your local community foundation, credit union, or regional small business development organization whether they have a small grant or partnership program to assist socially responsible for-profit microbusinesses and enterprising nonprofits (a.k.a. social enterprises). If you have the resources to do so, offer to work with these institutions to either set up a program or support an existing program.

- Make sure your sustainable purchasing policy includes a section on human rights and labor issues.

- Work with local and overseas suppliers to educate them about your policy and ensure that they take steps to comply with your policies.

- Consider relocating to an underserved area to help spark revitalization projects. Many big cities offer tax incentives for businesses to move in as part of their overall urban revitalization programs. *Note:* You may have to weigh this strategy in terms of easy access to public transportation and personal safety considerations for yourself, your employees, and your customers.

Conducting a "Community Impact" Cost-Benefit Analysis

If you're not sure whether some of the longer term strategies are a good fit or the right choice for your business, conduct a simple cost-benefit analysis before committing your valuable resources to going down a particular path. Assess the current state of your enterprise in terms of your finances, resources, mission, and sustainability goals, and ask yourself the following set of questions:

1.   Is it affordable given your current assets and cash flow?

2.   Does the action move you closer to your S-R goals or vision?

3.   Is it measurable? That is, do you have any way of showing that adopting a strategy produced a positive result? For example, if you sponsor or convene an Action Circle on reducing your carbon footprint, you could track how many people joined the circle, what actions they took each week, and calculate both individual and group totals for the amount of carbon emissions reduced.

If your answer to all of the above questions is "no," then clearly it isn't a strategy you want to pursue for the foreseeable future. If your response to all of the questions is "yes," then consider it a "green light" to go ahead with the initiative. If your response is mixed, you'll have to determine whether the costs (both financial and in terms of your company's brand, reputation, etc.) outweigh the benefits, or vice-versa.

For each S-R practice you decide to adopt, list the following:

• Necessary steps and strategies for each of the goals you want to meet.

• Potential challenges and obstacles to meeting your goals.

• Any support or cooperation from others required to successfully meet your goals.

• Positive or negative social/economic impacts of your actions.

Example: Evaluating the Impact of Sponsoring an Action Circle

Project Scope

Before you even solicit interest from others about starting or joining an Action Circle, there are a lot of details you'll want to figure out first: how big a time and financial commitment you're able and willing to give the group and what planning and logistics will be involved in running the group.

Participation and responsibility: Are you likely to find enough people who are interested in an Action Circle and will follow through for six to eight weeks? Who do you want to include in the group? What's the purpose of sponsoring the group? If you're a solopreneur, do you have the time and resources to manage all the planning details on your own? Are you going to purchase the reading materials and Action Guides for participants? Are you going to be the convener and facilitator for the group? How will you involve possible sponsors (to pay for food and refreshments, meeting space rental fees)? If it turns out to be a successful venture, are you prepared (and do you have the resources) to do it again? If so, how often?

Challenges and Key Considerations

Logistics: If you have meeting space on your work premises, you may have to check whether your insurance covers having additional people in the workspace. You may also have to check with the property management company (or strata bylaws if your business is located in a commercial strata building), especially if you plan on holding the group outside of office hours.

If you don't have space in your business premises, do you have access to an outside meeting space at a community center, coworking space, local restaurant, or church? If so, do you have the financial resources to take on that cost, or will you find sponsors? Is the space available for the time period that you'll need it for? Is the space easily accessible by public transit, as well as by car? Is there adequate parking nearby for people who have to drive? What will you do about making snacks and beverages (usually tea, coffee, and water) available?

Contingency planning: What happens if you're suddenly confronted with circumstances that prevent you from fulfilling your commitments? If you're called away on a personal or business emergency, is there someone else who can facilitate the group for that particular evening or week? Will they need keys or special permission to access the space in your absence? If you have to relocate the meeting space, can you give participants adequate notice?

If you're faced with an unexpected and large business expense prior to purchasing the reading materials or putting a deposit on the meeting space (for rented space), do you still have the financial resources to cover any commitments related to sponsoring the Action Circle? Do you have a contingency fund in place to cover both your planned and unplanned expenses? If not, how will you handle sharing the awkward news that participants will now have to pay for the reading materials themselves if the plan was that your company was going to pick up the costs for running the Circle?

What happens if the group falls apart for some reason? While I've never heard of an Action Circle falling apart, it's natural that there will be some people who drop out within the first few sessions. (The Circles are structured enough, however, that even if you only have four or five people left toward the end of the sessions, you can continue to run the circle smoothly; the remaining participants will just have more time to share.)

Support and Participation

Buy-in from others: Do you need the support or cooperation of anyone else—perhaps your property manager or the building security officer if you want to hold the meetings in the evenings? Some office buildings may prefer to have all business occupants leave by a certain time, or may have specific security concerns (depending on what other businesses are also sharing the building). The property managers may not allow for meeting times outside of regular business hours, or the building security services may not be keen on having to spend extra time signing a lot of guests in and out of the building.

If you're more comfortable co-convening or co-facilitating a group, you'll have to find someone who's willing to team up with you and be willing to follow through on sharing the responsibilities for organizing and convening an Action Circle.

If you have employees, will they be expected to participate in the Action Circle in some way—either as participants or as administrative support? You might think it's a wonderful idea to have your employees participate in or help organize an Action Circle, but if the time commitment is going to infringe on personal time or other work priorities, your employees may not feel the same way.

Make sure that your employees understand their participation is, in fact, voluntary on their part. If you're asking them to take care of some of the administrative details, make sure it doesn't impinge on the other work they need to complete for you. If any tasks related to helping you organize or run a circle spill into your employees' personal time, make sure they're more than adequately compensated for that time.

Positive Social Impacts

If your Action Circle is a success, you'll have introduced a group of citizens to a support network where they can find resources and ideas on making their own positive mark on the world around them.

CHAPTER CHECKLIST:

✔ Launch or participate in "buy local" or "local first" initiatives.

✔ Get to know other local businesses and support them by giving them your business as often as possible (e.g., pick the local café over the chain/franchised coffee shop if you have the choice).

✔ Find ethical investment funds that you and/or your company can contribute to; consider switching some of your existing portfolio to an ethical fund. If you have money available for a philanthropy fund, consider donating to a community foundation that provides grants to local social enterprises with a clearly defined social, economic justice, or environmental mission.

✔ Consider the variety of ways you can contribute to your community beyond financial donations, such as volunteering your time and expertise, leading or joining a community group, and forming partnerships with nonprofits.

✔ Identify and approach value-aligned local nonprofits or community development organizations and let them know you're interested in supporting them, whether by volunteering or offering in-kind donations (e.g., your services or products).

✔ Establish a sustainable purchasing policy and screening tool for vendors and suppliers.

✔ Create your own community engagement projects—and don't forget to invite others to collaborate with you on those projects.

✔ Consider joining a network like BALLE (livingeconomies.org). If there isn't a BALLE network in your area, talk to other business owners or the local business owners' network and suggest that you team up and start a BALLE network in your community. Explore other support groups such as Action Circles, Meetups, coworking spaces, or Jellies.

James Castro-Edwards, Greenstack Ltd.

Location: London, England

Product/Service: Greenstack Ltd. designs and sells an innovative wall planter made from sustainable, biodegradable materials. The wall planters enable people with limited outside space to grow plants on a vertical surface, such as a patio wall or balcony. The planters can be hung adjacent to one another to create a wall of plants, forming an attractive vertical garden, and can be used to grow everything from spring bulbs, bee-friendly flowers, or herbs, to salad leaves, vine tomatoes, or strawberries.

Company start date: 2008

Company website: greenstack.co.uk

Bio: James is a full-time intellectual property lawyer at a City law firm in London. He has advised innovators and entrepreneurs in developing sustainable products and services. He initially came up with the idea of a plant wall system as little more than a daydream. But the idea played on his mind for several years and ultimately led him to develop the product and set up a business to sell it.

Inspiration: James's inspiration for the planters came from living in the London Docklands area and commuting to work on the Light Railway every day. James explains that although the area has been gentrified from derelict docks and warehouses to a smart, modern residential area occupied by city professionals, the area is nonetheless, a hard, crowded, inner city landscape dominated by tall buildings of steel, concrete, and glass.

Traveling to work one day, he noticed how there was little in the way of open, green space, but plenty of open, vertical space: the sides of an apartment block, the walls of a housing development, or the sides of a railway bridge. James thought about how the area could be transformed by creating vertical green spaces—walls of plants.

James decided to create an eco-friendly product that would bring a multitude of environmental benefits to an inner city landscape, ranging from enhancing the visual appearance of the place and creating a habitat for wildlife, to creating an environmental buffer that absorbs carbon dioxide, pollutants, and noise, and offsets the "heat island effect" in cities.

Business philosophy: The overarching philosophy that drives Greenstack Ltd. is to offer a product that has environmental and social benefits and to make the product as good as it can be. The company also operates from a conscious decision to keep its operational expenses lean. Business partners then can ensure that their financial resources are invested in socially responsible initiatives and ensure that the product continues to be ethically made with sustainable materials. Looking to bring other social benefits to the community, James and his partners work with a local manufacturer. They also choose to invest their resources in socially responsible initiatives that promote their product, rather than in marketing or advertising campaigns.

Social Responsibility in Action

Overall: Greenstack Ltd. has adopted S-R strategies that primarily focus on the planet and giving back to the community. These strategies include paying attention to the entire lifecycle of their product, ensuring that their product is ethically produced by working with a manufacturer that gives back to its employees and the community, and investing its resources in S-R initiatives.

People: Keeping Greenstack Ltd. as lean as possible, James and his business partners choose to meet at his house, rather than putting financial resources into having a separate office. Each partner is also expected to invest their time for a share of any profits accrued. They also outsource every process they can. Maintaining a lean approach means that they aren't under pressure to make a profit just to cover overhead expenses, such as building leases, employees, and equipment.

This lean approach also gives them the freedom to use sustainable materials and ethical manufacturers, as far as possible, with the latter being a key priority for them. Their key criterion in finding suppliers is that they operate ethically. Their initial manufacturer was a social enterprise, established locally, where people out of work and not getting an education received training and pocket money (from the social enterprise) for making the planters. However, to meet increasing demand, they switched to a local manufacturer that operates on ethical principles, providing free, charitable schooling for its employees' children, and organizational funding through a percentage of product sales.

Their target customers are primarily those organizations that value a socially responsible approach. James and his partners feel that they've struck a chord and raised awareness about sustainable living and ethical production values through their company and its product.

Community: James and his partners are keen on using the Greenstack Ltd. to benefit the community, so they made a conscious decision not to invest their resources in marketing or advertising. Instead, they pursue socially responsible initiatives that promote their product by good reputation. One such initiative revolves around raising awareness about the declining bee population in the UK. Of the seventeen bumblebee species once found in the British Isles, now only six species remain. In 2011, Greenstack Ltd. started the Conserve B campaign (conserveme.org), where they donated planters and bee-friendly flower seeds to schools across the UK. Schoolchildren could then visit the planter each day and keep a log of the bumblebee species they saw. In addition to the national Conserve B initiative, James and his partners are in talks with local schools to donate planters.

Planet: One of the planet friendly actions taken by James and his partners is the conscious decision to pay attention to the entire product lifecycle and make the planters from sustainable, compostable materials. Their planet friendly strategies also extend to promoting community engagement projects specifically intended to raise awareness of environmental issues.

S-R advantage: Their passion and belief in what they're doing at Greenstack Ltd. is what has kept the venture moving forward despite numerous setbacks. "It has been a long road!" says James, "However, now we have reached the point where we are showing our product to potential customers and our focus on socially responsible considerations is starting to pay off. Feedback we frequently hear is, 'You really have thought this through.'" James and his partners are confident that the significant time they've invested in ensuring that the product is as socially responsible as possible will open a lot of doors for them in the future.

Transformative power of an S-R business: Greenstack Ltd. is just getting ready to launch their product this year, so it's too early to speak about their transformative power. "We don't think we're going to change the world singlehandedly," says James. "But if one school child participates in one of our projects and starts to think about the environment or the importance of sustainability and ethical production, we will be very happy!"

Words of wisdom: Consider your S-R values and how it may impact the sustainability of your business. "We found that people generally, in principle, agree with sustainable, ethical production. However, when in practice this results in a higher price and a less convenient product, there appears to be a significant drop in demand for that product or service," observes James. "This will result in a choice between standing by strict socially responsible values, or a compromise where socially responsible values are upheld as far as commercial reality permits. So, the question to small businesses is: How far do you want to take it?"

José Alejandro Flores, VOS Flips

Location: San Antonio, Texas, U.S.

Product/Service: Recyclable sandals and flip-flops made from sustainable materials.

Company start date: 2008

Company website: vosflips.com

Bio: José Alejandro Flores, the founder of the VOS brand, is an entrepreneur by nature. José's philanthropic principles, multicultural family background, ongoing life experiences in both the developed and developing worlds, and his first-hand awareness of the endless array of issues that our global communities face led to the simple but profound realization: Can we afford to care? José has applied his invaluable knowledge and experience gained through his International MBA and multinational corporate experiences to his vision of the VOS brand and his commitment to building an environmentally conscious, socially responsible company.

Inspiration: Wanting to help others and make a positive difference in the world is second nature to José. While traveling in developing countries, he would often give away pairs of shoes to people in need. Not surprisingly, José's passions for soccer along with his habit of giving away shoes coalesced into the inspiration to start a company that not only sold eco-friendly footwear—recyclable sandals made from sustainable natural rubber—but also made a positive difference in the lives of people.

Business philosophy: Broadly speaking, the philosophy at VOS Flips is to treat people with dignity and respect. "Social responsibility to me in particular comes back to humanizing everything, making everyone in the operation aware of the fact that we're working for something bigger than the bottom line," says José. "[It's about] finding ways to give more choices to those who don't have many choices." VOS Flips cares about the planet and communities, so the company is conscious of how the rubber plantations, production facilities, and products affect the planet, workers, and consumers. To that end, José is always looking for ways to minimize VOS Flips' carbon footprint by analyzing its logistics, sourcing, and by partnering with other organizations.

Social Responsibility in Action

Overall: In addition to being certified as a green business by Green America (greenamerica.org), VOS Flips has also partnered with the UN Global Compact, which means they voluntarily adhere to its "10 Principles" (unglobalcompact.org/AboutTheGC/TheTenPrinciples) related to human rights, labor relations, the environment, and anti-corruption. VOS Flips also voluntarily submits a report to the UN Global Compact outlining how well the company is adhering to its principles.

People: VOS Flips and their supply chain partners uphold human and labor rights related to equality and non-discrimination, personal security, the right to assemble freely, and the right to organize into collective bargaining units—all of which translates into higher standards and better working conditions for workers.

Community: VOS Flips collaborates and partners with other organizations to help translate a socially responsible vision into a viable practice. While the company also gives back to the community where its head office is located in San Antonio, Texas, José opted to make communities in Guatemala the focus of his community giving, since the materials for their rubber sandals are sourced there. José's eventual long-term plan is to expand its giving program beyond Guatemala to other underserved developing nations.

He has since developed a trademarked approach to social responsibility that he named, "Two Steps at a Time." The "Right Step" involves giving away one new pair of sandals—through their partner Soles4Souls (soul4souls.org)—for every new pair of sandals sold by VOS Flips. The "Left Step" provides health care and education services and improved living conditions for over five hundred rubber plantation workers and their families. They also provide potable water, build latrines, and provide garbage disposal systems for those communities.

To carry out its "Left Step," José partnered with Guatemalan NGOs Gremial de Huleros and AgroSalud. VOS Flips also provides various empowerment initiatives for production workers in the form of educational, healthy lifestyle, and spiritual harmony opportunities. Production workers have the opportunity (outside of work hours) to complete a high school education or get an undergraduate degree. Recreational and sports activities are available onsite for workers to help them maintain their fitness levels. Workers also have the opportunity to participate in programs that support their spiritual well-being and growth.

Planet: José set out to specifically produce an eco-friendly product. After some research, he realized that a sandal made from natural rubber would fit the bill on a number of points. First, the raw material is sustainable. Rubber trees are tapped for the latex and are often productive for over thirty years. Second, rubber tree plantations function as carbon sinks; meaning, they help to reduce the amount of CO_2 in the atmosphere and transfer it back into the earth. Third, because the sandals are made from 100% eco-friendly materials, they're recyclable. While it's true that recycling takes energy, it usually requires less energy than it takes to process raw materials.

S-R advantage: Having an S-R focused business is an advantage in itself, according to José, because it sharpens people's productivity and enthusiasm to know that they're working toward a good cause. "When you have staff members who really believe in what the company is doing, it leads to more productivity and positive outcomes in every aspect of the business," says José. "When everyone is on the same page and working for a bigger vision, the day-to-day tasks become more meaningful and people don't mind putting in the extra work."

Transformative power of an S-R business: VOS has not only further enlightened employees and workers about social and humanitarian issues around the globe, it has also shown them that business can be carried out in a positive manner and bring about social benefits on both a domestic and international scale.

VOS Flips is also helping some of their customers realize that there are affordable products in the marketplace that also have a positive humanitarian impact. "We're helping to shift consumer mindset through our products. [Consumers realize] they can buy products that make a positive difference somewhere else in the world."

Words of wisdom: "Don't ever think a business is too small to make a big difference!" says José. He firmly believes that it's vitally important for small business owners to keep in mind that even the smallest decisions along a supply chain can create chain reactions, so even a small operation can have a big impact on the world.

Patience is also of the essence. Whether you start out with a vision of creating an S-R business, or whether you shift your business practices in midstream—the process doesn't happen overnight. It took VOS Flips just over twenty-four months to identify both the right suppliers and community organizations to partner with to deliver the "Left Step" of their community giving program. "It takes time to find the right partners and make sure they're a good fit and can grow with your business for the long term," he says.

Joe Staiano, Meaningful Trips

Location: Seattle, Washington, U.S.

Product/Service: Socially responsible, adventure travel trips to exotic destinations in the developing world for small groups of four to ten people.

Company start date: 2008

Company website: meaningfultrip.com

Bio: Five and a half years into his first job after college, Joe Staiano went traveling. When he returned home from his travels, he got into the hospitality business. He enjoyed working in the field, generally, and in travel and adventure tours, specifically. During his tenure at REI, an outdoor clothing and equipment store, Joe participated in trips with a socially responsible and volunteer focus, though it wasn't the main focus of the work. After he left REI, eight years ago, he shifted to guiding more community-based trips, guiding travelers to learn more about local cultures. In addition to guiding trips, Joe also took on a number of consulting projects working with tour operators and other travel and hospitality professionals in developing countries to foster responsible tourism efforts in Africa, Asia, and Latin America. He also often speaks at industry conferences—most recently the International Conference on Responsible Tourism (ICRT) and Traveler's Philanthropy conference. Joe brings two decades of experience in responsible and adventure travel and personal knowledge spanning seventy-five countries on seven continents to his business and work.

Inspiration: The majority of Joe's travels have been to developing regions of the world and his experiences and observations inspired him to found Meaningful Trips so that travelers can both make a difference and give back to the global community while enjoying a well deserved vacation. "I believe that meaningful travel can change the world! I am passionate about the power that meaningful travel has in affecting positive economic, environmental, and social development. More importantly, we are creating an awareness, dialogue, and engagement on important issues in our everyday lives. To say that I am passionate about this industry is an understatement," says Joe.

Joe builds social responsibility into his tours at two levels: First, he applies stringent criteria for selecting partners, working with local tour operators and hospitality professionals based on their experience, professionalism, and S-R track records for environmental sustainability, hiring practices, and relationships with their communities, various nonprofits, and NGOs. Second, Joe builds experiences into the tours that provide travelers with the opportunity to learn about environmental and social justice issues relevant to the destination area through visits to (and sometimes hands-on volunteer work with) nonprofits and NGOs with whom Joe and his local tour operator partners have established relationships.

Business philosophy: For Joe, triple bottom line reporting is the minimum bottom line for businesses. In his opinion, it should be the entry ticket for running any kind of business. "It's a no-brainer that businesses should be more about values than profits. Every business needs to be paying attention to the social and environmental consequences of their business processes. For myself, there is no other option as to how I run a business," says Joe. A big part of running a socially responsible business, in Joe's view, is walking the talk—making sure that it becomes part of who you are, and ensuring that the talk is not just greenwashing.

The inequalities and poverty he has seen on many of his travels have also shaped his commitment to running a business that not only gives back to the global community by supporting projects that help to alleviate the inequalities and poverty, but also raises awareness and inspires his clients to take actions that make a difference.

Social Responsibility in Action

Overall: Joe's socially responsible business actions encompass people (community) and planet—both at home and abroad.

People: Where his customers are concerned, Joe realizes that many of his customers have never traveled outside of North America and may not know how to prepare for a meaningful trip to a developing country—or what to expect once they get there. His customers depend on him to ensure that their needs are met. Joe's customer service starts on his website where he provides potential clients with as much information as possible about the tour, including: the type of activities, level of fitness required for some of the outdoor activities, and whether travelers need a tourist visa to enter certain countries. In addition to providing the best in sights, activities, food, lodging, and guides at the destination country, Joe's trips address and lend support to global development issues, such as women's empowerment, youth, education, health, poverty-alleviation and social justice.

Joe offers his clients the best in terms of food, lodging, and guides, all provided by socially responsible tourism and hospitality operators in the host country. Joe has spent years laying down this foundation, establishing a wide network of trusted suppliers. Joe realizes how important it is to find the right partners, and he often meets, or hears about, potential suppliers at conferences on socially responsible travel or philanthropy. He asks suppliers about their environmental, social, economic, and labor practices. For example, he finds out how many women are employed by the company and whether the business has partnered with local community organizations or NGOs with programs related to supporting women's economic empowerment, social or environmental justice issues, or health programs.

Joe also notes that when it comes to working with suppliers, contractors, and vendors, it's never about price for him. He offers the following observation: "In the travel industry, a lot of people go down the price path, but it's bad for everyone, all around."

Community: Joe contributes to the well-being of the communities included in his trips by working with locally based partners. He also organizes hands-on volunteer activities (for some trips) and visits to local NGOs or community organizations to raise awareness of global development issues. Some of the proceeds of those trips are donated to the NGOs visited and a percentage of his net profits go to other international organizations (e.g., Global Giving, The Girl Effect) focused on global development issues.

Joe is also cognizant that social inequalities and poverty are also features of his own society in North America, so he also donates a portion of his net profits to programs that alleviate poverty and hunger in the U.S. In addition to financial donations, he also volunteers his time to nonprofits when he's at home. "In Seattle, I volunteer with an International Refugee Committee and Sierra Club Inner City Outings." Joe has also started a Meetup group (meetup.com/Meaningful-Trips) in Seattle to get people talking about both global development issues and local social issues.

He also involves his professional community and his customers in helping shape his policies and practices. As a member of the Global Sustainability Tourism Council, Joe uses the criteria established by the Council to make decisions about the tour and hospitality operators he partners with in destination countries.

Planet: When given the choice, Joe always chooses the vendor that has green, socially sustainable practices in place. But he also notes that it's important to look at the whole picture, and not just rely on the fact that a hotel or tour operator has attained various green certifications.

S-R advantage: Joe has a clear policy for selecting partners and vendors, and he screens them in regards to their values, policies, and practices. This has streamlined his decision-making processes and made his business more efficient. Another benefit of being a socially responsible business is the amount of positive feedback he gets from a variety of sources, including potential clients, colleges that are interested in placing student interns with his company, and individuals who offer to volunteer their services with the company.

Transformative power of an S-R business: A socially responsible tourism company, such as Meaningful Trips, not only has the power to bring about positive social and economic benefits to the tourist destinations in developing countries, it also has the power to raise awareness and inspire travelers from developed countries to start taking actions that bring about change either at home or half way across the globe. Says Joe, "This is exactly why I'm so excited about starting this business. It's not just taking someone to Nepal—it's exposing them to an entirely new culture and social issues (e.g., a 7% literacy rate among women and the inequalities that that entails). More importantly, it's about [keeping] them engaged in issues once they get back home. People come back from trips and do fundraising events for the organizations or projects they've seen."

One point that Joe tries to emphasize is how much difference can be made with small amounts of money. As an example, Joe refers to an e-mail he received from his tourism partner in Nepal. Next year, they're planning two trips—one using female guides and one that's a challenge trek to raise money for Save the Children. In Nepal, $2,500 will repair and maintain two birthing centers; $5,000 will train eighteen field health workers.

Words of wisdom: Learn as much as you can. "Seek out partner associations, industry associations, and experts that can provide you with guidelines and advice on socially responsible business practices within one's sector," advises Joe.

"Be on the lookout for who's doing the right thing; using locally sourced food, hiring women, etc. Watch to see what is actually happening beyond the official certifications."

Explore new avenues or areas where you can give back. "It's also important to look outside your market segment to find out about other ways of doing things." Although Joe's market segment is responsible tourism, he has also been involved with microfinance and other various nonprofit sectors.

Share your ideas and vision. "Think about how to engage your audience on your website or blog. Don't just see them just as customers. What I like to do is get other people's ideas. Run competitions, engage them, and get them thinking about issues even at home. Elicit ideas—put things out there for customers. Challenge them."

The sooner you start your S-R transformation, the better. "Start young! I received all this wisdom and passion to want to do things in my thirties, but it's great to see younger people getting involved...It keeps me optimistic when I see this."

FOUR: People Power – Employees and Business Networks

IN Chapter 3, I discussed how it isn't enough to just be mindful of how the businesses in your value chain treat their own employees, suppliers, and their own business networks. What's equally important is how socially responsible practices start with you and your business. As Toby Barazzuol of Eclipse Awards points out, "We're [engaging] in sustainability practices to create a better life, but why do it if we forget the human element?" How fairly do you treat the people who help make your business function, let alone, thrive? In this chapter, we'll explore what social responsibility looks like in the context of the people around you: your employees and contractors, vendors and suppliers, professional business advisors, and colleagues and other business contacts.

As a small business, there are various ways to empower others with your actions, advice, and values. Many microbusinesses are cautious about implementing people-focused, social responsibility (S-R) practices in the workplace because they imagine that those practices take the form of costly employee benefit packages, high wages, or formalized policies outlining the standards and expectations for your supply chain. Those things are no doubt important, but the truth is people-focused S-R practices can also be much simpler and more creative in the forms they take, especially for small businesses.

Consider how mentors or other well-meaning advisors can have far-reaching influence on careers and personal lives through small but well-timed suggestions. Think about the benefits of checking in with people who know the ropes or have your best interests at heart. Mentors like these can guide employees or interns in making strategic decisions in their career or life paths. For example, how might your personal finances have fared if during one of your first internships, the employer sat down with you and explained the power of compound interest and why you needed to start your retirement savings plan early? What if the employer helped you set up an RRSP (Canadian-speak for a 401K) and encouraged you to redirect part of your wages directly into that account? Would you now have a good-sized fund stashed away for your retirement? Not only employers, but customers, too, can provide feedback to help you work more effectively or efficiently. Don't underestimate the power of customers to provide motivation and acknowledgment that pushes you to do better and improves how you work.

We might not think of these kinds of behaviors as examples of socially responsible business practices, but they do reflect strategies you can undertake when working with others. Three entrepreneurs I interviewed for this book— Eileen Webb of webmeadow, Reesa Abrams of TechCycle3, and Lori Del Genis of Conscious Elegance—engage in exactly these kinds of strategies; they mentor and encourage young employees and interns, give these young workers feedback on their work performance, and praise and endorse suppliers and fellow businesses, respectively.

By taking small steps to improve working conditions and labor practices for your workers, for instance, or to provide opportunities and feedback to your suppliers or vendors, you can make a difference through your business. If you've made a positive difference in the lives of others—whether it's through finding ways to make the lunch hour less stressful for your workers or insisting that your suppliers' employees have safe working conditions and be paid a fair wage—there's a good chance those people will "pay it forward" in other areas of their lives and be more inclined to go the extra mile for you.

In this Chapter...

People-focused social responsibility is essentially philanthropy in the broadest sense: caring for and about others.[1] At its core, your business practices should reflect the following four qualities: fairness, respect, compassion, and generosity. No matter the scale and complexity of the policies and programs you implement, those core qualities should shine through. In this chapter, I'll go over simple but far-reaching strategies designed for the microentrepreneur. These S-R practices can work for a continuum of budgets, from shoestring to champagne. In fact, many of the S-R strategies described here don't require any money at all; they merely ask that we treat others with compassion, fairness, and respect—the same way we'd like to be treated by others.

In this chapter, we'll go over several strategies in detail:

- Sharing the wealth with employees or providing colleagues with opportunities to collaborate on wealth-generating projects within the community.

- Providing fair compensation and safe working environments free of discrimination for your employees and championing the same kinds of standards for your suppliers' employees.

- Treating employees, suppliers, vendors, and other key business associates with dignity and respect.

- Recognizing and appreciating employees for their work performance.

- Respecting employees' personal time and allowing for some flexibility in work arrangements (e.g., telecommuting).

- Providing opportunities for professional and personal growth whether through formal training or through mentoring relationships.

- Encouraging employees to share their feedback and ideas and rewarding them for their ideas.

Underlying many of these strategies is a genuine commitment to building relationships based on mutual respect and trust, empathy and awareness, and open communication and transparency. Developing these qualities and skills may take a bit of time, but it's time well spent if you truly want to cultivate a caring workplace and authentic professional relationships. Do consider investing some time and resources into learning or enhancing the skills that will help you become an effective leader and business colleague, whether that means attending workshops, finding a mentor or, as a starting point, reading up on these skills.[2]

Cultivating a Caring Workplace for You and Your Employees

Watching out for the best interests of your employees can be one of the most far-reaching S-R business practices you can undertake as a small business. In an ideal world, every business—and especially socially responsible businesses—would readily compensate its employees with a living wage and offer extensive benefits, including health insurance, some form of profit-sharing, and employee development.

These forms of compensation and benefits can be cost-prohibitive. The financial reality for many microbusinesses, particularly when they first start out, may make it impractical to pay a living wage, offer a comprehensive benefit package, and give out special bonuses. It can be a struggle for small businesses to stay ahead in an economic climate where the price of everything is going up. If your business falls into the boat where you don't currently have enough resources to support these practices, don't despair. With some careful planning and a bit of brainstorming, you may be able to find a way to bring your employees' salaries up to a living wage, even if you have to do it in small increments. The good news is that when calculating a living wage, benefit packages are also taken into account. Consider paying some benefits, even if it's "just" a percentage of health care insurance or a contribution toward bus passes.

While it's true that employees care a lot about salary and benefits, there are also other ways of cultivating a great work environment beyond just offering financial compensation. Indeed, for many workers, there are other aspects of the workplace environment or business relationship that they value as much or even more than high wages or having a dental plan. Consider a few perks that define a "good place to work" for many people:[3]

- Flexible work schedules and telecommuting options.

- Comfortable lunch room and the availability of filtered tap water, organic and fair trade beverages, and healthy snacks.

- Group activities that build an authentic sense of camaraderie and team spirit.

- Community engagement activities.

- Mentorship and opportunities for professional and personal growth.

- Management that listens to employee suggestions and appreciates feedback.

- Respect for work-life balance.

Fair Wages and Financial Benefits

In May 2012, the British Columbia provincial government implemented the last of a three-stage increase in the minimum wage from CAD$8 per hour to CAD$10.25 per hour. The increase was certainly an improvement for people struggling to make ends meet on CAD$8 per hour, but as the provincial Federation of Labour president pointed out, minimum wage earners' salaries are still below the poverty line.[4] If a number of small businesses (mostly in the retail and service sector) were grumbling about having to find an additional CAD$2.25 per hour in wages, one can just imagine how they might have responded if they'd been legally compelled to pay the living wage—CAD$19.14 per hour in Vancouver—to their employees.

Calculating the Living Wage

To get an idea of how to calculate a living wage, use the calculator at the Canadian Living Wage for Families campaign (livingwageforfamilies.ca/calculator/), or at the Massachusetts Institute of Technology (MIT) Poverty in America project (livingwage.mit.edu).

While businesses often cite concerns about rising costs as a reason for not paying better wages, this "concern" might turn out to be more of an excuse made out of a lack of long-term thinking than a valid fear. Business owners who offer this reasoning for not providing better salaries don't see the negative consequences of their choice. Paying low wages can work against the best interests of employers and the community and have deleterious economic and social impacts.

First, without a living wage (or one that approaches the living wage), employees often have to work two and three jobs just to make ends meet. When employees are holding down two or three jobs each, it crowds out an already tight job market.

Second, when you think about it, employee performance is intimately linked to business performance and revenues. People with multiple jobs are more likely to be chronically exhausted and stressed out, which impedes productivity at work. Low wages and poor working conditions also depress morale, which can, in turn, translate to bad customer service or sloppy work. In fact, a recent study by Zeynep Ton, an expert on retail operations, confirms what socially responsible employers have known for a long time: Choosing to invest in your employees by paying them well, providing sufficient training opportunities, and treating them well is correlated with lower prices, better customer service, and a more solid financial performance in the long run.[5] Unhappy employees are unhappy workers, and unhappy workers are bad for business.

Finally, low wage earners often have little choice but to shop at big box stores with low prices. As you know from the previous chapter, shopping at big box stores leads to less money circulating in the local economy. Less money circulating in the local economy has implications for the economic well-being of both the community as a whole and the individuals within that community.

As one large Vancouver-based employer pointed out, paying a living wage is a means of contributing to the long-term prosperity of both local economies and communities and the people who live in those communities. Paying a living wage is also a means of investing in the long-term sustainability of your business and increasing future success and prosperity. Several of the microentrepreneurs I interviewed understand that compensating your employees well and creating a caring, enjoyable work environment is a win-win-win situation for them, their employees, and everyone else (including customers) in their business network.

For Toby Barazzuol of Eclipse Awards, paying his staff a living wage was one more way of both increasing the quality of life for his staff and providing meaningful forms of recognizing and appreciating the contributions of his employees. When he decided in 2010 to commit his company to paying a living wage, he found his costs went down, not up.[6]

This may seem a bit paradoxical at first glance: How can overall costs decrease if you're spending more on labor costs? It works like this: First, paying your employees well signals to them that they're valued and appreciated for the work that they do for you. When employees are happy and feel appreciated, they're much more likely to be engaged with and take pride in their work; they're more attentive to the details and take pleasure in doing their work well. Having happy, engaged, and attentive employees results in fewer costly errors and wasted materials (and time) and a higher level of customer satisfaction that, in turn, results in more revenue through repeat business and referrals to new customers.

Second, if you pay your employees well and treat them even better, you not only attract great employees who can help your business grow, but you also retain many of these great employees over the long run. The hiring process—from advertising in a newspaper and conducting interviews, to following up on references and making a hiring decision—can be costly in terms of both money and time spent on the process. Likewise, continually training new hires gets to be costly, too. In the long run, recognizing

> **"**I pay as much as possible so employees will continue working with me at future events and be very happy doing so. In my job, the employees have to be happy, and that translates to the clients being happy.**"**
> - Joseph Hodgkinson, Foda Catering

your employees' value by paying them well yields returns on your investment that go well beyond just financial considerations.

Saul Brown of Saul Good Gift Co. had been running his business for three years when he hired his first employee. From the beginning, he decided he would pay a living wage either as the hourly rate or through some combination of the hourly rate and other benefits. Including himself, Saul now has three employees. In addition to paying a living wage, Saul's company also pays its employees' MSP coverage (the provincial medical services plan which is currently CAD$64 per month for employed adults), contributes toward a "Get Fit" program and a transportation program for employees who take public transit, and offers three weeks paid vacation.

Most of the U.S.-based microentrepreneurs I spoke to who had either regular or temporary employees also emphasized that they paid their employees a fair wage. Like Toby, Joseph Hodgkinson at Foda Catering recognizes the link between fair pay, morale, and customer service. "People who work with me are usually there because they enjoy working with me and helping make great food," he says. "I pay as much as possible so employees will continue working with me at future events and be very happy doing so. In my job, the employees have to be happy, and that translates to the clients being happy." At TechCycle3, Reesa Abrams makes sure that their employees get paid first and, when hiring, she works with the successful candidates to make sure they arrive at a win-win contract. Nancy Wahl-Scheurich of LittleFootprint Lighting pays for health insurance for her employees.

A Fun, Productive Workplace

Enliven your workspace by providing not only a pleasant office environment, but a fun one, too. Fun doesn't have to equate to visions of frivolity and people shirking at their desks. Studies have shown that a happy workplace is also a more productive one.[7] The more outlets there are to relieve stress and promote bonds among workers, the harder and more efficiently everyone works. Try holding a few fun activities during the week: contests, team lunches, outings, or even mini-social breaks. If you have contract workers who work remotely, try to schedule casual Skype chats and talk about other topics aside from work. If your contract workers are in the same city, why not invite them to a casual meeting over tea or coffee and learn what makes them tick.

Nurture innovation through open floor plans and flat management structures. The old, hierarchical, top-down structures that dominated corporate life are antiquated in today's dynamic work environment. Collaboration and openness are the much-touted ingredients in the magic alchemy to enhance worker well-being and productivity and nurture the spark that makes companies more innovative and creative. Many large companies now promote "open office" designs where cubicles and walls are knocked down and people work alongside each other. Remove the physical and psychological separation between bosses and employees and watch workers thrive. The thinking is minimalist: Take out the dividers and people may naturally become more collaborative.[8]

Do note that while an open floor plan will work for your extraverted employees, your introverted employees may not appreciate some of the by-products of increased collaboration—more noise and more interruptions. Your introverted employees will feel more appreciated if you give them a quiet space to hang out in when they need to recharge their energy levels or concentrate on a project. Aim for a balance between open spaces and private workspaces. The key is providing your workers workspace flexibility, where they can choose how to engage with one another in open, collaborative spaces, and can retreat to private spaces when needed.[9]

Smaller businesses should also consider rethinking their space and management structure. Choosing to adopt a more open style of management or democratizing the company, as Hans Hassle of Plantagon did, inspires greater levels of participation and innovation from employees, managers, and shareholders alike. At Plantagon, collaboration between workers and management is encouraged, and employees tend to think of themselves as "managers" with a real stake in the organization's well-being. The nonprofit organization part of their "companization" business model also holds quite a bit of power and has a say, through their board of directors, about the running of the for-profit part of Plantagon.

Reesa's TechCycle3 is located in a local coworking environment at NextSpace (nextspace.us/nextspace-santa-cruz). This means that employees and interns affiliated with the various companies within the space get lots of opportunities to network with other companies, participate in organized events, and get specific feedback on their work. In the same way, the open floor plan at "Strawberry Fields"—the nickname for the building where Saul Good Gift Co. and Eclipse Awards are located—stimulates all kinds of collaborative efforts from sharing ideas and resources to working on new community projects.

Employee Development and Well-Being

Provide incentives for your employees to practice social responsibility in their everyday lives. Toby Barazzuol of Eclipse Awards encourages the use of environmentally sustainable modes of transit. Eclipse Awards pays up to CAD$450 towards the purchase of a zero emissions vehicle (e.g., an electric scooter or hybrid vehicle) or bicycle that will be used as the primary means of transportation between work and home. Toby also pays 50% toward a bus pass, encouraging employees to use mass transit. He also pays employees to walk or bike to work, and, as you read in an earlier chapter, he even rewards people for bringing their lunch to work.

Saul of Saul Good Gift Co. gives his employees the opportunity to spend one workday afternoon per month volunteering for a community organization. After they have been full-time employees for a set period of time, they're eligible for a sabbatical to explore various personal interests. Saul's employees also get the perk of sampling the various edible goodies that are brought in by their artisan snack and food product suppliers.

Nancy Wahl-Scheurich (littlefootprintlighting.com) offers several perks such as flexible schedules and telecommuting. These perks don't cost her a cent, but they ease her employees' expenses and give them back some time. Not having to commute to work every day frees up both time and money for employees.

Workers also appreciate the opportunities to learn new skills and tackle more challenging jobs and tasks. Toby invests in his employees' professional development through formal and informal educational opportunities. Giving his employees opportunities to learn and grow is a priority, whether it's through giving employees a chance to obtain professional certifications, attending conferences, or arranging field trips to meet suppliers.[10] Reesa Abrams works with her employees and interns, providing learning opportunities and encouraging employees to share—and implement—some of their ideas and suggestions. For example, interns get first-hand experience honing their business development skills.

Finally, show that you value the well-being of your employees. You may not have the resources to support a sophisticated wellness plan for them, but you can implement a few policies and practices that make it clear you place a high value on their health and well-being. If you can't afford to financially contribute to a fitness pass or equipment, figure out how you can give them some time to participate in their favorite fitness activities at their preferred locale rather than what happens to be conveniently located near the workplace.

Emphasize the importance of taking scheduled breaks and having one or two minute "mini-breaks" at the end of each hour spent in front of a computer screen. It seems that humans are just not meant to either or sit or stand in the same position for too many hours at a time, so be vigilant about ensuring that your employees take adequate breaks to stand up and walk around, do a few stretches, or sit down. If you have access to a pleasant walking path or trail, why not consider incorporating a weekly walk-and-talk meeting (on nice days) instead of sitting at a table?[11] Make it a policy to respect employees' personal time while on their breaks and definitely after work, on weekends, and during their vacation time.

Leading by Example

Demonstrate to your employees that you practice what you preach when it comes to policies you promote at work. Your employees, interns, and contract workers aren't likely to buy into your S-R philosophy about the importance of taking breaks, using their weekends to rest rather than work, and being compassionate with themselves and others if they see you skipping breaks or working through lunch hours, failing to balance work and leisure, and being your own worst critic.

Remember, your own well-being is also vitally important to the sustainability of your business. You are a key asset in terms of human and intellectual capital; if you burn out or become ill, what will happen to your company and your employees? "You as the business owner are every bit as important and worthy of care as your employees and colleagues," says Lori Del Genis of Conscious Elegance. "Be gentle to yourself and give yourself the best work environment you can give. It will reflect not only in your products but in your quality of life."

Contract Workers

Don't forget that many of the socially responsible practices that you would apply with your employees are also applicable to the independent contractors you might hire. Neither Kate Sutherland of Kate Sutherland & Associates nor Mia Kalef of Emerging Families employ full-time or part-time staff, but they do hire contract-based workers for specific projects. Both women noted that they pay the fees established by their contract workers, which is often the equivalent of paying them a fair wage.

Paying Contract Workers – What's Fair Pay?

Many businesses that can't afford full-time or part-time employees decide to hire an independent contractor to help them on a project-basis. These workers provide an invaluable service for small businesses, assisting microentrepreneurs with their finances, taxes, customer outreach, media and promotional efforts, and more. Whether or not your independent contractors are local businesses, they deserve to have their skills and time respected and to be recognized and appreciated, too. The same dynamics and behaviors that nurture engaged, loyal employees—clear communications, specific feedback, an easy-going attitude, and respect for their personal time—will also do wonders for your relationships with contract-based workers. Here are other ways to cultivate a rapport:

Agree to pay a fair rate. Contractors have to pay their own business expenses (operating costs, taxes, professional fees, and so on) out of their earned revenue, and their rates reflect this. Just as you would strive to pay your employees a living wage, pay your contract workers in line with standard industry rates. Note: The exceptions to this guideline would be if (1) the standard industry rates are abysmally low, or (2) your contract workers have already established the fees they charge for their services.

Pay on time. Because they take on fewer clients than bigger businesses, many freelancers and independent consultants depend on their projects to meet their monthly business and living expenses. Delayed payments can be an unnecessary burden for your contractors. Pay your invoices on time.

Recommend their services. If you're happy with their work, spread the word and tell others about them. Contract workers often have small advertising budgets and depend mostly on word-of-mouth referrals to generate new leads. They're often looking for new clients, and your kind words can generate some much-needed business opportunities.

Show your appreciation. If your contract workers went out of their way and provided service well above and beyond what was required of them, provide some extras: a handwritten note and a gift basket filled with non-perishable organic and/or fair trade goodies, a small cash bonus, a gift card, or some other meaningful token of your appreciation.

Sharing the Wealth with Employees

How you share your company's wealth with your employees will depend upon the legal structure of your business. For example, while you might be able to provide a year-end bonus to employees if you're a sole proprietorship or LLC, you wouldn't be able to provide stock options or shares of the company to your employees unless you changed the structure of your business. On the other hand, if you're structured as a C Corporation, you may be able to share the wealth through a bonus system or through options to buy shares or equity in the company. However, like Mal Warwick, coauthor of *Values-driven Business: How to Change the World, Make Money, and Have Fun*, you may also have to contend with board members who aren't so keen on sharing the wealth through sharing the profits with employees.[12] You could also give bonuses as prizes for work place "contests"—especially if the behavior being recognized is tied to your core S-R values.

Setting the Bar: Worker-Owner Co-Ops

The worker-owner co-op is often considered the paragon of social responsibility and workplace democracy. A co-op structure is based on the values of self-help, democracy, equality, equity, solidarity, honesty, social responsibility, and caring for others.[13] It also aspires to uphold certain social and economic justice principles, including democratic member control, member economic participation, cooperation, and concern for the community. In effect, owner equity and profit-sharing are built into its core at a co-op.

This business model provides a great template for what many people-oriented S-R practices look like in action. A worker-owner co-operative is expected to share profits among its members since all have invested in the company. There's usually a minimum amount that a member must invest, often a combination of financial investment and "sweat" equity. Worker-owner co-ops not only share the profits and the decision-making responsibilities, they also strive to pay their members a living wage, provide meaningful work, and empower their members through skill-building and leadership training.

While some of these practices may be difficult to replicate exactly in other types of for-profit business structures, it shouldn't deter microbusiness owners from striving to uphold many of the co-op principles and values. Ideally, you want to find a means of sharing the wealth with your employees through an avenue that is readily accessible and available to you in your current business structure. You also want to be very sure that you choose a method that, in fact, is going to benefit rather than unintentionally harm your employees' financial security. For example, depending on the type of profit-sharing plan you set up, your employees may also find that not only are they not getting a bonus in a lean year, but that they might also be letting themselves in for a loss of regular income due to decreased revenues over the year (or quarter) due to factors over which they had no control or decision-making power.[14] Also, remember that however you share the wealth, it will be considered as taxable income for your employees.

Sharing the Wealth When You're a Solopreneur

As a solopreneur, you won't have employees with whom you can celebrate and share the financial success of your business, but that doesn't mean you can't find other ways to share the wealth within your community and your business network. Try investing some of your wealth back into your community. We'll discuss a few suggestions in this section.

Collaborative Projects

Reach out to colleagues and competitors alike and suggest engaging in collaborative projects that generate both shared wealth and shared expertise. As a consultant with a variety of interests, Kate Sutherland often approaches her colleagues to collaborate on various consulting projects, especially if she and her colleagues have complementary skill sets or areas of expertise that would increase the value of the outcome for her clients. Linh Truong of The Soap Dispensary reaches out to other small businesses with opportunities to collaborate on the various workshops she offers on-site at her store.

Networking

Act as a connector and pass on business to others. Whether you do this on a one-to-one basis, or you adopt Tim Sanders' suggestion to organize small networking meetings to introduce your suppliers or service providers to each other, sharing the wealth by making introductions or directly passing along business to a colleague or competitor will be greatly appreciated.[15] If you're a natural connector, this is an easy strategy to adapt and use as you go about your daily interactions and projects. For example, if you know you can't possibly take on a project, ask a colleague whose workflow has temporarily slowed down whether he or she would be interested in taking it on.

Minority and Women-owned Businesses

Despite the fact that women and ethnic minorities have made notable strides toward securing equal rights over the past fifty years, it seems that neither public nor private sector organizations got the memo about giving minority and women-owned businesses equal opportunities as suppliers or business associates. Consequently, businesses owned by these two demographic groups in the U.S. are defined as historically underused businesses by the U.S. Small Business Administration.[16] Look around your local business community and seek out opportunities to forge business connections with historically underused businesses in your neighborhood. Later, refer them to other contacts if you receive good service. Joe Staiano of Meaningful Trips has a preference for working with partners that support women's employment in developing countries. When he looks for tourism and hospitality partners in trip destination countries, Joe makes a point of asking about how many women they employ. Joe supports women's employment and businesses at home, too—over 80% of his support team is comprised of women.

In addition to giving a financial boost to historically underused businesses in your community, you might also consider partnering with social enterprises in your city. Many social enterprises provide employment training for individuals who face multiple barriers to employment. Through choosing to partner with these organizations, you not only increase business for the social enterprise, but you also give individuals facing a variety of social or economic barriers an opportunity to regain their dignity and confidence and a chance to reclaim their lives.

Choosing Your Suppliers with Care

By now, it probably wouldn't surprise you to learn that the microentrepreneurs featured in this book put a lot of thought into choosing their suppliers. Nearly two-thirds of the microbusiness owners specifically mentioned shared values as one of their top criteria for working with suppliers.

Reesa Abrams of TechCycle3, Kate Sutherland of Kate Sutherland & Associates, Joseph Hodginkson of Foda Catering, Jane Faye of Gaia Noir, José Alejandro Flores of VOS Flips, and Nancy Wahl-Scheurich of LittleFootprint Lighting all emphasized the importance of working with suppliers who shared their values.

Whether they make decisions based on their "inner wisdom" or intuition, use some combination of a "gut feeling" or a mental list of criteria that are important to them, or have a formalized policy they use for deciding on suppliers and procuring materials or services, they all know what they're looking for and won't compromise on criteria that are central to their S-R values or business processes.

> **Choosing Your Suppliers with Care:**
> - Aligning your values: prioritizing what matters
> - Quality and delivery come first
> - Code of conduct with suppliers and vendors

Kate chooses local, Vancouver-based suppliers with whom she has a rapport and kinship of values. José devotes time for doing serious research into the process of selecting and building a relationship with his suppliers based on their compliance with the principles set out in the UN Global Compact. Nancy also spends considerable time looking for like-minded suppliers for the major components of their task lamps. While Nancy won't work with suppliers "who don't get it" (and don't want to understand), she'll work with suppliers who are open to improving their business processes and implementing sustainable practices.

Eileen Webb of webmeadow explained that since they work closely with their graphic design partners, they start mostly with finding people with whom they get along. "We have partners who we work with on a very regular basis—like people I call up at home and talk with all the time—our graphic design partners," she says. "For partners, the most important thing has always been people we click with personally because we work very closely with them. And then, of course, it works out perfectly that the people we click with are the people who share our values."

Juan Gallardo of California-based Greyka prefers to deal with socially responsible suppliers and vendors for his company because they generally offer better customer service. "Vendors that provide a good work environment tend to produce employees who are more productive and responsive to our needs," explains Juan. "Employees at companies who are socially responsible tend to have higher morale and retention because the employees feel a deeper bond—they feel that they are making a positive impact."

Aligning Your Values: Prioritizing What Matters

Each business will have different priorities as to what it values most in a vendor. If you have little choice when it comes to suppliers and vendors, start by making a list of S-R practices you value the most. This may be a never-ending laundry list of S-R practices and values, but the brainstorming process will get you thinking about what matters the most to you. Now, take that list and circle the top five items that are the absolute requirements for you and your business. Once you have a short list, you'll feel less intimidated about making a hiring decision.

Find suppliers with whom you have an affinity. Saul Brown has a preference for choosing local businesses and social enterprises for his suppliers. Linh Truong prefers to work with suppliers who are willing to send their products in bulk, refillable formats. Plantagon's Hans Hassle requires that their suppliers have a shared set of ethical principles and practices with the company. Going one step further, the partners at Plantagon have formalized a company charter that governs how they do business with others; the charter is based on the principles drawn from the UN Global Compact and the Earth Charter. Here are other factors to consider when deciding on suppliers and vendors to hire:

Cost Shouldn't Be the Only Factor

While most businesses might consider cost as the overarching factor in choosing vendors or suppliers, socially responsible businesses look beyond price. Several microentrepreneurs I interviewed were adamant that cost shouldn't be at the top of the priority list when making a selection. According to Joe Staiano, "In the travel industry, a lot of people go down the price path, but it is bad for everyone all around." Julie Beyer of For the Love of Food observed that "a lot of businesses in the food industry shy away from investing in the higher quality and higher priced ingredients" to everyone's detriment. When it comes to purchasing edible goodies for his corporate gift baskets, as far as Saul Brown is concerned, quality outranks price as the more important consideration. "There's a big difference between mass produced goods and items produced in small batches, especially when it comes to edible products," he says.

Quality and Delivery

When it comes to finding vendors to host their customer websites, Eileen Webb of webmeadow always prefers to work with vendors that use alternative energy, but she has found that being green doesn't always translate into quality. In the past, webmeadow tried working with both solar-powered and wind-powered suppliers for their web hosting needs , but when the companies fell short in providing the quality of service Eileen needed for her clients, she chose to go with a commercial provider. Eileen describes her current provider as "a huge hosting company [that does] green stuff the way corporate America does green stuff…", but, she notes, "the quality is good." As you make your selection, remember that quality and delivery come first. "It doesn't make sense to [stay] with someone who doesn't give good service just because they're green," says Eileen.

Suzanne Akin of Akinz Clothing in Fort Collins, Colorado, chooses her suppliers based on three criteria: location, price, and customer service. Suzanne appreciates the importance of supporting her local economy as much as possible. Like Eileen, Suzanne prioritizes quality of service over other factors. If there are recurring issues with suppliers that affect the quality of her products, she changes suppliers. "I had a U.S.-based business that I worked with exclusively for my first couple years in business," Suzanne explains. "They supplied blank t-shirts that I loved at a good price…but every time I put in an order, there seemed to be an issue that would arise either with shipping times, incorrect products, or something else."

Sometimes compromising on quality becomes a liability. "After a while, it becomes a business risk to continue working with people like that," says Suzanne. She's optimistic, despite her negative experiences with suppliers, and takes the experience as a lesson in how to manage her own business. "It reminds me that others expect the best in customer service out of me for my business, and I try to keep that in mind when handling my outgoing orders."

If your suppliers or vendors are making mistakes, offer them specific feedback and constructive criticism so they can learn from their mistakes. Find out if there is anything else they need in order to implement your feedback. You may choose not to continue doing business with them, but your pointers can help them improve their business practices and customer service. Consider it a gracious act to help strengthen the small business community.

Code of Conduct with Suppliers and Vendors

Think about all of the other people who work with you and contribute to your company's success: suppliers, vendors, delivery and courier services, just to name a few. How a company treats other companies in its supply chain is a measure of ethics and can play a significant role in determining a company's social reputation.[17] What S-R principles and practices apply in your dealings with business associates? As you might guess, most of the practices are just plain old common sense and courtesy. Let's go through a few below:

Pay on Time

Pay the invoices from suppliers or vendors promptly. Don't make people wait for payment. You risk your own reputation and being dubbed a problem client when you don't pay others promptly. It's bad for your business (word may get around about your tardy practices) and makes life difficult for those companies that rely on a steady cash flow. If you're having difficulties paying your bills on time because some of your own clients are tardy about paying you, then it's time to examine your operating reserves and to implement some new payment policies with your clients. No one should have to spend their valuable time chasing after tardy clients and getting frustrated when payment is past due.

Respect Others and Play Fair

Always treat people with respect. Try not to make unreasonable demands such as asking for extras, bonus services, or expecting regular discounts on services or products.[18] As a socially responsible business, one of the best ways to show your commitment is in how you treat others. If you're always trying to undercut others just to save a few bucks, it will cost you in the long run when those businesses decide to cut ties or refuse to renew contracts with you and your business.

Be Willing to Work with Others.

Support and mentor others. Give others the knowledge and feedback that would help them work with you more effectively.[19] This is an important consideration if you discover a supplier or vendor's S-R practices don't measure up. Educating others on your vision can go a long way. Lori Del

Genis of Conscious Elegance argues for mutual respect and politeness. "Always say 'thank you' in every business interaction possible. Give honest but constructive feedback and ask for the same," says Lori. "Praise others' excellent work lavishly. Put your praise in writing and make sure it's sent to where it would do the most good." Offer to write testimonials for good work, or recommend the services or products of favorite vendors or suppliers to others.

Small Steps to Nurturing Your People Power

If you're still with me after all of the prescriptives for how you should ideally treat your employees, suppliers, and others in your business network— wonderful. If you're still wondering how you're going to pay your employees a living wage, mentor suppliers, prioritize your criteria for choosing suppliers, *and* still get your work done—relax. Remember that it's all about small, incremental steps at a pace that works for you and your company's resources.

As you've seen, microentrepreneurs can incorporate many of the suggestions listed into their business practices in various ways. Now, it's your turn. Look through the following list and figure out which small steps you can take right now to nurture your people power and which steps will need some advanced planning and preparation.[20] Don't forget to consult with your mentors, accountant, or other professional advisors to make sure you get the information that's right for you.

Business Hearth Basics: Within 3 months

- Invite a financial planning expert to talk to your employees about socially responsible investment portfolios and how to set up self-directed retirement savings accounts.

- Acknowledge your employees (or independent contractors) regularly. A reminder from Toby at Eclipse Awards: Be generous with giving professional and personal recognition to all the people who work for you and make your business a success, not just the super achievers.

- Allow for some flexibility in work schedules and arrangements based on what's appropriate for your business. Offer flex time, telecommuting, and other remote work options.

- Stress the importance of taking scheduled breaks throughout the day. Encourage off-site contract workers to follow the same practices.

- Encourage staff to take frequent mini-breaks if they spend a lot of time in front of a computer.[21] Make sure their workstations are ergonomically correct for them, and ensure they aren't spending extended periods of time sitting in front of their computer.

- Have some healthy treats and beverages available in your lunch room for your employees. Stress the importance of staying hydrated and nourished throughout the day. Be doubly good and choose organic and/or fair trade tea, coffee, sugar, and chocolate. By choosing fairly traded items, you're contributing to better pay and working conditions for the producers in developing countries.

- Respect employees' personal and family time. Don't make a habit of contacting employees (or other business associates) about work-related matters during their free time, and don't ask them to give up their free time without finding some way to compensate them for their work outside of working hours.

- Give your employees time off to participate in community engagement activities of their choosing.

- Start mentoring your employees. Sharing your wisdom, experience, and expertise, and informally coaching others to excel in their jobs, to learn more about your industry, and so on, are all cost-free yet immeasurably valuable alternatives to formal professional development.

- Encourage your employees to share their ideas on how to make your business more socially responsible.

- Pay your employees, contract workers, suppliers, and other business service providers on time.

One Step Further: Within 1 year

Within Your Business:

- Draft core guiding principles and policies that will govern wages and working conditions, benefits, professional development opportunities, etc. in your company.

- Investigate professional development opportunities that will help your employees to build their skills and career path; encourage your employees to pursue professional development options.

- Be a champion for fair wages and safe working conditions both in your own operation and those of your suppliers.[22]

- Promote a workplace wellness program. Consider collaborating with other micro or small businesses to develop an affordable, win-win package for everyone.

- Ask your employees which employee benefits they would find most useful and valuable, and implement them according to priority and when financially possible.

Outside Your Business:

- Make a list of contractors, vendors, and suppliers that serve your business. Prepare a short questionnaire regarding employment practices or matters regarding diversity, inclusion, labor conditions, sourcing for ingredients/parts, and other S-R concerns.

- Make others aware of your company's mission, vision, values, and policies in a formal document or statement. Emphasize which values and policies will affect your business relationship. Help others identify what changes they need to make to meet your conditions.

People Power Advocate: Long term

Inside Your Business:

- Aim to pay your employees a living wage. Remember, it can be a composite of both the hourly wage and benefits.

- Help your employees set up a retirement savings plan so that a small percentage of their paycheck goes directly into the account.

- Put in place a profit- or gain-sharing plan that sets aside a meaningful share of annual profits for all of your qualified employees.

- Find a way to provide employees equity (i.e., shares) in the business if the business' legal structure allows it.

- Set up a philanthropic matching gift program that allows your employees to choose where they want to make a financial donation. Better yet, give your employees some paid time off to offer a hands-on contribution, such as volunteer hours, to a local organization or cause they support or would like to support.

Outside Your Business:

- Look into joining up with other micro and small businesses or business associations to see if it's possible as a group to purchase basic or extended health care insurance for employees.

- Reach out and connect with colleagues and competitors to identify and create wealth-generating collaborative projects with them.

- Share your network and host small networking events for your business contacts and colleagues.[23]

- Support equal opportunity by seeking out and developing partnerships with under-utilized businesses and social enterprises.

- Treat your suppliers, vendors, and other business associates and professionals in your network as equals; listen to and seek out their point of view, and ensure that their businesses are also benefitting from the relationship.[24]

- Don't expect deeply discounted prices and demand "extras."[25]

- Be loyal to your suppliers and other service providers and be willing to forgive non-serious, honest mistakes.[26]

Conducting a "People Power" Cost-Benefit Analysis

If you're not sure whether some of the longer term strategies are a good fit or the right choice for your business, conduct a simple cost-benefit analysis before committing your valuable resources. Assess the current state of your enterprise in terms of your finances, resources, mission, and S-R goals, and ask yourself the following set of questions:

1. Is it affordable given your current assets and cash flow?

2. Does the action move you closer to your S-R goals or vision?

3. Is it measurable? That is, do you have any way of showing that adopting the strategy produced a result? For example, by partnering with a social enterprise as a supplier or service provider, how did that money support the organization's social mission?

If your answer to all of the above questions is "no," then clearly it isn't a strategy you want to pursue for the foreseeable future. If your response to all of the questions is "yes," then consider it a "green light" to go ahead with the initiative. If your response is mixed, you'll have to determine whether the costs (both financial and in terms of your company's brand, reputation, etc.) outweigh the benefits, or vice-versa.

For each S-R practice you decide to adopt, list the following:

- Necessary steps and strategies for each of the goals you want to meet.

- Potential challenges and obstacles to meeting your goals.

- Any support or cooperation from others required to successfully meet your goals.

- Positive or negative social/economic impacts of your actions.

Example: Boost Networking Connections

Project Scope

You've decided to support the people in your business network by giving them opportunities to expand their network and passing along business to them when appropriate. You want to introduce various individuals in your business network who might benefit from talking to each other, and now you just need to figure out how to turn this idea into a meaningful and useful event.

Connecting people: Will you connect people on a one-on-one basis as opportunities present themselves? Or, will you coordinate regular group meetings and invite half a dozen people for an informal get-together? How well do you know your business contacts? Are most of them extroverts who love any opportunity to meet with new individuals, or are they introverts with a marked dislike for any kind of unnecessary meetings? Your colleagues will be more likely to appreciate your efforts if you keep in mind what seems to work best for them. (Yes, that means you have to be observant, curious, and sensitive to the cues you get from the people in your business network.)

Logistics and planning: If you opt for holding small networking meetings, you'll have a number of logistical and financial issues to sort out. First of all, where are you going to host your event? Do you plan to invite your guests to your business premises? If so, do you have adequate meeting space and resources (e.g., a place to prepare refreshments and snacks)? If you're a home-based business, it could get a little awkward inviting business associates into your home for meetings, especially if you want to hold them during business hours. If you arrange to hold the meetings at a coffee shop, restaurant, or coworking space, are you, as the host, prepared to pick up the tab for refreshments? Does the venue have a small meeting room you can book so that you and your colleagues aren't struggling to be heard over the dull roar of a busy location?

Communication: Make sure you're clear on the purpose, expectations, and anticipated outcomes of such a group, and convey the purpose and expectations to the others in the group. You might want to spend some time mapping out who would be useful to whom and why. (This would be a useful exercise even if you choose to do the connecting on a one-to-one basis.) Like any good matchmaker, once you've made the introductions, you need to get out of the way and not impose your preferred outcome on any collaborative ventures or new partnerships that arise out of the introductions.

Challenges and Key Considerations

Conflicting schedules: How will you work around everyone's busy—and often conflicting—schedules? Are there enough individuals with complementary skills or businesses in your network who could actually help one another out? Are your various connections even interested in expanding their network at the moment? Your support and interest from others will determine how you proceed.

Keeping the group at the right size: What will you do if your guest list starts getting out of hand? If you specifically wanted to keep the meeting small because that's what works best for your temperament and resources, how will you handle guests' requests to bring more people into the mix? You'll have to be firm but decidedly diplomatic as you don't want to offend any key business contacts. Also, if you choose not to invite (or inadvertently overlook) one of your key business contacts and your event gets back to him or her via a mutual acquaintance you didn't know you had, how will you handle that situation? You might be surprised by who knows whom in your network, whether directly or indirectly.

Triumphs and Tribulations of Fostering Connections

Connecting people can lead to both positive and negative outcomes. In the worst-case scenario, it could be a disaster if those relationships and partnerships go sour as it may reflect on your credibility and affect your reputation. In the more likely scenario, the strategy can be immensely positive when it results in new alliances and partnerships that generate increased prosperity for everyone involved.

If you're comfortable with a bit of uncertainty about how your experiment might turn out, and you have the resources to give this strategy a try, why not float the idea past a few of your key business contacts. If you get a warm response, set up a meeting as a test run. Choose a locally owned coffee shop or restaurant as your venue; if nothing else comes of the event, at least you know you've supported one local business and the local economy in your experiment. Just remember the mantra: Start from where you are and take small steps.

CHAPTER CHECKLIST:

✔ Read up on co-op values and evaluate how many of the values or dimensions you already bring to your workplace. What additional values could you introduce?

✔ Establish clear policies around workplace issues—compensation, working conditions, etc.—based on your company's values. Make sure your employees and your suppliers are aware of and know how to abide by or uphold your policies and practices.

✔ Incorporate your values and standards into an ethical or sustainable purchasing policy for your company. Talk to your suppliers and other business partners so they're aware of your policy and know what they need to do to continue working with you.

✔ Learn how to mentor others effectively. Cultivate an awareness, sensitivity, and openness to collaboration that will help you nurture your key business relationships.

✔ Create a healthier work environment for you and your employees.

✔ Sit down with your employees and find out what kinds of benefits or wealth-sharing options are most important to them.

✔ Depending on your company's finances, investigate the different kinds of wealth-sharing options available to or allowed for your business structure. For example, if you're a C Corporation, meet with your Board of Directors (and business lawyer) to establish whether you might be able to give your employees equity or shares in the business. Alternatively, you can find less "formal" ways of sharing the wealth and simply award small bonuses throughout the year.

✔ Look into professional development opportunities for your employees and put aside a fund to pay for at least one opportunity per employee per year.

✔ Find out where colleagues and competitors in the same line of business gather in person and online; reach out and make contact.

✔ Identify and follow up on a collaborative project with a colleague. (For the risk-averse, start with a small project with someone you know and trust.)

Saul Brown, Saul Good Gift Co.

Location: Vancouver, British Columbia, Canada

Product/Service: Corporate gift baskets made from environmentally friendly or recycled materials and filled with high quality, artisan-made items from local businesses within British Columbia that also adhere to sustainable business practices.

Company start date: September 2006

Company website: itsaulgood.com

Bio: Drawing from his background in environmental studies, an MBA in sustainable business, and Paul Hawken's books, Saul recognized the potential to bring about social and environmental change through business. He founded Saul Good Gift Co. as a B Corporation. Saul sits on the board of LOCO, an organization that supports local businesses, and participates in the Strathcona Business Improvement Association's Sustainability Committee and the Strathcona Green Zone Initiative.

Inspiration: For some time prior to starting his business, Saul had contemplated the market of gift baskets, but he knew he couldn't do it the conventional way—that approach seemed wasteful to him. Saul describes such "traditional" gift baskets as being "filled with tiny little jam jars (made to look big) that usually sat [unused] in the back of someone's fridge."

In the interim, Saul started working in the field of industrial ecology and then began an MBA program in sustainable business at the Bainbridge Graduate Institute (BGI). Halfway through his studies, Saul realized that gift giving was about relationship building, not stuff. Gifts are more memorable (and meaningful) when the items not only have a story behind them but also support other local businesses and organizations within the community. Saul decided to start a gift basket business—and to do it the socially responsible way. "I designed the boxes (made from recycled material), and sourced local suppliers to fill the gift boxes with the best local, artisanal products," he says. Picking the name of the company was easy. "Saul Good was a nickname I'd had for many years, so I went with it for my company name."

Business philosophy: For Saul, a commitment to socially responsible values and practices is the only way he wants to run a business. From Saul's perspective, "It's irresponsible as a business not to be part of the solution. Just making a lot of money in the business doesn't mean you're successful—it has to be about more than money." This underlying philosophy that businesses need to be part of the solution and have a bigger, more socially minded purpose than just making profits translated into the decision to not only structure his business as a B Corporation but to take the steps to become, and remain, a certified B Corporation. For Saul, the existence of a third-party certification process for socially responsible businesses "helps to separate good businesses from good marketing."

On a day-to-day basis, the core driver of his business is developing relationships with and supporting other local businesses. He recognizes that there are many intricate relationships between businesses within a local business area.

Saul is also highly conscious about using environmentally sustainable materials and reducing both waste material and his company's carbon footprint. His values and practices are evident in his core operational practices, from using gift boxes made from 100% recycled cardboard and repurposing offcuts from a local printer as filler, to sharing space and resources (e.g., utilities) with another socially responsible business.

Social Responsibility in Action

Overall: As a certified B Corporation, Saul's company is expected to demonstrate a high level of social responsibility across a number of areas, including accountability, employees, consumers, community, and environment.

People: Saul's company not only pays its employees a living wage, it also covers their Medical Service Plan (MSP) payments—the health care plan administered by the provincial government in British Columbia—and gives employees three weeks of paid vacation per year. Saul has also implemented a "Get Fit" program that provides funds for up to CAD$500 to contribute to fitness classes or equipment, a transportation benefit for employees who take public transit or cycle to work, and a sabbatical program for full-time employees available to them once they've worked at Saul Good Gift Co. for a specified length of time.

When it comes to working with suppliers and vendors, Saul chooses local businesses (i.e., within the province) that meet the base level standards in his "Supplier Code of Conduct." This code serves as a starting point for discussion rather than a means of auditing suppliers. Saul's commitment to working with and supporting other local businesses is evident in his preference for choosing social enterprises and suppliers located in impoverished areas, such as the Downtown East Side of Vancouver. "Ten percent of my products are sourced from impoverished areas."

When Saul first started his business, he had envisioned his customer base being mostly green corporations. In practice, most of his clients are local or regional businesses from a variety of sectors. What they share is a set of strong community values and an appreciation for both the stories behind the gifts and the suppliers who are making a positive difference in their communities through their products.

Saul's company engages with customers both in person and through social media, including Twitter and his blog, *Stories from the Gift Box*. When Saul and his employees meet with new clients, they make a point of learning about the clients' values and organizational culture, and discovering what's meaningful to them.

That information is then used to develop a gift program tailored to those clients. The care that Saul and his staff put into developing gift programs for their customers means that, in turn, their clients look to his company for the best gift ideas.

Community: Saul's company contributes to community partners, local businesses, and social enterprises in a number of ways. First, he doesn't just do business with other socially responsible, local businesses, he also promotes them by talking about them on his blog and on Twitter. Second, he's found innovative ways to partner with other local businesses to share resources and even repurpose other companies' waste products. For example, Saul partnered with a print shop, using its paper scraps and offcuts as filler for his gift boxes. This helped reduce the print shop's recycling and waste stream and replaced Saul's need to use new paper products or plastic shreds. The two businesses then brought in a third organization, a nonprofit and social enterprise that provides job training for individuals with multiple barriers to employment. Later, a member of that organization was given a job delivering paper shreds from the print shop to Saul Good Gift Co. every two weeks.

Saul has also implemented a "Gifts that Give Back" program where a donation of 1% is integrated into the gift. The gift recipient chooses among three nonprofits to make the donation: SOLEfood Farm (1sole.wordpress.com), an inner city urban farming organization; Canopy (canopyplanet.org), an environmental organization that saves old growth forests and works with the forestry industry; or Engineers Without Borders (ewb.ca), the Canadian chapter of the organization that designs sustainable engineering projects around the world.

Planet: Some of the eco-friendly operational practices in place at Saul Good Gift Co. include reducing waste, using recycled materials, and reusing other materials (e.g., the paper shreds from the printing company). Working with suppliers that are mostly local or from within the province helps to reduce the company's carbon footprint, as does sharing space and resources with another socially responsible business in a green building. The building features large windows, a skylight to maximize the amount of natural light (thus reducing the need for electric lighting), and a green roof. Furthermore, the building is fully powered by an alternate energy source through a local company.

S-R advantage: Saul readily acknowledges that running any kind of business is hard work, and when you start integrating sustainability practices, it creates more work. But he's also quick to point out that in the long run, socially responsible business practices can result in greater operational efficiency. "I think being conscious of materials and waste—eliminating waste—allowed us to be more efficient and to reduce costs," he says. "Standardizing our policies around using recycled, reclaimed paper has also simplified processes. [For example,] we get the reclaimed paper shreds from the local printer every two weeks and it doesn't cost us anything."

Transformative power of an S-R business: Saul encourages employees to get involved with activities that make a difference in their communities. The company offers a volunteer program for full-time employees, which allows them to take half a day per month to volunteer for a community program.

When it comes to his customers, Saul observed that as community-minded customers learn more about the stories behind the goodies in the gift boxes they receive or buy, they also become more interested in environmental issues.

Relationship building and supporting local businesses and organizations are the engines that drive Saul's business. It's also helped to transform the Strathcona community where Saul's business is located into a zone characterized by socially and environmentally responsible businesses, more green spaces, and collaborations between businesses and community organizations to help reduce some of the social challenges within the area.

Words of wisdom: "You have to be passionate about your business and really love what you do," advises Saul. "It takes a lot of work and commitment, so if the passion and commitment aren't there, you're not really likely to succeed. Also, it's your passion for your business that helps you sell it."

Mentors are key: "Get as many mentors as you possibly can who can help you with the areas where you need help," he says. "Along the same lines, tap into others' expertise; focus on what you do well and delegate the other stuff."

Finally, don't rush into implementing a business strategy or cut corners. "You get what you pay for, so it's wise to spend the time and money to do something right the first time," Saul warns. "If you [don't have the resources to do it right], then wait until you can afford to do it right. Be patient."

Hans Hassle, Plantagon

Location: Stockholm, Sweden

Product/Service: Vertical greenhouses and indoor vertical cultivations or "green walls." Consulting services on urban agricultural design, as well as lectures and workshops on urban agriculture and sustainable business practices.

Company start date: The project started in 2002, though the innovation for the idea of vertical greenhouses goes back to another farmer who first had the idea in 1992. In January 2008, the company was formed as a joint partnership between Hans Hassle (then CEO of SWECORP Citizenship) and the Onondaga Nation.

Company website: plantagon.com

Bio: Since he was a teenager, Hans Hassle has been involved in a variety of projects that were intended to make the world a better, more democratic place. For the past twenty-five years, he has worked in the business sector specializing in corporate social responsibility and citizenship. In 2012, Hans was named CEO of the Year, Sweden by European CEO. He's the author of *Business as Usual is Over* (2012).

Inspiration: Plantagon's products and services have been inspired by the realization that in order to meet future food demands for increasingly urban populations in a sustainable manner, we need to change how and where food is grown. Vertical farming is about growing as much as possible, while taking as little ground space as possible, resulting in a smaller ecological footprint. Additionally, growing food closer to where most people live (in urban environments) reduces or eliminates long distance transportation and its associated problems.

Plantagon is also recognized for its unique organizational structure known as a "companization." It's a model that partners a for-profit company with a nonprofit organization. The inspiration for the organizational structure grew out of the recognition that corporations should have a purpose beyond simply maximizing profits, and that corporations need to bring more long-term thinking and transparency to their business decisions, as well as adopt a more democratic structure. As inspiration, Hans cites Anita Roddick, founder of The Body Shop, whose vision was to create a company that would change society for the better.

Business philosophy: With his extensive experience working as a corporate social responsibility consultant, Hans realized that if he was going to lead a company that was not only financially sustainable, but also environmentally and socially sustainable and transparent in its processes, he and his partners would have to create a different kind of business. They decided to institutionalize the company's guiding ethical principles. Plantagon's ethical principles, embodied in its Articles of Association, are based on the UN Global Compact and the Earth Charter, which both set out the standards for governance pertaining to human rights, labor standards, the environment, and anti-corruption.

Hans emphasizes that the company's Articles of Association translate into real responsibilities. At shareholder meetings, managers and partners have to show that they have met their fiscal, environmental, and social responsibilities. "If 10% of shareholders think a manager didn't meet [his or her] responsibilities, [he or she] can be sued or fined, or lose [his or her job]," says Hans. "Equity, ethics, and sharing are major principles in Plantagon, and our managers and board members are personally responsible for executing their work within these guidelines."

Social Responsibility in Action

Overall: With its business aligned with both the UN Global Compact and the Earth Charter, Plantagon shareholders and managers know that they're responsible for ensuring that their actions are both planet and people friendly. The organization's mission is to show that a company can be both profitable and responsible.

People: Plantagon's democratic structure has fostered a more collaborative workplace. Managers and employees collaborate with partners on both sides of the organization. The management style is responsible and transparent, and employees are given the option of choosing not to work with external partners if they feel that working with the partner company would violate their personal ethics and values.

A unique feature of Plantagon's companization model is that 50% of the board is comprised of individuals from the nonprofit side of the organization. In fact, the nonprofit side owns 10% of the company, and under Swedish Law, 10% gives a shareholder enough power to raise questions and challenge the business side of the organization on social responsibility-related issues.

When it comes to choosing and working with external partners, suppliers, and vendors, Plantagon looks at whether they follow the same ethical principles. Plantagon does its own research to find out about their prospective partners' S-R practices. Hans notes that it gets challenging when a partner is very good with its technology, but is involved with an industry sector that's questionable from an ethical perspective and conflicts with Plantagon's philosophy.

Hans notes that Plantagon tends to attract two types of clients: those whose values are genuinely aligned with Plantagon's values and are interested in finding viable solutions to long-term problems, and those who are looking for assistance in demonstrating that they're socially responsible but aren't really committed to solving problems. Managers must walk a fine balance between meeting the wishes of their customers and the larger good of the community, particularly if it appears that a client is more interested in having a fancy building that incorporates green architectural features than in how a vertical garden or green wall would affect the surrounding community.

Community: When Plantagon reviews project proposals or requests from clients, managers consider the potential impacts on the community where a garden or wall site would be built. If building a vertical greenhouse would bring about negative economic or social consequences, then project managers must either turn down the project or work with the client to modify the request so that the outcome becomes a win-win-win for the community, the client, and Plantagon. If the project is a go, the project managers invite feedback from the growers and then bring in the universities and schools within the community to weigh in. Plantagon also makes a point of trying to recruit locally for all of its projects.

Plantagon reaches out to its members and stakeholders through various social media platforms (e.g., Twitter, Facebook, YouTube), an e-newsletter and blog, and various discussion forums. Anyone can join Plantagon's nonprofit and become a member. Hans is hoping the membership will grow to 100,000 people.

Planet: Plantagon researches and practices the most cutting-edge, sustainable greenhouse design and engineering techniques. The designs have evolved over the years. "First, we looked at geodesic domes, and using a helix inside the dome to get as much space as possible. But then we needed a way to get to the plants at the tops of the helixes, and we needed energy systems [to do that]," Hans explains. "The biggest challenge is to control air flow and energy without taking too much in energy demands. We are trying to [figure out] how to build it so we have a ventilation system that isn't an intensive energy draw."

S-R advantage: According to Hans, their companization model helps to keep innovation fresh because the partners and staff interact with more people with different perspectives on a day-to-day basis. Furthermore, democratizing the corporate structure has increased the productivity, effectiveness, and efficiency of Plantagon employees and workers.

Transformative power of an S-R business: Through its innovative approach to urban agriculture, Plantagon is working toward finding sustainable approaches to agriculture that move food production closer to where people live. Plantagon raises awareness about urban agriculture and its benefits and advocates for alternative solutions that work better for both farmers/growers and consumers. Through their work and mission as an organization, Plantagon is shifting mindsets about what it means to be socially responsible and sustainable. With its companization business model, Plantagon has pioneered a more democratic way to structure a business for others to emulate.

Words of wisdom: "If you want to grow a company (especially an S-R business), you need to understand the game and how to play it," Hans points out. "If you want to make it as a business, you have to learn about the business, what it means to run a company—accept what it is. If you want to protect it from becoming like any other company (focused on profits only), it is important to constitutionalize the objectives and values from day one, so you're not tempted by power and profits. It's also important to share power and develop partnerships."

To create lasting change through your business, a shift in mindset is key. "At the philosophical level, the current challenge with society is that we value wealth over doing social good, but we have to do the whole thing differently if we want to see lasting change."

FIVE: Value, Values, and Valuing Your Customers

MOST people have a favorite store where they like to shop, or a service professional that they have been loyal to over many years. Stop and think for a minute about your favorite places to shop, eat, and do business. Why are those particular places your favorites, and why are you a loyal customer? Most likely, it's because the business owner or its employees go the extra mile to ensure that you not only get what you want but what you need, or because the owner is clearly more interested in developing a long-term business relationship with you based on mutual respect and trust, rather than making a sale in the short run. This level of attention to customer preferences and demands is what makes companies thrive and encourages loyalty and return business.

Among the various types of active wear that Suzanne Akin designs and makes for her company, Akinz, is a line of beanies—also known as "toques." Along with her standard beanie designs, Suzanne also gives customers the option of purchasing custom-made beanies. Suzanne goes out of her way to listen to her customers and understand their preferences. "I go the extra mile to make sure people are getting the exact colors, fit, and style they want," she explains. "People love the opportunity to own something unique to them, so I will try anything new or different if it means making my customers happy."

Affinity with your customers can and should go beyond the simple business transaction. Customers not only care about your products, but also how you take your stated values about the environment, sustainability, and community and use them as guiding principles throughout your business processes—from hiring and work conditions for your employees, to compensation and community engagement. More and more, people choose to shop at particular stores and venues because those businesses share their customers' values and concerns about sustainability and social justice. According to MS & L's Global Values Study, 77% of survey respondents indicated they took into consideration a company's values when deciding whether to give their business to a company, and 78% of respondents stated they wouldn't do business with a company if the company's values didn't align with their own personal values.[1]

In this Chapter...

Whether your customer base is comprised entirely of value-aligned individuals that have supported you from day one, or a mix of value-aligned individuals and clients who just want to know that they're still going to get the best value for their money, your social responsibility (S-R) mission must include practices that clearly show you value your relationships with your customers.

In this chapter, we'll go over several S-R practices that show you value your customers and adhere to your S-R mission:

- Talking to your customers and getting them talking to each other; helping to create a community around a shared concern or interest.

- Listening and responding to your customers.

- Engaging your customers in a social cause.

- Offering matching donations (or a percent of each sale) for any cause marketing campaigns.

- Introducing your customers to other great, local businesses.

- Showing your customers that you care about local and global issues.

Following those broad areas of practice, we'll explore the relationship between S-R practices and your customers. First, we'll look at how you should approach your S-R practices with your customers. Second, we'll focus on the opportunities and challenges in how you involve your customers in shaping your S-R strategies. Finally, we'll look at how you can inspire your customers to engage in social change activities themselves.

Promoting Customer Satisfaction through Your Values and Value

Your customers are vital to the success of your business. In fact, you wouldn't stay in business without them, so it's just good business sense to develop strong, ongoing relationships with your customers and ensure they continue to find value in your product or service. The microbusiness owners interviewed for this book recognize this and have proactively built socially responsible values into their companies' missions

Expressing Value and Values:
- Setting a fair price
- Customer engagement
- Going beyond the financial transaction
- Customer feedback
- Customer appreciation

with their customers in mind. They understand that taking the time to develop authentic, respectful relationships ensures that their interactions are positive ones. They go the extra mile to ensure that their customers get top quality products and customized service because they understand that this level of attention creates lasting value beyond the price tag.

While some of the S-R strategies we'll discuss in this chapter do have a financial cost attached to them, most of the strategies for developing good long-term customer relations don't cost a lot of money. They do, however, require time, patience, sincerity, integrity, and a genuine desire to listen to and learn from your customers.

Setting a Fair Price

Emerging Families owner Mia Kalef offers healing sessions and understands that her fees may be prohibitive to some people. Rather than exclude those who need her services but can't afford to pay the full fee, she finds ways to make the burden more manageable. "One way I do that is through my community clinic days. Another way is that I will let people pay what they can afford." Mia also makes house calls to clients who are new mothers "so they don't have to disrupt their time with their babies or rearrange their schedules to get here for an appointment."

Lori Del Genis of Conscious Elegance also does her best to keep her prices reasonable and fair for her wedding tailoring services. She's committed to being transparent about her prices and policies relating to shipping, returns, and repairs. On her website, she states upfront: "We impose no huge mark-up to inflate profits despite the typical 300%-700% wedding industry standard (sadly, those numbers aren't exaggerated). We give you a clear and honest price upfront, not some evasive 'range' that allows middle-men to pile on their share of profit without contribution."

Troy Van Beek of Ideal Energy Inc., a company that designs renewable energy systems for both individuals and corporations, makes every effort to provide systems to clients even if it means practically giving away their services. The impact has been "worth its weight in gold," says Troy. "We understand that if we continue to put out a good product and allow it to be seen by the community, it will catch up to us." This flexible model of pricing generates more visibility for his business while at the same time giving customers a chance to try out his product and get to know his business for a reduced or low cost.

Customer Engagement

Since the majority of consumers (75%) think that corporations aren't currently doing a good job of engaging their customers, there is a real opportunity for microbusiness owners to take the lead on fostering and following through on customer engagement.[2] Webmeadow owners Eileen Webb and her partner hold lengthy consultations with their clients (primarily nonprofit organizations) before they launch a website project. "We do a lot of talking with people, especially to help them make sure they spend their money well because they're spending a lot of money if they're working with us," says Eileen. "We don't want them to spend money and then a year down the road, say no one has ever used this part of the site. We want them to say, 'Wow this was a great investment. Look how well it's working for us.'" Investing the extra time to work with customers has led to better business and more revenue for webmeadow. "Our clients like us a lot. Most of them are repeats; they have us come back and enhance their site, or add a blog, or add a new program section," says Eileen.

Linh Truong of The Soap Dispensary takes the time to explain her products—what they are, what they contain, how they work—to customers when they first come into the store. She'll also bring in recommended products, or research and source products for clients. For example, several customers had asked for more eco-friendly alternatives to toothpaste. In response, Linh and her partner did some research and eventually found a local company that agreed to let [them] bring in the product in a refillable format. Linh's customers asked, and she enthusiastically delivered.

Going Beyond the Financial Transaction

If you've ever been at a store and come away with the distinct impression that you were nothing more than a financial transaction to them, you know how depersonalizing or mundane it feels. Joseph Hodgkinson, the owner of Foda Catering, recognized this risk and saw a chance to change the way he treats the business transaction. Where his customers are concerned, Joseph intentionally sets out to ensure that the sales process isn't just a financial transaction but an opportunity to create positive interaction with his clients. "My approach is with meaning and substance beyond the tangible goods/services provided. This is done with a genuine recognition that our lives have meaning and each moment is important to all of us," he explains. "We are sharing our lives in this interaction and I hope it is memorable in a good way. This promotes genuine feelings of mutual benefit."

Joseph also connects with his customers by recommending various products and businesses to them. If you know of other great products or services offered by local businesses, find a way to introduce your customers to these other businesses and earn double the number of good karma points.

When I asked Kate Sutherland how she satisfied clients beyond price considerations, she explained her approach: "When I have a client, I'm serving the client, but I'm always attuned to serving life in the bigger picture." Helping clients see the big picture is part of how she helps organizations. As a consultant running her own firm that specializes in helping organizations improve their group processes and dynamics, Kate Sutherland understands how important communication skills are. "You pay attention to what the client wants, but you give them what they need," Kate says. "I'll make recommendations based on what I think serves the highest [good]. I feel like I'm working for life through my clients. For Kate, connection is about listening. "I listen really deeply. I listen behind the lines—really deeply—to what's below the surface, as well as what I'm hearing," she explains. "I'm listening for what's trying to emerge. [I ask myself] where are the double signals between what's being said, and what is going on at a deeper level."

Committed to always going the extra mile for her customers, wedding dress designer Lori Del Genis offers a couple of unique services. She provides her clients with private, online access to her workshop logs so that they can see their gown in progress in real-time. She also offers to repurpose the wedding dress (either as a party dress or a baby's christening dress) after the big day so that her clients can get more than one day's use out of the garment. In the same spirit, Troy Van Beek's team at Ideal Energy Inc. not only designs and installs the alternative energy systems for their clients, but also helps them with completing grant and rebate applications. With their corporate clients, Troy and his team collaborate with PR experts to promote clients' sustainability credentials and efforts that, in turn, raise awareness and attract business.

Customer Feedback

According to a 2010 survey, over 70% of customers want to be engaged on key pillars of business responsibility, and almost as many consumers are prepared to spend time and money participating in surveys or research-related to these key pillars.[3]

Show your customers that you value their input by making it easy for them to be heard and responding to their feedback promptly. It's as simple as responding to e-mails and phone messages in a timely manner. If you want to collect feedback in a more systematic way, send out customer satisfaction surveys with invoices, or provide short survey forms (and a box to collect them) for your in-store customers to complete and submit. Here are other survey tips:

- When designing your survey, make sure you keep your questions short and sweet (no more than five questions if open-ended; eight to ten questions if close-ended questions).

- Be discerning about how often you administer surveys. Once a business quarter? Every six months?

- Have a policy and practice in place for protecting the privacy of the information you collect.

- Give your clients the option of filling out a web-based survey. Survey Monkey (surveymonkey.com) is a flexible survey generator that also compiles the survey results for you.

- Be sure to read through the surveys at the end of each business week or month to make sure you catch any concerns or complaints and respond to them quickly. Make sure you respond to questions or concerns promptly, but hold off on looking for trends in responses until you have collected several months' worth of data.

Customer Appreciation

Show your customers that you appreciate them. Find ways to hold customer appreciation events throughout the year that work for your business model. However you structure these events, be sure to demonstrate how highly you value your customers. For example, if you have a retail business, have an open house or a sales event combined with some other event or promotion. If you're a service-based business, you could offer a slight discount on a particular service, or bundle selected services together in a specially priced package. If you don't have a large clientele, you might also consider sending gift cards for other local businesses as a way of saying thank you to your key clients. (If you can give your clients gift cards for socially responsible local businesses, so much the better!)

Find monthly or quarterly ways of showing appreciation for your customers' loyalty, wisdom, and business. Showing appreciation doesn't always have to take the form of a discount or freebie. Acknowledging your customers with a quick but sincere comment through social media channels or periodically organizing an event (either online or in person) where you can involve your customers in providing feedback or offering suggestions related to your S-R strategies is a great way to show your customers you value their loyalty and wisdom. José Alejandro Flores of VOS Flips uses social media both to get feedback from customers and to engage them in two-way conversations. José's team also interviews customers to get their feedback and to learn about what's going on in their local communities.

Getting You and Your Customers on the Same S-R Track

If you originally set up your business with a specific social or environmental mission, it's likely that your customers chose to do business with you on the basis of your aligned values. Several of the entrepreneurs interviewed for this book remarked that most of their customers already shared the same values as them, and in some cases used online green directories, such as Green America's National Green Pages (greenpages.org), to find them.

James Castro-Edwards of Greenstack Ltd. acknowledges that their target customers "are primarily those organizations which value a socially responsible approach." But, whereas a few years ago only a minority of consumers was concerned about ethical and sustainable production, "there seems to be a growing awareness of the need to move away from finite to sustainable resources, and to move towards ethical production values," says James. "While a few years ago these concerns appear to have only mattered to a few [customers], sustainable, ethical values certainly appear to be moving towards the mainstream."

Troy Van Beek of Ideal Energy Inc. observes that living in a community with a strong commitment to being as green as possible provided a ready-made base of support for the company's vision and mission. "When Ideal Energy first began designing and installing renewable energy systems in the Southeast Iowa area, the uptake was phenomenal. Our clients are pioneering the sustainability industry by choosing to use clean, renewable energy."

If your company has found its market niche and fan base already, count yourself as lucky. In many cases, you already have an eager audience and motivated market for your goods and services, but don't discount the possibility that some of your most steadfast customers may come from an unexpected sector. When Saul Brown started his gift basket business in 2006, he had anticipated that most of his customers would be from green corporations, but as he discovered, that wasn't the case. "I have clients from a variety of sectors, and what they really like [about the product] is the local community and the stories behind the gifts," Saul says. "The clients are mostly local or regional businesses with strong community values. It makes people feel good to give or receive a gift with a story behind it about how the supplier makes a positive difference to the community."

Skeptics and Doubters

It's important to remember that not all of your clients have to share your values to appreciate the value or quality of your service or product. Julie Beyer of For the Love of Food observed that some of her customers "are in it more for the health benefits and not so much about the shared values." However, Julie has also found that through talking to and educating this group of clients, they "come to value the values as one of the benefits of the product."

If you decided later on in the life of your business that you wanted to incorporate more S-R practices, a few "old guard" customers may be skeptical about supporting your sudden shift in your business practices and wonder how the changes will affect your pricing. Here are a few strategies that might help you to win over the skeptics in your customer base:

Don't Preach

How you convey your S-R philosophy with customers makes all the difference, especially if their first contact with you is through your website. Skip the pedantic tone, and project a welcoming attitude that won't frighten away customers who might think they don't "belong." Rather than getting too preachy about your values, take a light-hearted, friendly approach to explaining your S-R philosophy.

Emphasize the Value (Beyond Price) to Customers

Your customers want to know that they're getting the same quality and value in your services or products in addition to the value added through any newly minted S-R practices. If you need to, conduct the research and run through some calculations to figure out whether any of your S-R strategies are going to increase the cost of doing business and how many of those expenses can be legitimately passed on to your customers. Ideally, you want your planet-friendly strategies from Chapter 2 to not only benefit the planet, but also reduce the cost of doing business. For example, less waste and a choice to use reclaimed or recycled materials (for non-edible goods, of course!) should help to reduce overhead costs. Track the outcomes of your decisions and the cost savings, and if many of your S-R initiatives start to yield savings in the long run, you may be able to give your clients a small discount.

What might be a little trickier is convincing (or educating) some customers to appreciate both the aesthetic and environmental value of using reclaimed, recycled, or repurposed materials in making your products. However, if the end products are well-made and backed by excellent customer service, your customers may readily embrace the idea that eco-friendly and aesthetically pleasing can co-exist harmoniously.

Enlist "Ambassadors" Among Your Customers

A few of your customers might actually be so enthused that you're starting an S-R initiative that they sing your good graces from the rafters. With a little public relations savvy, you can marshal these "ambassadors" who applaud your decision to incorporate more socially responsible practices. If they have an especially strong interest, encourage them to participate in shaping your S-R strategies. Collaborate with these motivated customers to generate ideas and find out what they think are high priority S-R issues. It's a great way to strengthen relations with them and to start creating a community where others engage in activism that creates positive social change.

Like many of the entrepreneurs I interviewed, Linh Truong of The Soap Dispensary uses social media and a blog to reach out to customers and find out what's important to them. In addition to engaging customers through social media, Linh also engages her customers and their interests in reducing their plastics footprint through tracking the number of plastic bottles they bring to the store. In June of this year (2012), her customers helped to keep 418 containers out of the landfill or recycling system!

Take advantage of social media outlets, such as Facebook, Twitter, Pinterest, Yelp, or Foursquare, and don't forget about your company blog. Chronicle your journey to becoming more green or community-oriented. Share stories and advice, and ask your customers to share their experiences, too. As Joe Staiano of Meaningful Trips points out, "Think about how to engage [your] audience [online]—don't see them just as customers."

Take a Customer Poll

One approach to collecting feedback is to design and send out a survey to your customers. Surveys can help you get ideas on S-R practices that might be feasible for your business. Better yet, invite your customers to participate in a focus group. If you can't afford a professional facilitator, see if you can find a friend or colleague with excellent group facilitation skills who would be willing to moderate the group for you. Here's what you should find out from your customers:

- What are the top five S-R strategies they think should be rolled out in the first year? (Though indicate that while their input will be considered, you'll have to make the final decision on what's feasible for you at this point in time.)

- What causes would they like to see you support? Will they support cause marketing?

- What is their preferred format for communications from you about your progress on your S-R transformation?

- What other ways can you work with customers to help them engage more fully with community issues and social activism?

Deliver on Your Promises

Once you decide to venture along the S-R track, your customers will most likely expect to see ongoing evidence of transparency in your business policies and practices and alignment between your values and practices, both personally and professionally. They may be interested in your values as well as the value they get from your services or products. The business benefits are potentially enormous. If you repeatedly demonstrate transparency, consistency, and accountability, your customers will likely reward you with loyalty and referrals.

Own Up to Mistakes

If, for some reason, you or someone in your supply chain does something that doesn't align with your customers' values or that violates your customers' trust in your company, you may well discover what it feels like to be on the losing end of the deal when your customers opt to vote with their wallets. Recent surveys show that customers are increasingly willing to punish companies for engaging in objectionable behavior, and it may take more than a public apology and an announcement of policy changes to win them back.[4] For many customers, it might even take a complete overhaul of a company's business practices after engaging in objectionable behavior.[5]

While accidents and mistakes do happen, a company's willingness to be accountable, own up to its mistakes, and take all reasonable—and possibly some heroic—measures to correct problems will lessen the negative fallout. Ideally, having a clear set of S-R guidelines to steer your business decisions should greatly minimize the likelihood of any epic blunders. In Chapter 6, we'll offer some insights and suggestions for dealing with some of the struggles and pitfalls you may encounter along the way to transforming your microbusiness into a socially responsible enterprise.

Small Steps to Promoting S-R Values with Your Customers

Implementing some of the following S-R strategies should help you to keep your customers happy and engaged. As with the other chapters, the strategies are divided into short, medium, and long-term projects.[6]

Getting to Know Your Customers: Within 3 months

- Talk to your customers about your S-R strategies and find out what matters to them.

- Design a survey or organize a focus group to collect customer feedback and ideas on what S-R strategies customers would like to see you implement.

- Touch base with your customers on a regular basis through social media, direct mail marketing, and other means.

- Produce a short customer satisfaction survey (keep it to about five items) you can send out with your products or invoices.

- Invite customers to send their questions, comments, or feedback through your website, social media outlets, or by phone, and be sure you respond promptly to their questions or comments.

- Be interactive with your customers; create an online community for them, and find ways to get them engaged in social activism.

- Produce an e-newsletter that tells customers about various social or environmental issues that are of concern to them (and you) and what actions they can take to make a difference.[7] Send your e-newsletter out on a regular basis, like every quarter or on major holidays.

Deepening the Relationship with Your Customers: Within 1 year

- Put a small blurb on your packaging that directs customers to your website or social media site to learn more about issues that are important to you and your company.[8]

- Hold "Customer Appreciation" events on several occasions throughout the year. Be creative about organizing events that not only recognize your customers' loyalty, but also demonstrate that you're attuned to their values.

- Invite new clients to your office and give them a tour of the building if, like Toby of Eclipse Awards and Saul of Saul Good Gift Co., you have some interesting green features in your building.

- Participate in community events that raise awareness about social or environmental issues that are important to you and your customers. Consider adopting this strategy suggested by Ben Cohen and Mal Warwick: Set up an exhibit or information booth with materials explaining why an issue is important to you and what customers can do to help out or get involved.[9] *Note:* Be discerning about how you present the problems and solutions; you don't want to appear as though you're exploiting a social issue or cause just to generate PR or business opportunities for your company.

- Invite representatives from a local nonprofit (or local branch of a national or international NGO) to set up a table for a day or evening (if you have a brick and mortar retail business) and raise awareness about their cause. Explain to your customers that a portion of their purchases that day or evening will be donated to the organization.

- Consider hosting an Action Circle for your customers (Action Circles are discussed in more detail in Chapter 3). *Note:* This strategy will work better for some kinds of businesses (e.g., those that have a community of regular clients, already offer workshops/group events, and don't have privacy/confidentiality as an issue) than others.

Ongoing Customer Relationship Advocate: Long term

- Be transparent and proactive in the face of problems. For example, recall faulty products and fix errors. Offer a refund or discount on future services/purchases to make up for any inconveniences to customers.[10]

- Whether your product is mass-produced (in a sustainable manner, of course), made in small batches, or is custom-made, establish a refund policy that finds a fair balance between meeting the needs of your customers and of your business. The same goes for service-based businesses.

- Provide matching donations or give a portion of each sale to a specific cause. Use your online community to find out from your customers which cause(s) they'd like you to support.[11]

- Introduce your customers to other great products and businesses. Remember that the best customer relationships thrive on two-way communication, so be willing to learn about other products, businesses, or processes from your customers, too.

Conducting a "Customer Relationship" Cost-Benefit Analysis

If you're not sure whether some of the strategies are a good fit or the right choice for your business, conduct a simple cost-benefit analysis before committing your valuable resources to going down a particular path. Assess the current state of your enterprise in terms of your finances, resources, mission, and sustainability goals, and ask yourself the following set of questions:

1. Is it affordable given your current assets and cash flow?

2. Does the action move you closer to your S-R goals or vision?

3. Is it measurable? That is, do you have any way of showing that adopting the strategy produced a result? For example, if you decide to provide matching donations or give a portion of each sale to a specific cause, be prepared to tell customers how much money you raised for that cause, and how the associated nonprofit or NGO used that money to advance their programs.

If your answer to all of the above questions is "no," then clearly it isn't a strategy you want to pursue for the foreseeable future. If your response to all of the questions is "yes," then consider it a "green light" to go ahead with the initiative. If your response is mixed, you'll have to determine whether the costs (both financial and in terms of your company's brand, reputation, etc.) outweigh the benefits, or vice-versa.

For each S-R practice you decide to adopt, list the following:

• Necessary steps and strategies for each of the goals you want to meet.

• Potential challenges and obstacles to meeting your goals.

• Any support or cooperation from others required to successfully meet your goals.

• Positive or negative social/economic impacts of your actions.

Example: Create an online, interactive community for your values-minded customers

Project Scope

You've decided you want to support your social activist-minded customers by creating an online, interactive community for them. Before you launch a viable platform, you'll need to assess what kind of resources you need and how resource-intensive this activity will be as a long-term strategy.

Choosing a platform: As a starting point, what kind of social media platform will you use to create this space? Will you use Facebook or Twitter? Will you set up a discussion group on LinkedIn? Will you start a blog and invite guest posts? Do you want to make your online community open to everyone or restrict membership to your list of client contacts?

Deciding on your goals: Do you want to encourage people within the community to initiate discussions and respond to items that you post? Do you want to alert your community to emerging issues and offer suggestions for how they can take action? Alternatively, would you rather just discuss social or environmental issues in more general terms and offer some strategies for how your customers can make a difference? If you choose the former approach, you'll have to be vigilant about staying on top of current events and alerting your online community in a timely fashion. After all, it doesn't do much good to urge people to take action on issues that aren't timely or are "old news."

Comfort-level: You'll also have to consider your comfort level with using various social media platforms and their associated applications. Do you know how to make the most effective use of Facebook or Twitter to reach a large audience? Do you know how to set up and moderate a LinkedIn discussion group or a blog site? If you don't have much experience with these social media tools, do you have the time and resources to get up to speed on them and make sure your online community functions smoothly for your customers and online followers? If you don't have the knowledge or skills to moderate discussions and comments or update information, do you have someone on your staff who could take this on for you? Do you have the financial resources to hire an "online community manager," if necessary?

Commitment level: Do you have the time (and patience) to maintain an online community, whether that means committing to writing a blog post on a regular schedule, responding to comments, or keeping up with Twitter?

Challenges and Key Considerations

Learning new skills or hiring help: If you don't have the skills to easily set up an online, interactive community, you'll either have to learn these skills or find (or hire) someone who does have the skills and can manage this part of the project for you. Do you have the financial resources to pay for either getting the training you need, or hiring someone who has the skills to achieve your vision without taking on debt to do so? If you don't have the financial resources, you may have to decide that for the time being, this S-R action has more costs than benefits attached to it. Even if you can afford to pay for someone to handle the technical details or moderate the site for you, what happens if your "go-to" person moves on or is otherwise no longer available to help you? Will you have to put the community on hold, or will it be able to run itself to some extent? If you have to go on hiatus, whether on a temporary or indeterminate basis, what will that do to your company's S-R credibility or reputation for customer service?

Triumphs and Tribulations

If you plan it well, you'll build a thriving online community of socially conscious customers who take their social activism beyond just being a green consumer to actively engaging in their community to bring about the changes and values they want to see in the world. It takes time to build your community and have it gain momentum, especially if you don't already have an established online presence and following. It can be frustrating and disheartening to send out a tweet, post a blog or comment on Facebook, and get no response at all.

If you're consistently seeing a lack of responses, consider getting some feedback from a colleague or mentor who is social media savvy, asking some of your loyal customers for their feedback, and then modifying your strategy or content, accordingly. (Ideally, you'll have started the process by first getting input from your customers about what would work for them.)

CHAPTER CHECKLIST:

✔ Talk to your customers about the S-R practices you are/will be incorporating. Find out what interests them and how they perceive the decision if this is a new direction for you.

✔ Keep your customers in the loop about your decision to incorporate more S-R practices into the business. Let them know if/how the S-R practices will affect them (particularly, if there will be changes to your pricing) and assure them that they're still getting the same high-quality product or service—and more.

✔ Go the extra mile for your customers and make sure that your interactions with them contribute to positive, meaningful experiences for them and you.

✔ Expect your customers to demand transparency and consistency on your part and encourage them to ask you questions.

✔ If you send out a newsletter or periodic updates to your customers, show them how the S-R practices you've put in place have benefitted people, the planet, and your business. *Tip:* This is where your tracking system comes in. Create a few quick little charts and combine it with some qualitative data (People love anecdotes and stories!) to create a company narrative that supports your claims.

Joseph Hodgkinson, Foda Catering

Location: Mountain View, California, U.S.

Product/Service: Personalized fine dining and catering services.

Company start date: December 2001

Company website: fodacatering.com

Bio: Joseph was born in San Francisco, CA and grew up in the South Bay Area. Joseph had a passion for cooking from an early age and started working in restaurants at fourteen years of age. Joseph studied at the California Culinary Academy and graduated from the Culinary Institute of America. He gained additional professional experience at a variety of restaurants, including The Campton Place, before starting Foda Catering when he was twenty-two years of age.

Inspiration: Joseph was first inspired to start his own company after doing some private parties and getting some great results. This led him to ask, "Why can't I do this all the time?" About one year later, he committed to starting his private chef business.

Business philosophy: For Joseph, social responsibility is about helping to sustain the regenerative benefits of a self-sufficient network, as well as supporting local economies and sustainable agriculture. Joseph puts his philosophy into practice by shopping locally as much as possible, and buying from small businesses, local manufacturers, or local farms. Joseph started his business with the intention of running it as a socially responsible business. Because the focus of his business was fine dining, it naturally led him to think in terms of sustainable agriculture. He knew that where food is concerned, buying from organic local farms/manufacturers results in a better product and in a product that is better for the environment.

Social Responsibility in Action

Overall: In addition to his support for local economies and local, sustainably grown food, Joseph gives back to his community through various volunteer activities, partners with like-minded chefs and suppliers, gives his services to fundraisers and charities, speaks at high school career days, and makes sure that his customers remain satisfied by ensuring that interactions are meaningful and go beyond a simple business transaction.

People: Although Joseph doesn't have any full-time employees, he does have a group of chefs that regularly help him with events. Joseph pays his temporary workers a good wage and makes the work experience positive and enjoyable for these workers. On occasion, Joseph will take high school students who are interested in cooking under his wing and hire them if they show promise. Joseph also collaborates with other chefs and seeks to learn from, as well as teach, others.

Joseph recognizes that real customer service goes beyond just providing great service; it's about seeing his customers as people with whom he can build relationships, not just complete business transactions. "My approach is with meaning and substance beyond the tangible goods/services provided. This is done with a genuine recognition that our lives have meaning and each moment is important to all of us. We are sharing our lives in this interaction and I hope it is memorable (in a good way)," says Joseph. In keeping with this philosophy, Joseph shares information about great products and stores that he likes with his customers, and he listens to the ideas that his customers share with him.

When it comes to engaging customers in his socially responsible business practices, Joseph has an advantage in that many of his clients in the Bay Area are already socially responsible and can afford to pay the higher costs that are sometimes associated with choosing local, sustainably produced food or goods from small-scale suppliers. A commitment to supporting sustainable agriculture and a willingness to pay for these goods results in a win-win-win for Joseph, his clients, and local businesses: "I get to buy the best products, my clients get the best quality, we support sustainable living, and [suppliers] make money to keep the cycle going."

Joseph also reaches out to interested customers through his website: He provides a variety of links to other sites that promote healthy living through sustainable agriculture, social/economic justice, buying organic food, and a culinary skills training program for high school students.

When it comes to choosing his suppliers and vendors, Joseph gives high priority to shared values and origin when buying products. For him, that means buying ingredients that are organic/chemical free, free-range, sustainable, and local, whenever possible. Joseph notes that most of the producers/businesses he partners with share the same socially responsible values that he does, and that makes his job easier. He explains that "through this shared mentality, we form a network bigger than just ourselves (hopefully one that grows exponentially). Not only does this cultivate a healthy society, but it also makes for healthier food, planet, and individuals. I could further elaborate on the benefits of a healthy society, but that could be a whole book of its own!"

Community: In addition to supporting local businesses directly (through his purchases) and indirectly (referring clients and others in his professional network to local businesses that he likes), Joseph gives his services to various local fundraisers, donates time to charity, and speaks at high schools on career days. He donates time to the El Cajon Project, a program that helps at-risk and disadvantaged students graduate from high school through its culinary arts program (for credit). Joseph will occasionally take some interested students from this program under his wing. Joseph also collaborates with other local chefs who share the same socially responsible outlook to further connect with and expand a network of like-minded people in the Bay Area.

Planet: Joseph incorporates planet-friendly actions into his business activities in several ways. As already mentioned, he makes a point of choosing local, organic, sustainably produced food—all of which help to reduce his and his customers' carbon footprint. He prefers to use reusable plates, cups, and cutlery, but when that isn't possible, he chooses disposable products that do the least amount of environmental damage, and makes sure that everything that can be recycled is recycled.

S-R advantage: In Joseph's business, seeking out specialty producers often takes more time, money, and effort, so choosing to be socially responsible is often less efficient. However, for Joseph, there are many subtle intangibles that add up to a distinct advantage. Like other socially responsible entrepreneurs, Joseph acknowledges that it's true you work with more passion when you believe that what you're doing is for the greater good.

In addition to the personal satisfaction he gains from being able to align his personal values with his professional activities, there's also a clear business case for putting the extra time and resources into his choice to use sustainable, local food sources as much as possible: This is what his clients want and are willing to pay for, and he wouldn't get return business without these practices. "If I did not think and work this way, I would not get their business," Joseph explains. Fortunately, as more individuals and business sectors are accepting that we live on a planet with finite resources, and that we must create a more sustainable human presence, they're embracing a socially responsible approach to living and doing business.

Transformative power of an S-R business: For Joseph, the transformative power of a socially responsible business is partly in its ability to support and expand a network of like-minded individuals, and partly in the expanded knowledge and desire to keep improving that comes from sharing information back and forth with others in his network. As he points out, "There are a great many intelligent and socially conscious people [living] in the Bay Area. This [the transformative power] is a constant process of me learning and teaching—from my customers as well [as my colleagues]."

Words of Wisdom: Joseph recommends establishing a strong business network. "Look to work with people who share your values," he says. "Seek them out and get in their network. It will not only create the best product, but should also help you get referrals/clients."

Mia Kalef, Emerging Families

Location: Vancouver, British Columbia, Canada

Product/Service: Holistic healing using Craniosacral Therapy, Pre and Perinatal Therapy, and other healing modalities for adults, babies, and families.

Company start date: 2006

Company website: emergingfamilies.com

Bio: Mia Kalef is a Vancouver-based doctor (DC) and holistic healer, and is the author of *The Secret Life of Babies: Decoding the Cultures of Birth, Love, and Violence* (2011). She runs a private practice for people of all ages using Craniosacral Therapy and Pre and Perinatal Therapy. Her research in these areas has brought about an understanding that experiences from preconception through the first three years shape our bodies, brains, and behaviors. She gives workshops internationally and is dedicated to rebuilding the "village life in the modern day." Mia is also a lifetime member of the Association of Pre and Perinatal Psychology and Health.

Inspiration: Like many healers, Mia's path as a healer emerged out of a series of experiences and observations that catalyzed an act of self-discovery and learning. When she was in her late teens, a sports-related injury resulted in a diagnosis of "tissue irritation" and a vague prognosis that the condition might go away one day. When medical specialists weren't able to give her clear answers on how to heal the pain and stiffness, she started researching natural and complementary healing modes to deal with the discomfort. At the age of nineteen, she learned that unresolved emotions could create physical pain and disease, and it took another decade for her to finally learn what was at the root of her challenges and fully heal her injuries. In the interim, her experiences inspired her to work with knowledge traditions that support holistic healing. With guided therapy, she helps clients access early childhood memories—and often as far back as their time *in utero*. She uses this knowledge to help individual families—including couples who are planning to conceive or already expecting a child—ensure that their children feel fully wanted and accepted by their family, as well as their village and culture.

Mia's vision is to bring about a more accepting, peaceful culture and planet where everyone matters. "My business is around "mattering" [i.e., supporting and educating people to understand that all of us on the planet matter]." Mia notes that "being wanted and accepted... affects babies and people as they're growing up" and helps to "bring about a more accepting, peaceful culture/planet." She is at the forefront of a movement that recognizes that we all have it within us to do the healing needed to achieve this vision.

Business philosophy: When Mia thinks of sustainability, she thinks of "coherence." Her philosophy is based on an innate drive/need to see things as a coherent whole: to see and understand how the separate pieces of a system fit together, interact with, and affect each other. Her philosophy has evolved out of her own experiences when she was studying medicine, and out of her Authentic Leadership studies: "I learned to think of nature as a model for systems and the body. One of my biggest 'A-ha moments' occurred when I was studying medicine, and I was amazed by the complexity of the body and its systems. The truth is that anatomy and healing unfold according to a self-organizing pattern."

Mia also extends this "mattering" view to nature, as well as people. Because every being needs to feel welcome on the planet, it becomes an ecological conversation, too. She asks, "What would we be doing differently if we listened to the voice of nature as if it mattered?"

Social Responsibility in Action

Overall: In keeping with her philosophy and belief that every being on the planet matters, Mia is mindful of how her actions and choices affect both the planet and people. While her focus is on working with individuals or small groups, she also ensures that her actions benefit the community, as well as the individuals within it.

People: Mia is a solopreneur who works with community partners and other professionals on a contract basis. When she works with contractors, she pays the fee set by the contractors, based on their estimate of what it will cost them to complete the project. At the interpersonal level, Mia's commitment to making her partners and contractors feel welcome plays out as an opportunity for them "to bring their whole self to the conversation and work from their leading edge in a dynamic that is supportive, patient, and compassionate."

Mia finds ways to make her fees more manageable for those clients who really need her services but can't afford the fees. One option she offers is to let people pay what they can afford, a practice that's inspired by the Buddhist practice in which a teacher gives a lecture and students pay what they think the lecture is worth. Mia has adopted this practice for her Community Clinic days.

An added customer service that Mia provides for some of her clients is offering to make house calls to new mothers, so that they don't have to disrupt their time with their babies. She's also flexible about rearranging her schedule to try and get to an appointment, if needed.

Mia also helps her clients tune in to their feelings and instincts. Among new parents, Mia notes that they "seem to appreciate the coping tools they learn for responding to inconsolable babies. I get parents to think about what the inconsolable baby is saying that she or he can't put into words. Parents start to feel more empowered as they learn to listen and tune in to their intuition, and they feel more love and intimacy with their babies."

The work she does with young families and babies to help parents foster stronger bonds and better communication with their children increases overall health and well-being that translates to long-term savings on health care spending for families.

Community: Mia gives back to and engages with her community and clients in several ways. She offers a Community Clinic, gives free talks for post-natal groups, and provides answers for free through e-mail. She supports her professional community and belongs to APPPH (Association of Pre- and Perinatal Psychology and Health) and attends their conferences.

At the local level, Mia supports Seed Stock (villagevancouver.ca/forum/topics/seedstock), a group within Village Vancouver that is exploring developing a community currency and is launching a campaign to fund the project.

Planet: Mia ensures that all of the materials she uses are biodegradable and eco-friendly. She strives to achieve low or zero waste standards and plans to launch several green, S-R initiatives, including: continuing to support the local economy; managing her carbon/ecological footprint; and having a building or clinic that goes beyond being LEED-certified.

S-R advantage: Mia started out with the intention of being socially responsible in her business. She notes that while it isn't always the easier path, it's the better path: "It's the higher ground—better for everyone—and is more rewarding for the soul," says Mia. For her, being adaptable and responsive to situations and seeing cohesion between people and the planet are the only ways forward.

Transformative power of an S-R business: For Mia, the transformative powers of her business extend to herself, as well as her clients and the planet. She notes that while the adult clients she works with already share her values, some of the younger families she works with who are referred by Doulas and midwives don't always share her values. There is a bit of a learning curve at first, but the parents understand the value of communicating with and bonding with their babies and gain the awareness of how parental health affects infant well-being. More generally, Mia believes that even those individuals who are destructive can be healed and transformed if they have someone sit with them in a compassionate and non-judgmental way.

Entrepreneurship is also transforming Mia as she navigates a business path that both allows her to scale up her business and, at the same time, remain compassionate, emotionally regulated, and grounded in the present. With her commitment to collaboration over competition in business, Mia is part of a larger movement of entrepreneurs who are transforming how business is done. "It's nice to know that people have each other's backs," says Mia.

Words of wisdom: "Social capital is not just a great asset, it's essential for survival," asserts Mia. "It's important to find a community of people where everyone matters and has each other's back. It's important to find that within one's self, as well. For example, believing that we matter and that we are there for ourselves at the individual level."

Kate Sutherland,
Kate Sutherland & Associates

Location: Vancouver, British Columbia, Canada

Product/Service: Kate's services include facilitating transformative processes for individuals and groups, organizing conferences, convening and facilitating board retreats, consulting with community organizations to develop innovative and collaborative projects, and coaching individuals to align with their true purpose using tools for "inner knowing."

Company start date: 1994; Make Light Work projects since September 2010

Company website: katersutherland.com and makelightwork.com

Bio: Kate Sutherland is a social entrepreneur who helps change agents and community organizations to be more innovative and effective. As an inspiring leader and in-demand consultant, trainer, and coach, Kate has helped hundreds of leaders and organizations become more nimble, resilient, and aligned with their core purpose. In 2010, she created the *Make Light Work* blog, an online meeting place for people to use their "inner work" approaches to increase their effectiveness. Kate is also the Regional Director for "What's Your Tree" Action Circles in British Columbia, co-founder of the Two Block Diet, and founder of the Daphne Lane Plastics Recycling Depot—all pioneering, grassroots, citizen engagement projects. She's also the author of *Make Light Work: 10 Tools for Inner Knowing* (2010) and *Make Light Work in Groups* (2012).

Inspiration: Kate's inspiration for the work she does comes from a personal desire to change the world. Kate has always seen herself as having a vocation or calling—rather than simply a business. It's only in recent years that she has come to see a synergy between social purpose and a positive role for business.

Business philosophy: For Kate, being socially responsible means running her business in alignment with her life. She chooses to live as close to her life purpose as possible. "I feel the larger purpose is to be [of service to] the Great Turning—[the shifts we're seeing and experiencing in the world right now]," says Kate. Living in alignment with her purpose means that Kate aims to be generous to those around her, that she pushes herself out of her comfort zone to improve herself and her business, and that she's always mindful of the impact of her business and personal decisions on the world and communities around her.

Social Responsibility in Action

Overall: With her commitment to a sustainable lifestyle, an orientation toward social justice and equality, and her passion for being engaged in collaborative community-based projects, Kate's S-R focus seamlessly encompasses people, the community, and the planet.

People: Although Kate doesn't have any employees working for her, she does hire other professionals on a contract basis and she pays their established rates. When Kate works with clients, she's mindful of how she treats them. In consultations, she pays careful attention to what clients are saying and not saying, making sure she gives her clients both what they want and what they actually need. "I'll make recommendations based on what I think serves the highest [good for clients]. I listen really deeply. I listen behind the lines to what's below the surface, as well as to what I'm hearing. I'm listening for what is trying to emerge because that's where there are double signals between what's being said and what's going on at a deeper level."

Prior to taking on projects or requests for her services, Kate checks to see if they fit with her values and purpose. Kate notes that she often takes on work on a *pro bono* basis when a project excites her and aligns with her purpose: "I take on projects for free when they align with my purpose, and when I know I can bring all of my networks and skills to the project. A lot of my work feels mission-based or mission-driven."

When it comes to choosing suppliers, contractors, or vendors, Kate favors local suppliers. Kate also tends to go with suppliers and vendors with whom she feels a personal rapport and shares S-R values. She may work with people based on intuition and the potential for fulfilling interaction. She notes that she doesn't have to like a person to work with him or her—although she usually does—but she distinguishes between the times when it's important to like the person and the times when it's good to have differences because those differences can also generate a strong, dynamic synergy.

Community: Connecting with others, whether at the individual level or at the community level, is a big part of Kate's work. She volunteers in civic elections, is active in local neighborhood events, goes to farmers' markets, and votes with her dollar. For Kate, connecting with others is also tied to the integrity of what she does. "How do I talk to my clients about being in community," she asks, "if I'm not in connection or in a community/circle with others in a way that is co-creative?"

Planet: When Kate has to travel and fly to her destination, she buys carbon credits. At home, she often bikes or takes the bus as an alternative to driving her car. When she does use the car, she's mindful of the fossil fuel she burns. She explains that during the winter season, she has a love-hate relationship with the seat-warmer feature in her car, but she also tries to be compassionate with herself about her choice.

Kate is a dedicated recycler of items that can't be reused, and since her business is home-based, it's easy for her to extend her personal practices to the professional sphere. When Kate was looking into envelopes to ship copies of her first book, she spent many hours researching which kind of envelope had the lowest environmental impact.

She has recently decided to take on another socially responsible action that's both planet and people friendly. She is developing workshops that can be delivered by phone or Skype. And, in the interests of both minimizing her carbon footprint and keeping the cost of her services affordable for everyone, she's looking at doing more of her work by phone than in-person.

S-R advantage: Kate's definition of social responsibility is tied to being in alignment with her life purpose. Says Kate, "I'm accountable to my life purpose not so much at the level of practices but in making commitments and following through based on what is really important. I'm accountable to showing up."

When she feels aligned and on purpose, she feels highly motivated—and this has been an advantage for her business. She explains that when she's aligned with her purpose she's filled with joy, she has more fun, and she's more effective in the work she does. The benefits of being connected to her purpose also spill over to those around her. For Kate, part of being in that alignment is "gift giving, trust, and love" directed to others. She says, "More magic happens when I'm in alignment."

Transformative power of an S-R business: For Kate, one of the most potent ways of transforming others through her work is by cultivating a sense of possibility and ownership in people for their own lives and communities. Kate offers the following example of how her work transforms and builds capacities. "I called a meeting in a small, rural community and made it open to everyone who cared about making it a better place for children. I facilitated the group in a certain way, and out of that process they formed another group that went on to do amazing work. I invited people to show up and engage—and they stepped up and owned the work."

Kate also sees the power of transformation in her coaching clients who are learning to use the "Make Light Work" tools to access their inner wisdom and find their own answers. "I get excited about watching light bulbs go off in people as they access that inner wisdom and shift from seeing everything as problems to seeing situations as opportunities. I see it as literally helping people make light work of navigating all the shifts we're going through in the world [right now]. There is a lot of power in seeing people and knowing without question that they each have a potent purpose and being curious about what that purpose is." Kate's most recent book, *Make Light Work in Groups*, was written specifically to help groups transform their dynamics, and nurture the power of a group to align with and live their purpose.

Words of wisdom: Kate advocates for cultivating a life purpose. "Listen to your heart and your inner knowing—cultivate that," she recommends. "Ask to be in alignment with life; ask to be true to your essence. Trust life: Be willing to go outside your comfort zone if that's where your purpose is calling you."

Kate advocates for connecting with others to make light work of both personal transformations and projects we're called to do as social change agents. Her advice in two sentences: "Ask for help. Don't do it alone."

SIX: WHEN VISION AND REALITY COLLIDE – UNPACKING THE FIRST-AID KIT

IT seems to be an inevitable fact of life that, at some point, our plans to carry out an ideal vision of a cherished dream or carefully thought-out plan are derailed by that impersonal force known as "reality." Whether the collision produces or results from a major catastrophe or a "merely annoying" fender bender that is more of an inconvenience than a calamity, the first reaction is often a mixture of dismay and stunned disbelief. If you're running a business, you can't afford to remain stunned and dismayed for too long. You need to figure out what happened and how to resolve the problem so it won't jeopardize your vision and your business.

Webmeadow, a New Hampshire-based web development company, runs on solar energy. As much as Eileen and her partner would love to work with web hosting companies that are fully green and run on sustainable, renewable energy, they've often had to accept that sometimes it's not feasible without compromising their quality of customer service. They've tried using green energy hosting companies in the past, but when those suppliers fell short on providing excellent customer service, Eileen and her partner had to make a choice: either maintain their ideals or compromise the quality of their customer service. For now, they've opted to scale back on the ideal and go with a company that comes through on the level of customer service they expect. While the hosting company does have some green strategies in place, such as going paperless, its overall green strategy isn't as all-encompassing as Eileen and her partner would like.

Entrepreneurs committed to social responsibility often feel as if they're working with a double-edged sword. They want to uphold their values about the environment or social issues, but they also need to keep an ever-watchful eye on their bottom line. Just like Eileen and her co-owner, many microentrepreneurs find that running a healthy, socially responsible small business is sometimes about making carefully considered compromises.

In this Chapter...

It's disappointing and frustrating when cold, hard reality intrudes on our ideals and the vision that we want to create for our businesses or ourselves. Whether your S-R venture has been thwarted by insufficient resources (e.g., time, money, people power) or insufficient (or too much) enthusiasm from key stakeholders, you need some solutions—preferably those that soothe the pain of bruised ideals and still offer a glimmer of hope or encouragement. This chapter considers some of the challenges you might encounter along the path of becoming an S-R business and offers some practical solutions. I'll help you to modify your S-R goals in ways that respect your concerns about financial sustainability and continue to help you make strides towards becoming more socially responsible.

Most of your challenges are likely to emerge from the following:

- Conflicting relationships, false expectations, and misunderstandings among people connected to your business.

- A lack of funds or other resources that prevent you from carrying out your plans on the scale you dreamed about.

- A sense of being overwhelmed or disillusioned with the process that makes you want to call it quits.

While it's beyond the scope of this book to anticipate and respond to every challenge that microentrepreneurs might encounter on the path to becoming (more) socially responsible businesses, I'll discuss a few key examples of the types of problems you might come face-to-face with along your S-R journey. There may not be any "easy" or "quick" solutions for some of these problems. Some of them may, in fact, pose painful dilemmas in which you have to weigh competing interests or values. In this chapter, I'll take one or two examples from each of the main areas outlined above and walk you through them to give you some general ideas on the problem-solving process. Where appropriate, I'll also identify and point you in the direction of some resources that might either offer tangible resources or inspire you to approach the problem from a different perspective.

Your Customers Are More Interested in Value than Values

You may be passionate about greening your business and giving back to the community, but you may have a few customers who don't care about your passion. Their main concerns are getting the best value at the lowest price point, and now they're wondering whether your decision to become a more socially responsible business is going to translate into higher prices and inconveniences for them.

If you're just starting out, or have only been running your business for a few years, you may not have the luxury of working only with clients who are fully aligned with and support your business philosophy and practices. That's okay. As we pointed out in the last chapter, it isn't necessary for all of your customers to share all of your values as long they're happy with the quality of your product or service and believe they're still getting good value for their money. However, if you want to work mostly with your ideal clients but find yourself continually dealing with customers who could care less about S-R business practices and their only value is getting the most for the least, you may need to revisit your marketing strategies. Eventually, you'll have to figure out where and how to reach out to your ideal market so you can start building a customer base that's more value-aligned with your company's vision, mission, and values. File this "re-visioning your ideal market" project under your long-term to-do list, and then identify what you need to do *right now* to keep your existing customers and make them happy, regular patrons.

Solution 1: Empathize and Educate

Listen and respond to customer concerns, correcting any misunderstandings or erroneous assumptions they may have about what being socially responsible means for them and what it means for you as a business. As Jane Faye of Gaia Noir observes, "Psychologically, people have a tendency to think [that] any option [which] is new or different will involve extra expense or effort for them than a regular, mainstream option. It's up to you to take the hard labor out of the situation and make it easy."

In 2007, a study found that the barriers to customers buying green products or supporting green businesses, in practice, are usually a lack of information, higher prices, reduced availability and accessibility, and wariness of corporate greenwashing.[1] Researchers found that the burden often falls to

businesses to educate their customers about the benefits of their products or
S-R vision, and try to keep the price as
affordable as possible.

While it's true that increases in
your cost of doing business in an S-R
framework may be passed along to
customers, it doesn't mean foisting
sticker shock on them. Try to be as
conservative as possible with price
increases. Troy Van Beek of Ideal
Energy Inc. often finds that his pricing
is heavily determined by market
volatility; as a result, he's had to remain
flexible in his approach to pricing.

> **"**Psychologically, people have a tendency to think [that] any option [which] is new or different will involve extra expense/effort for them than a regular, mainstream option. It's up to you to take the hard labor out of the situation and make it easy.**"**
>
> - Jane Faye, Gaia Noir

If you do have to increase the price
of your products, be upfront about the
estimated increase, why it's increasing, by how much, and when it will occur.
If you can give your customers ample lead-time, it will help them to budget
appropriately for your services or products. Make your pricing policies
transparent by publishing them on your website or posting them clearly in
your business premises (if you're not a home-based business).

Solution 2: Give Your Customers Options

If your new price points really are out of your clients' reach, you might
need to go back and rethink the assumptions you used to arrive at your price
points. What are the sources of your information? Did you solicit feedback
from your customers or do other research to guide your decision-making? If
your data show that most clients were indeed willing (in theory) to pay the
higher price points, you may just have to accept that sometimes there is a
disconnect between what customers say they would support and what they
actually do. You may find that customers grumble about the price increase but
continue to patronize your business. Head off any customer resentment by
making sure you're transparent about your reasons for increasing prices
(solution 1), and try to explain what customers will get with that price increase.

Also, consider whether you're willing or able to give clients a small break
on the price. Can you offer a discount or special on a product and still make
sure you're doing a little better than breaking even? If your business is service-

based, can you find a way to accommodate customers who would really benefit from your service but can't afford the full fee?

Recall that Mia Kalef of Emerging Families offers several options to make her services more affordable for financially strapped clients. One option would be to offer a sliding scale for your services. Another option would be to allow for a payment plan. A third option, especially if you're providing a service like Ideal Energy Inc., which offers solar and wind energy installations, is to identify government grants or rebates clients can get to reduce their costs. By helping clients get financial aid upfront, Ideal Energy Inc. makes it affordable for clients to use their services and to see a return on their investment sooner rather than later.

Solution 3: Get Buy-In from Employees

Sometimes, it isn't only your customers who are reluctant about your S-R strategies to transform your business. Your employees may also be a bit baffled at your change of direction. Getting buy-in from employees can be a challenge if they perceive the process as entailing a lot of disruption to their work. Just like with your customers, listen to your employees' concerns and try to work around their schedules. Find ways to engage your reluctant employees and help them to see the benefits of being associated with a socially responsible business. If your employees are enthusiastic about your business decisions, their motivation will translate to better performance and customer service. Happier employees can do wonders in singing the praises of your products and services to others and can serve as "ambassadors" for your S-R strategies.

The S-R Practices of Your Suppliers Fall Short of Your Expectations

In a world where increasing numbers of companies and manufacturers are branding themselves as "green" and certification by an independent body is largely a voluntary decision, you may just meet a vendor or supplier that has dabbled in greenwashing, whether or not it was intentional.

Reesa Abrams of TechCycle3 advises that all businesses should "do [their] due diligence," vetting and checking all green claims. Linh Truong of The Soap Dispensary asks for a disclosure statement listing the ingredients for the eco-friendly cleaning and personal care products she stocks. Saul Brown of Saul Good Gift Co. has a written "Code of Conduct" that he gives his suppliers, and Jane Faye of Gaia Noir prefers to deal with small, local suppliers who are well informed and more than happy to tell her where the supplies come from and how they're made.

If you discover that your suppliers' practices leave something to be desired when it comes to their green or labor practices, you have a few options—and responsibilities—before showing them the door. In Chapter 4, I mentioned that when it comes to dealing with your business network, loyalty and a willingness to work with your suppliers or vendors to troubleshoot an issue or help them improve their practices are characteristics of socially responsible businesses.

Solution 1: Give Your Suppliers a Chance

If your suppliers are willing and able to get their practices up to par, the next step is to sit down and discuss a timeline, the costs that suppliers will have to pass along to you and their other customers, and the process of how your suppliers will be able to offer proof that they've made the changes requested. Will it require that they get certification from a third-party? If you're requiring this step from your suppliers, are you willing to do the same for your company? You may have to accept that working with your existing suppliers so they meet S-R standards will be a long-term and potentially costly project.

Solution 2: Look for Suppliers that Fit Your S-R Vision

Sometimes, you really can't "teach an old dog new tricks." Large or well-established suppliers may not be able to make changes to their systems. If your suppliers are unable or unwilling to change their practices in the near future, then you may have to start looking for new suppliers who are a little more flexible about meeting customers' needs or have already demonstrated that they adhere to S-R business practices.

Linh Truong says that one of her biggest challenges was finding companies that were willing to sell in bulk and refill the containers for her. "There are a few companies that we'd love to work with, but they don't or won't refill," she explains. "We've got around this by finding smaller, independent companies that are more flexible, more environmentally [friendly] and community-minded. The benefit is that we get to support other local, small businesses."

Melissa Cartwright of Mellifera Bees has also encountered some challenges finding sustainable suppliers for some of the products she needs, such as glass jars for the honey produced by her bees. Melissa thinks a lot about her business processes and is constantly on the look-out for better and more sustainable ways to do things that align with her values. However, she has also realized that it's a delicate balance between meeting your business needs and upholding your S-R values. "Sometimes, you have to make compromises on some issues, but not if it compromises your core values or the quality of the product," she says.

When Toby Barazzuol decided to develop a line of green recognition awards made from reclaimed and recycled materials, it meant researching and developing an entirely new network of suppliers; it's a process that is anything but instantaneous. The process of changing suppliers is also likely to take longer than you might expect. José Alejandro Flores of VOS Flips remarked that it took his company two years to find their suppliers and other business partners.

If you're not sure where to start looking for a green supplier and no one in your immediate business network has any leads, start by approaching local business associations (especially if they're affiliated with BALLE [livingeconomies.org]), or check out B Lab (bcorporation.net) or Green America's Green Business Directory (greenpages.org) for

> If your suppliers are unable or unwilling to change their practices in the near future, you may have to start looking for new suppliers who are a little more flexible about meeting customers' needs or have already demonstrated that they adhere to S-R business practices.

suggestions or ideas. These sources of information are most likely to refer you to companies that are not only more socially or community-minded in their values, but also more likely to walk their talk.

You Can't Share What You Don't Have

You want to share your good fortune with others, but you can't spread the wealth when there's nothing or little to share. If there's a little bit to share and the choice is between your employees and the community, the best idea would be to share the wealth with your employees as they are the people who help you keep the business running smoothly. They deserve to have their hard work on your behalf recognized through tangible rewards and warm sentiments. Even a small bonus as a way of saying "thank you" or as a prize for a contest would likely be appreciated.

Solution 1: Offer Shoestring Budget Benefits for Your Employees (that Still Show You Care)

If you're on a very tight budget, there may be other ways of giving or contributing to the quality of life for your employees by improving their working conditions that don't strain your finances. If you really can't afford to pay for group health coverage, and you only have one or two employees, consider setting aside a small sum as a "wellness spending account" for your employees. You could also collaborate with other small business owners and organize a series of wellness seminars for your employees that help them to proactively maintain their health and reduce stress. You might even look into partnering with a community-owned recreation center. If your employees enjoy cycling and there are some relatively safe bike paths near your workplace, you could even adopt one of Toby's strategies and invest in one or two "company bikes." (Don't forget to supply the bike helmets, too!)

Another shoestring option that might greatly improve the quality of your employees' work lives (and bank accounts) might include allowing employees to telecommute a couple of days a week. For some employees, such an arrangement may translate to significant savings on transportation and childcare costs. If your business is located in a place that requires a vehicle, allow employees to telecommute two days a week: Telecommuting will not only help them cut down on their gas expenses, it will also lower both their carbon footprints and the overall carbon footprint of your business.

Solution 2: Provide Non-Monetary Gifts to Your Community

If you can't afford to share the wealth with your community through philanthropic giving, there are ways of adding value that don't involve finances. For example, Eileen Webb of webmeadow and Reesa Abrams of TechCycle3 support their communities through providing in-kind donations of older computers to public libraries and various nonprofit organizations, respectively. It doesn't just have to be electronic equipment; donations of other kinds of office equipment, such as furniture or desk supplies, are also usually appreciated.

Giving your time and expertise to support a local cause or project, or giving other value-aligned organizations some free publicity are also greatly valued and appreciated and often more helpful than a one-time donation.

Just remember not to get too carried away and give away so much time that you're not getting any paid work done. Yes, you want to add value to your community, but you also want to grow the overall value of your business by generating long-term financial prosperity—that's good karma for the long term.

You're on a "Lemonade" Budget

You've probably heard the expression about having "champagne tastes and a lemonade pocketbook." It's often used to describe individuals who have expensive ideas or plans but don't have the budget to match the dreams or aspirations. If you're facing a disconnect between what you would like to do to make your business more sustainable and what you can afford to do, don't throw your hands up just yet. Remember, this book is grounded in the philosophy of starting where you are and taking small steps with the resources available to you now. Figure out how you can make the best lemonade possible with the ingredients you have on hand. It's also useful to remember that sustainability is about conserving and caring for resources—including your financial resources—to ensure long-term viability.

Solution 1: Look for Partners to Share the Benefits and Costs of "Champagne" Items

First, take a look at the results of your S-R Assessment (Chapter 1). If you haven't already prioritized the items based on importance and cost, go back and do that now. If there are actions that you have identified as urgent or vitally important but are too expensive to implement, consider contacting your municipal or provincial/state government or your local power supplier to see if they offer grants (or tax credits) to small businesses for any particular green fixes you need to make.[2]

A second option might be to consider partnering with local governments, other local businesses (through any business associations you belong to), or schools or community organizations to share costs (and resources) and create community-wide rather than just company-wide green solutions.[3] An example of this in action is the partnership between Climate Smart and municipal governments and corporations to provide grants to fund training and provide subsidized or low-cost environmental audits for small businesses (discussed in Chapter 2).

If there are no options for sharing costs or applying for grants or rebates, there's always the old-fashioned but reliable way of achieving the goal: Plan ahead for the purchase through tighter budgeting and savings. Specifically, set aside money in a designated "green fund" that will be used to finance S-R initiatives that are currently outside of your budget. The next couple of suggestions will provide you with some ways to think about boosting your green fund through some S-R friendly, cost-cutting measures.

Solution 2: Choose Green Measures that Also Save You Money

Boost your lemonade budget with measures that are green and cut costs. Think about choosing a few reduction-themed, money-saving S-R initiatives like reducing your energy and resource use (lowering your utility bills), and reducing or eliminating purchases (eliminating or cutting back on disposable cutlery and plates, bottled water, printer paper, etc.). Then, redirect the saved money into your green fund.

Toby Barazzuol of Eclipse Awards points out: "If you're going to make being sustainable possible and accessible, you have to be creative... [Becoming socially responsible] doesn't have to be costly."

Also, remember that lemonade costs less to produce than champagne—and lemonade probably has a smaller water footprint than champagne.[4] In a culture that seems to equate spending money and having the latest, best, or biggest model of an item with being successful, choosing initiatives that are low or no-cost might feel like an insignificant contribution compared to implementing the bigger ticket initiatives included in this book. In fact, there are plenty of low-cost or no-cost strategies you can implement that do contribute significantly to reducing your energy and resource use and carbon footprint. Reduce or banish disposables such as paper, paper coffee cups, and water bottles. Consider turning off all of your electronics and appliances before closing shop for the day. Your desktop computer and CRT monitor left on all day, every day uses nearly 1,000 kilowatts a year.[5] Think about the amount of energy used (wasted) by other office equipment that is either left on twenty-four hours a day or doesn't have the energy saving features activated. Remembering to switch off lights and unplug (or switch off from a power strip) equipment at the end of the day will not only save energy, but will also save you money. In my corner of the world, saving 1,000 kilowatt-hours by remembering to turn off computers and other office equipment translates into cutting CAD$55 from the utility bill.[6] A savings of that amount every month could help to grow your green fund in no time.

Saul Brown of Saul Good Gift Co. points out that certain socially responsible business practices can also result in greater operational efficiency, saving you money in the long run. "Being conscious of materials and waste—eliminating waste—allowed us to be more efficient and reduce costs," he says. At Saul Good Gift Co., they standardized policies around using recycled and reclaimed paper that simplified processes. They now use reclaimed paper shreds from a local printer as filler for their gift baskets, which also reduced costs.

Be discriminating about what green initiatives you launch because some may be deceptively costly. Replacing big ticket items can be costly. Keep in mind that replacing an old item with a newer version means that you not only have to figure out how to dispose of the old appliance or fixture, you also have to take into consideration the resources and embodied energy used to manufacture the new item, as well as the energy and resources needed to recycle or dispose of the old item. So while it's true that replacing old, energy or water greedy appliances and fixtures will reduce your ecological footprint, it's just as true that reducing your use of scarce resources in the first place will also shrink your footprint—and conserve your budget. Think about it: Is it really sustainable to replace an old, functioning toilet with a new, low-flush toilet if you can reduce the amount of water used per flush simply by placing a brick or plastic container filled with sand in the cistern?

Likewise, depending on the type of business you're running, do you really need an office at all? Several of the entrepreneurs I interviewed for this book made a conscious decision to keep their footprint and overhead costs low. True to the name of her business (LittleFootprint Lighting), Nancy Wahl-Scheurich keeps the company's carbon footprint small by maintaining a virtual office: No energy is being used to run a separate office, and since everyone telecommutes, no one uses fuel or generates carbon emissions commuting to work. James and his partners at Greenstack Ltd. also made the choice to keep their operations as lean as possible. For James, a lean approach means they aren't "under pressure to make profit just to cover overheads…" James points out that this gives [them] "the freedom to use sustainable materials and ethical manufacturers as far as possible."

Stay flexible and lean. Remember Linh Truong's comment that small, local suppliers are often more flexible in working with their clients? Well, the logic applies to you, too. Eileen Webb of webmeadow praises staying small. "Small or microbusinesses [should] embrace the smallness…[they] can be more flexible," she says.

You Don't Know How to Find the Time and Set Priorities

You want to contribute to your community in meaningful ways, and if you're service oriented, both by profession and temperament, the number of community engagement projects and volunteer hours you take on could quickly get out of hand. It can also pose some problems if the time and energy spent on nonprofit activities is encroaching on activities that contribute to your business' short- and long-term sustainability.

Solution 1: Check the Balance on Your Time Account

How much time you and your business can realistically devote to activities that support your local business and civic communities depends on a number of factors, including: how long you've been in business; how many hours per week or month you need to work to generate enough income to meet your financial commitments; how much time you need to set aside for administrative activities, and; how much time you need to set aside for your personal life and self-care. You may find you have less time left over to engage in volunteer work than you had anticipated.

Solution 2: Set Personal Limits

First, set some limits. Perhaps for you, one clearly defined, short-term project on a monthly or bimonthly basis works better than an on-going activity, such as working with a committee. Or, perhaps you might find that promoting local causes and businesses through a monthly newsletter or blog is better suited for your temperament and your schedule. However you choose to contribute to your community through your business, remember that choosing one project that aligns with your values should energize and inspire you.

Solution 3: Choose Projects that are Regenerative for You and the Community

With so many volunteer options to choose from, it can be a challenge trying to decide where to invest the time into social commitments that yield the most value—in the short and long run—for your community. Reesa Abrams advises going for quality not quantity when it comes to donating your time and energy. "Focus… and find [projects] that provide a real difference," she says. Toby Barazzuol expresses a similar point of view and added that his company tries to invest in hands-on projects such as creating community gardens or green roofs that have real, lasting value.

Give some thought to what other kinds of revitalization projects you could contribute to that would produce tangible, positive changes in your community. If you would rather sow and tend to intellectual seeds and gardens, there is, as Toby points out, plenty that needs to be done in terms of working to change the current unsustainable business model from competitive to cooperative and collaborative. Seek out groups that are committed to creating change through revitalizing communities, and explore how you can contribute your skills and experience to planning or implementing projects that will result in lasting social and economic improvements in your community.

You're Suffering from Analysis Paralysis and Option Overload

If you feel paralyzed just thinking about how to choose and set measurable goals—never mind figuring out how to find and consistently track information that will show you whether you're on target with meeting your goals (see Chapter 1)—you might understandably feel like shrugging off the whole exercise. Before you succumb to analysis paralysis or run for the hills, step back, breathe, and keep the following fixes in mind:

Solution 1: Be Selective in What You Take On

Be selective. First, not all of the S-R initiatives discussed in this book will apply to your business, and you don't have to implement the relevant strategies all at once. If some of the relevant S-R initiatives don't quite fit for your company, by all means feel free to modify the details to suit your resources and circumstances. If, at second glance, it seems that you've overestimated how many S-R initiatives you can feasibly implement within a given time frame, give yourself a break. Revise your time line for some of the projects, break them down into smaller steps, or reduce the number of projects on your S-R "to-do" list. You'll be better off for succeeding at one or two actions than struggling and missing the mark by taking on multiple projects at once—or not getting started at all.

Solution 2: Simplify the Data Tracking Process

Make life simple for yourself by tracking information that you already have or could easily find. For example, if you want to reduce the amount of electricity you use, you would use your utility bill to track how many kilowatt-hours you're using on a monthly or bi-monthly basis. To track the changes, set up a table with two columns—month and total kilowatt hours used—in a software program like Microsoft Excel. Every month when you get your utility bill, simply enter the information into the table at the same time you pay the bill. Decide on a quarterly or yearly target number and timeline to meet your goal. At the end of the time period, check whether you have achieved your target. You may want to start with just one energy reduction action and a clear target so you know exactly what kind of savings you should expect to see. For example, if you know that turning the computer off at the end of the day saves "x" amount of kilowatt hours over a six-month period, then you know that your target usage should be reduced by "x" amount at the end of six months.

If your strategies include switching off the computers, equipment, and lights at the end of the day, create a visible checklist that you can post near the office door so you can note how often you remember to practice the new behavior.

Solution 3: Ask for Help and Get Support

Saul Brown of Saul Good Gift Co. noted that one of the biggest challenges for him when he started out was the lack of readily accessible mentorship and a network of experienced individuals to call on for advice. Indeed, one of the reasons Saul started the group LOCO BC was to create a network of local businesses with similar values.

If you're a solopreneur, find like-minded microentrepreneurs by either joining an existing group or forming an S-R transformation group, through a Meetup (meetup.com) or Action Circle. It's easier to follow through on goals when you have some accountability or a supportive group you can commiserate with. Your fellow group members can celebrate with you when you meet a goal, and they can help you identify and solve challenges that might be preventing you from meeting your goals.

If finding or starting a group isn't feasible, check out the Green Business Directory (greenpages.org) or the B Lab website (bcorporation.net) to find microentrepreneurs who have similar businesses to yours and who might be willing to mentor you or give you some tips on prioritizing and choosing S-R strategies if you're feeling stuck.

You Worry About Postponing or Downsizing Your S-R Vision

You want your business to be socially responsible and environmentally sustainable: a model S-R business for the long haul. At the same time, you're watching out for the organizational and financial sustainability of your business. You also don't want to deplete your personal energy reserves if you want your business to thrive. While

> Opting to defer implementing S-R strategies that are too much of a stretch for our current resources is the wise course, and reduces the likelihood of failure or defeat in the long run.

businesses are increasingly expected to operate in a socially responsible manner, they're still expected to generate sufficient revenue to make profits and meet their financial obligations.

What do you do when you're faced with competing expectations and clashing demands on your time and resources? What if you realize that your business doesn't have—and, for the foreseeable future, likely won't have—the resources to support a comprehensive S-R overhaul? Should you try to please everyone and stretch the resources so you can do a little of everything, even if that means being less effective, overall?

Solution 1: Plan for Long-Term Value Rather than Instant Success (Don't Confuse Deferral with Defeat)

In a culture where we expect to get almost everything instantly, where we're told to pursue our passions and trust that the money will follow, and where we roll our eyes at the quaint notion of deferred gratification, it would be easy to get caught up in setting ambitious goals with unrealistic timelines or budgets so that we appear to be on top of our game. If we can't do or have it all instantly, should we just give up and not bother at all? The answer, of course, is no.

Opting to defer implementing S-R strategies that are too much of a stretch for our current resources is the wise course, and reduces the likelihood of failure or defeat in the long run. As Melissa Cartwright points out, "It's great to have an ultimate goal, but acknowledge when you can't make it happen."

Both Saul Brown and Eileen Webb also suggest that, in some cases, it's better to be patient and wait until you have the funds to get what you really want and do it right the first time. That might look like waiting until you can afford to build a website that meets all of your needs, or waiting to upgrade or replace equipment.

Skip the "all or nothing" thinking. We can choose not to buy into the "play big or go home" thinking. We can decide that the better strategy is to start from where we are, work with what we have, and scale down our S-R vision. We can take small, manageable, and incremental steps that lead to lasting changes. We can demonstrate that small businesses can, indeed, create big change.

Solution 2: Expect Delays and Bumps in the Road—and Enjoy the Journey Anyway

You're bound to run into some delays and bumpy patches along the way to becoming a full-fledged, socially responsible business, but these aren't causes for giving up. You'll likely experience less stress and far fewer headaches if you accept where you are on your journey and figure out how to make the best use of the "down time." You might want to try emulating Julie Beyer of For the Love of Food and treat your business as a spiritual practice, or take the approach of Kate Sutherland and be intentional about ensuring that your actions serve the highest good.

When it seems as though things are going wrong, take the time to step back and appreciate what you have been able to achieve. Remind yourself that small changes make a difference—and doing them right makes a bigger difference.

There is, of course, no magic cure that will work for everyone, but if you're still finding that the collision between your S-R vision and financial reality is giving you a headache, consult the chapter checklist and try the remedies outlined in this chapter.

CHAPTER CHECKLIST:

✔ Balance the long-term sustainability of your business with your ability to successfully run an S-R focused business. Be patient and wait to do things right the first time. If you catch yourself falling into all-or-nothing thinking, remember the mantra: Small, incremental steps can lead to big, lasting changes.

✔ While you don't want to compete solely on price, you also don't want to lose valuable customers. Look into finding ways to offer your customers a bit of a break. If many of your customers are remarking that your price increases are now out of their league, re-examine your figures and assumptions and rethink prohibitive increases.

✔ Re-examine your costs and see if you can reduce expenses rather than raise prices.

✔ Seek out small, local partners who are more willing to be flexible and more environmentally focused and community-minded.

✔ Find creative, low-cost ways to show your employees that you value their work and contributions to your business.

✔ As one business alone, you may not be able to afford health insurance or other benefits for your employees, but if you collaborate with others, you might be able to purchase some benefit packages as a group or through an organization.

✔ Consider sharing or exchanging resources and materials at a community level.

✔ Find strategies that fit within a "lemonade" pocketbook: Look for green cost-saving measures and use the money saved to finance your big-ticket items.

✔ Value your time and set some priorities and limits when it comes to adding value to the community through volunteering.

✔ Simplify your life by simplifying your data-tracking.

✔ Seek out mentors, experts, and like-minded colleagues from whom you can learn more about running a socially responsible business.

✔ Don't forget to have fun and take care of yourself.

Suzanne Akin, Akinz

Location: Fort Collins, Colorado, U.S.

Product/Service: Casual clothing line and custom-made beanie hats

Company start date: November 2007

Company website: akinz.com

Bio: Suzanne is a fashion designer turned retail manager, turned professional wanderer, turned freelance graphic designer who has finally found her way back to fashion design. She started her clothing line as a hobby and has had the opportunity to watch it grow into a viable business through persistence, hard work, and word-of-mouth.

Inspiration: Suzanne had always wanted to be in the clothing industry and studied fashion design in college, but she hadn't quite found the right niche to work for in the fashion world. She wanted the opportunity to create fun and unique clothing for people with an active lifestyle, so she started Akinz—inspired by the wakeboarding community in Texas. When she moved to Colorado several years ago, she switched her focus from wakeboarding to snowboarding.

Suzanne's move to Fort Collins, Colorado, with its huge focus on participating in local activities and supporting local businesses, inspired her to extend her personal values about social responsibility to her business. Suzanne got involved with a group called 'Be Local,' which focuses on getting people to support their local community. She notes that "in Fort Collins, there are some really great examples of medium and big businesses—New Belgium Brewing and Otterbox—who still give back locally."

Business philosophy: For Suzanne, being socially responsible as a business means thinking about how to help and change the world immediately around you, instead of just focusing on what's best for your bottom line. To achieve this with Akinz, Suzanne hand-makes a lot of the clothing items herself using local products and the help of other, local businesses. Says Suzanne, "I get all of our promotional products printed through local businesses, support local nonprofits and city programs, and get the rest of my items produced in the U.S. instead of outsourcing overseas."

Social Responsibility in Action

Overall: While Suzanne's S-R initiatives emphasize engaging with and supporting her local community, several of her business decisions, like using organic and recycled fabrics, and choosing local manufacturers whenever possible, are also planet friendly and help to reduce her company's carbon footprint.

People: Suzanne chooses her vendors and contractors using three criteria: location, price, and customer service. Her first preference is to get her products (or the materials for her products) made locally, if the quality is the same as what she could get from a manufacturer out of state or overseas. "Even if it costs slightly more than it would elsewhere, you're putting money back into the local economy, and that, in turn, supports you," says Suzanne, "as well as avoids shipping costs."

Suzanne has often found it challenging to find local and U.S.-based manufacturers. She would like to be able to work with a manufacturer for her products and create a manufacturing process for other businesses that would prefer to have their products made locally but currently have to outsource. "Price," as Suzanne points out, "is always a concern for any business." She notes that she would love to make all of her decisions without price as a factor, but she acknowledges that "businesses have to make money," too.

Suzanne also places a high priority on customer service. She describes a situation with a U.S.-based supplier that sold blank t-shirts that she loved at a good price. When the customer service fell short, Suzanne had to find a new supplier. "Every time I put in an order, there seemed to be an issue that would arise either with shipping times, incorrect products, or something else," she says. "After a while, it [became] a business risk to continue working with people like that." The experience serves as a reminder to Suzanne that "others expect the best in customer service out of me from my business, and I try to keep that in mind when handling my outgoing orders."

Community: Suzanne participates in and contributes to a number of programs intended to support the local economy and her community. She donates to a local bike co-op that provides free bike maintenance—the sole form of transportation for many people who live in Fort Collins. She also helps out with a bike donation program to support the city's free bike rental program for people who temporarily need a bike, or for those who have friends and family visiting from out of town.

Given her connection to and love of outdoor activity, Suzanne also gives time and resources to sports activities and campaigns intended to encourage people to become less sedentary and more active. Her company has sponsored the local Ultimate Frisbee leagues for the last couple of years and manages a local snowboarding club. She also offers discounts to a local art club called Articulate City, and organizes a local shopping marketplace on Black Friday to encourage people to shop at their local businesses.

Planet: Suzanne's preference for using local businesses and manufacturers helps to reduce her carbon footprint, as does using organic and recycled materials for some of her product lines.

S-R advantage: Suzanne notes that both people within the community and company get excited when they hear about what her company is trying to do to help the local environment. Operating a socially responsible business serves as a motivator for creativity, too. Suzanne is constantly thinking of new and creative ways to help the local scene, which in turn drives better, newer ideas, and more sales for her business.

Transformative power of an S-R business: Suzanne uses her community engagement activities through the bike and snowboarding programs to promote a healthier lifestyle by encouraging people to get out into nature and be more active.

Words of wisdom: Small steps can make a difference. "One thing I realized as I got more involved and motivated in helping our local economy and improving our business practices is that it doesn't take huge steps to make a difference," says Suzanne.

For example, host an event. "You could simply host a local event that doesn't cost you a lot of money and that gets the community members out of their homes and socializing with one another," suggests Suzanne. Or, commit to wasting less and choosing to recycle when you can't reuse. "Recycle your paper instead of throwing it away. Any little change makes a difference. I promise: The more small steps you take, the more business changes you will want to make."

Eileen Webb, webmeadow

Location: Littleton, New Hampshire, U.S.

Product/Service: Solar-powered website design and development

Company start date: 2005

Company website: webmeadow.com

Bio: Eileen and her partner are professional web developers who spent many years living in Silicon Valley (i.e., the South Bay area of San Francisco) developing websites and managing servers and databases of large corporations before moving to Littleton, New Hampshire. She and her partner work primarily with clients whose mission is to make the world a better place.

Inspiration: Tired of the crazy, long hours at their Silicon Valley jobs, never having time for themselves, and feeling exhausted, Eileen and her partner opted for a major lifestyle change and moved to New Hampshire where they had a family home and some land. At first, they ran a bakery, but they soon discovered the hours were just as crazy and the work was still exhausting. They started developing websites on an informal basis for friends who needed websites, and soon realized that it would be a good way to make a living since they could work from home and not have to commute to the nearest big city. The work would also allow them to continue enjoying their lives on the small farm that they started.

Business philosophy: Webmeadow's business mission and S-R philosophy is grounded in helping clients and the earth at the same time. They do this by building websites that meet their clients' business and organizational performance needs and by reducing their carbon footprint using solar power to run their home and business.

Social Responsibility in Action

Overall: Their socially responsible business practices include taking steps to minimize their carbon footprint; giving back to their community; engaging with their customers and potential customers through their blog; and treating vendors and contractors fairly. Eileen and her partner run their business with the same values by which they live.

People: Because webmeadow is so small, they don't have any regular employees. However, they do occasionally hire interns and they do regularly partner with freelance web designers for their projects. They pay a living wage for all of their workers. With their younger interns, Eileen and her partner take the time to teach and promote financial literacy. They give lessons on the power of compound interest, and why it's important to save early. Eileen and her partner encourage workers to set up retirement accounts and offer to pay a portion of salaries directly to those accounts.

When it comes to choosing suppliers, contractors, and vendors to work with, Eileen starts mostly with finding people with whom they get along. For partners they work with on a regular basis, such as their graphic design partners, they look for people with whom they have a personal rapport or shared values. As Eileen points out, "It works out perfectly that the people we click with are the people who share our values." Their two design partners are Pixels and Pulp (pixelsandpulp.com), located in southern Maine, and Rock and Feather (rockandfeather.com), located in San Francisco, California. Both of these companies are committed to green business practices, such as using Forest Steward Council certified paper and vegetable-based inks for print jobs, and undergoing the Green Business certification process (Rock and Feather).

As for working with green web hosting companies, Eileen notes that while they prefer to use a company that uses alternative energy (or, at the very least, buys credits for wind power or other alternative energy sources), they haven't had the good luck to find a vendor that meets both their sustainability goals and their business needs. For now, they've settled for using a larger web hosting company that does green stuff "the way corporate America does green stuff," but does provide high quality service, which in turn means they're able to fulfill their customer service responsibilities. As Eileen points out, it doesn't matter if you have wind-powered hosting if the server isn't up and running. Although they're not able to rely on green-powered web hosting companies for their clients' websites, they can at least guarantee that their clients' websites are developed using solar power.

Eileen and her partner also engage in extensive consultations with their clients who are mostly nonprofits. "We do a lot of talking with people, especially to help them make sure they spend their money well, because they're spending a lot of money if they're working with us. We don't want them to say, 'No one has ever used this part of the site.' We want them to say, 'Wow, this was a great investment. Look how well it's working for us.'"

Community: Eileen volunteers with the local library a couple of hours per month to do Q&A sessions on using technology and e-readers. Eileen explains, "There are a lot of older people who've been given iPads and Kindles but can't figure out how to get their library books on them, so I help them figure it out." They also donate monitors and computer equipment to libraries and other organizations that are using energy-draining, outdated technology. "We give the libraries our outdated computers, which are still only a couple of years old. That helps them reduce their energy usage. Our lifestyle also allows us to… share our more technologically minded ideas with them."

Planet: In addition to relying entirely on solar power to run their home, business, and small farm, Eileen and her partner also offset the power used by their suppliers and vendors by purchasing renewable energy credits, finding ways to work as efficiently as possible, and composting, reusing, or recycling everything possible.

S-R advantage: "It's much easier to work on something when it's really awesome and you really want to help the client make a positive difference," says Eileen. "Even if I won the lottery, I'd still want to do what I'm doing." While they took on a wider array of clients when they first started their business, they now get to work more with their ideal clients: organizations that want to make the world a better place and that want to work with socially responsible businesses. "Now," says Eileen, "our clients are self-seeding. Others see that we work with nonprofits, so we get more calls from those kinds of organizations." But where they see the transformative power of their business is in how they get to educate others about the issues that they care about. With clients, they often discuss the environmental impacts of technology, particularly how much energy is used to design a website.

Transformative power of an S-R business: Eileen notes that many of webmeadow's clients already share the same types of values as theirs around wanting to make a positive change in the world. Many organizations have implemented the three S-R strands into their own business processes. "A lot of our clients are networked together—a good chunk of them are in the Bay Area and are very much in the S-R end of the spectrum already."

Words of wisdom: Eileen believes that small can be a good thing. "One thing for small businesses or microbusinesses is to embrace the smallness of your company," she advises. "There are so many things that small businesses are good at where they can be more flexible [in their business strategies and processes]." For example, she points to not having to commute or rent a commercial space. "Working from home means not having a lease, which is better, financially, for the business."

Eileen also recommends watching your workload. "Don't pretend to be bigger than you are. That includes taking on larger clients if it isn't a good fit for where you are at. If it's not a good match, it's not a good match, and it won't work," she warns. "Be genuine and know your niche; it's better for long-term business."

ONE LAST WORD:
THE JOURNEY
CONTINUES

YEARS ago, when I graduated with a Master's degree in Criminology and a set of social justice-tinted lenses, I wanted a career that would enable me to help create a more socially just world. I thought I'd be making that difference either through an academic career or at a nonprofit organization—not by working with social enterprises and social entrepreneurs to help them achieve social good through their business practices.

Back then, in the mid-1990s, I knew of only a few businesses that seemed to care about something in addition to profits, and I figured they were the exception rather than the rule as far as the business sector went. I hadn't heard of the terms "social entrepreneur," "social enterprise," or "socially responsible businesses," and back then it wouldn't have occurred to me to work with these kinds of enterprises, let alone write a book on social responsibility for micro-entrepreneurs, or become an accidental microentrepreneur, myself. After working as an institutional research analyst for many years, my career path branched off in a different direction that led me toward working with social entrepreneurs and consulting with them to help them achieve social good through their business practices. *Small Business, Big Change* represents a continuing desire to use my background to help social change organizations and businesses that want to make a positive difference in the world.

After reading this far, I hope you've come away both sobered and inspired by what it takes to become a socially responsible business. As you read, you may have noticed a recurring theme: Many of the entrepreneurs I interviewed freely admitted that operating a business from a socially responsible stance is often more work and requires more patience than doing business "the usual way." You'll also have noticed that not one of those socially responsible entrepreneurs would dream of doing things any differently. Even those who stepped up to the social responsibility (S-R) plate a bit later in the lives of their businesses are consistently re-inspired when they see how even the small steps they take can add up to big changes.

Even though the S-R journey won't always be easy, my hope is that the material and resources in this book have given you the tools to navigate the choppy waters and have inspired you to keep going forward at the pace that best serves the highest good for everyone. By following the "small steps" mantra, you'll be able to pace yourself, be effective, and enjoy the journey as you transform your business, your people and community, and the planet. Remember to have compassion for yourself if you fall short of your goals at times, find your community of like-minded entrepreneurs and changemakers, and celebrate all of your successes along the way.

Goals by S-R Strand (People, Planet, and Profits/Prosperity) – A Recap

People: Treating Employees, Suppliers, and Others in Your Business Network Well (Chapter 4)

Within 3 months

- Invite a financial planning expert to talk to your employees about socially responsible investment portfolios and how to set up self-directed retirement savings accounts.

- Acknowledge your employees (or independent contractors) regularly. A reminder from Toby at Eclipse Awards: Be generous with giving professional and personal recognition to all the people who work for you and make your business a success, not just the super achievers.

- Allow for some flexibility in work schedules and arrangements based on what's appropriate for your business. Offer flex time, telecommuting, and other remote work options.

- Stress the importance of taking scheduled breaks throughout the day. Encourage off-site contract workers to follow the same practices.

- Encourage staff to take frequent mini-breaks if they spend a lot of time in front of a computer. Make sure their workstations are ergonomically correct for them, and ensure they aren't spending extended periods of time sitting in front of their computer.

- Have some healthy treats and beverages available in your lunch room for your employees. Stress the importance of staying hydrated and nourished throughout the day. (Be doubly good and choose organic and/or fair trade tea, coffee, sugar, and chocolate. By choosing fairly traded items, you're contributing to better pay and working conditions for the producers in developing countries.)

- Respect employees' personal and family time. Don't make a habit of contacting employees (or other business associates) about work-related matters during their free time, and don't ask them to give up their free time without finding some way to compensate them for their work outside of working hours.

- Give your employees time off to participate in community engagement activities of their choosing.

- Start mentoring your employees. Sharing your wisdom, experience, and expertise, and informally coaching others to excel in their jobs, to learn more about your industry, and so on, are all cost-free yet immeasurably valuable alternatives to formal professional development.

- Encourage your employees to share their ideas on how to make your business more socially responsible.

- Pay your employees, contract workers, suppliers, and other business service providers on time.

Within 1 year

Within Your Business:

- Draft core guiding principles and policies that will govern wages and working conditions, benefits, professional development opportunities, etc. in your company.

- Investigate professional development opportunities that will help your employees to build their skills and career path; encourage your employees to pursue professional development options.

- Be a champion for fair wages and safe working conditions both in your own operation and those of your suppliers.

- Promote a workplace wellness program. Consider collaborating with other micro or small businesses to develop an affordable, win-win package for everyone.

- Ask your employees which employee benefits they would find most useful and valuable, and implement them according to priority and when financially possible.

Outside Your Business:

- Make a list of contractors, vendors, and suppliers that serve your business. Prepare a short questionnaire regarding employment practices or matters regarding diversity, inclusion, labor conditions, sourcing for ingredients/parts, and other S-R concerns.

- Make others aware of your company's mission, vision, values, and policies in a formal document or statement. Emphasize which values and policies will affect your business relationship. Help others identify what changes they need to make to meet your conditions.

Long term

Inside Your Business:

- Aim to pay your employees a living wage. Remember, it can be a composite of both the hourly wage and benefits.

- Help your employees set up a retirement savings plan so that a small percentage of their paycheck goes directly into the account.

- Put in place a profit- or gain-sharing plan that sets aside a meaningful share of annual profits for all of your qualified employees.

- Find a way to provide employees equity (i.e., shares) in the business if the business' legal structure allows it.

- Set up a philanthropic matching gift program that allows your employees to choose where they want to make a financial donation. Better yet, give your employees some paid time off to offer a hands-on contribution, such as volunteer hours, to a local organization or cause they support or would like to support.

Outside Your Business:

- Look into joining up with other micro and small businesses or business associations to see if it's possible as a group to purchase basic or extended health care insurance for employees.

- Reach out and connect with colleagues and competitors to identify and create wealth-generating collaborative projects with them.

- Share your network and host small networking events for your business contacts and colleagues.

- Support equal opportunity by seeking out and developing partnerships with under-utilized businesses and social enterprises.

- Treat your suppliers, vendors, and other business associates and professionals in your network as equals; listen to and seek out their point of view, and ensure that their businesses are also benefitting from the relationship.

- Don't expect deeply discounted prices and demand "extras."

- Be loyal to your suppliers and other service providers and be willing to forgive non-serious, honest mistakes.

People: Showing Customers You Care (Chapter 5)

Within 3 months

- Talk to your customers about your S-R strategies and find out what matters to them.

- Design a survey or organize a focus group to collect customer feedback and ideas on what S-R strategies customers would like to see you implement.

- Touch base with your customers on a regular basis through social media, direct mail marketing, and other means.

- Produce a short customer satisfaction survey (keep it to about five items) you can send out with your products or invoices.

- Invite customers to send their questions, comments, or feedback through your website, social media outlets, or by phone, and be sure you respond promptly to their questions or comments.

- Be interactive with your customers; create an online community for them, and find ways to get them engaged in social activism.

- Produce an e-newsletter that tells customers about various social or environmental issues that are of concern to them (and you) and what actions they can take to make a difference. Send your e-newsletter out on a regular basis, like every quarter or on major holidays.

Within 1 year

- Put a small blurb on your packaging that directs customers to your website or social media site to learn more about issues that are important to you and your company.

- Hold "Customer Appreciation" events on several occasions throughout the year. Be creative about organizing events that not only recognize your customers' loyalty, but also demonstrate that you're attuned to their values.

- Invite new clients to your office and give them a tour of the building if, like Toby of Eclipse Awards and Saul of Saul Good Gift Co., you have some interesting green features in your building.

- Participate in community events that raise awareness about social or environmental issues that are important to you and your customers. Consider adopting this strategy suggested by Ben Cohen and Mal Warwick: Set up an exhibit or information booth with materials explaining why an issue is important to you and what customers can do to help out or get involved. *Note:* Be discerning about how you present the problems and solutions; you don't want to appear as though you're exploiting a social issue or cause just to generate PR or business opportunities for your company.

- Invite representatives from a local nonprofit (or local branch of a national or international NGO) to set up a table for a day or evening (if you have a brick and mortar retail business) and raise awareness about their cause. Explain to your customers that a portion of their purchases that day or evening will be donated to the organization.

- Consider hosting an Action Circle for your customers (Action Circles are discussed in more detail in Chapter 3). *Note:* This strategy will work better for some kinds of businesses (e.g., those that have a community of regular clients, already offer workshops/group events, and don't have privacy/confidentiality as an issue) than others.

Long term

- Be transparent and proactive in the face of problems. For example, recall faulty products and fix errors. Offer a refund or discount on future services/purchases to make up for any inconveniences to customers.

- Whether your product is mass-produced (in a sustainable manner, of course), made in small batches, or is custom-made, establish a refund policy that finds a fair balance between meeting the needs of your customers and of your business. The same goes for service-based businesses.

- Provide matching donations or give a portion of each sale to a specific cause. Use your online community to find out from your customers which cause(s) they'd like you to support.

- Introduce your customers to other great products and businesses. Remember that the best customer relationships thrive on two-way communication, so be willing to learn about other products, businesses, or processes from your customers, too.

Planet: Being More Eco-conscious and Green (Chapter 2)

Within 3 months

- Check the size of your carbon, water, and ecological footprints using one of the D-I-Y tools listed earlier in this chapter. Most of these online calculators and mobile-based apps also provide you with tips on how to reduce your footprint and assess your environmental impact.

- Turn off room lights and appliances when you're not using them. Use a central power strip and switch off appliances and electronics from the strip. (*Note*: If your phone line is through your internet connection, make sure your modem and router are plugged into a separate outlet, or you'll inadvertently disconnect your phone service!)

- Activate the energy-saving settings on your computer.

- Switch to rechargeable batteries, and remember to unplug rechargers when they're not in use.

- Invest in a stainless steel water bottle and a travel mug to replace all of your disposable beverage containers.

- Reduce your paper use; be selective about what you print. If you must print, select the double-sided print setting on your printer/photocopier.

- Choose 100% recycled paper when you must print documents. If you must use mixed source (e.g., 30% recycled content), make sure it's certified by a third-party organization such as the Forest Stewardship Council (FSC).

- Use e-mail and cloud-based tools like Dropbox (dropbox.com) or Google Drive (drive.google.com), rather than faxes or snail mail to share documents.

- Reuse paper. Turn your junk mail into scrap paper. If you printed a rough draft using one-sided printing, use the other side as scrap paper.

- Cancel the junk mail and catalogs. Phone the catalog companies to be removed from their mailing lists, and sign up for the Mail Preference service through Direct Marketing Association (dmachoice.org).

- Refill (first choice) or recycle ink cartridges and toners.

- Encourage employees to bring their lunches in reusable containers or wrappers. Make it easy for your employees to bring their lunch from home: Make sure they have a fully equipped lunch room. Adopt one of Toby's strategies and implement a contest to reward sustainable behavior.

- Replace disposable cups, plates, cutlery, etc., with reusable items. If you must use disposable items, find environmentally friendly options that are biodegradable.

- Fix leaky faucets or problem toilets right away, or notify the building maintenance workers if you're in a leased office space.

- Consider letting your employees telecommute one or two days a week.

- Opt for virtual meetings (e.g., teleconferences or web conferences) over long distance travel.

- Buy carbon credits when you do have to travel by air.

Within 1 year

- Be proactive: Solicit feedback or conduct a customer survey to gauge your customers' environmental values and figure out how you can respond to their concerns through your S-R practices. Better yet, engage your customers when planning your planet friendly S-R actions.

- Include environmental information about your product on the labeling. Alternatively, keep printing and packaging to a minimum: Post environmental information about your product on your website, and provide a link to your website on your packaging.

- Switch to environmentally friendly packaging; work with a labeling vendor that uses recycled paper and vegetable-based inks. Go one or two steps further: Minimize packaging as much as possible, and make it easy for clients to recycle or reuse the packaging materials.

- Switch to reading newspapers, magazines, and other materials in digital formats. Also, instead of printing an article or story you see online, save it using a program like Read It Later (readitlaterlist.com) or Instapaper (instapaper.com) that lets you collect all of your online reading material for review later on the device of your choice, such as a tablet, laptop, smart phone, or e-reader.

- Take paperless notes using apps such as Evernote (evernote.com) or Zotero (zotero.org).

- Repair equipment rather than automatically replacing items when you experience problems. When you absolutely must replace something, find out if the manufacturer takes the product back for disassembly, remanufacturing, or recycling.

- Consider using Freecycle (freecycle.org) or Craigslist (craigslist.org) for letting go of equipment that is still in good condition but that you no longer need. Likewise, you could also use Freecycle or Craigslist to find "gently used" equipment that you need rather than buying the items new.

- When it's time to replace your computer, consider switching to a laptop computer as it uses less energy than a desktop computer.

- Replace incandescent light bulbs with more energy-efficient bulbs such as compact fluorescent light bulbs (CFLs) or light-emitting diodes (LEDs). LEDs are ultimately the biggest energy and money-saver because they're the most efficient and last for ten or more years, but they're an expensive investment upfront. (The average cost for one bulb is about US$35). The next best bet is a CFL bulb at a fraction of the cost (around US$4), though CFLs do pose some environmental concerns due to the small amount of mercury present in the bulb.

- Find low-tech, low-cost ways to conserve water and avoid replacing plumbing equipment unnecessarily.

- Choose cleaning products that are environmentally friendly and free of harsh chemicals. If your office relies on the services of a janitor, ask the janitorial services company to switch to eco-friendly products. Alternatively, ask the janitor to use eco-friendly products that you will supply for your office. (*Tip:* Read labels carefully and make sure you know the difference between an authentic eco-label and an impressive looking but meaningless label. Also, baking soda, distilled white vinegar, water, lemon, and either tea tree or pine essential oils are handy ingredients for making your own inexpensive, yet effective, cleaning products.)

- Set up a program of incentives to encourage your employees to opt for sustainable modes of transportation for their daily commute (assuming your employees live within biking or walking distance from work).

- Look into carbon neutral options for local deliveries (e.g., bicycle couriers, delivery tricycles) and purchase carbon offsets for long-distance shipping, if applicable.

Long term

- Develop a sustainable purchasing policy and work with your current suppliers to help them meet your standards. Make a commitment to screen all future suppliers and vendors on their sustainability practices. For some ideas on what types of questions you should be asking, consult the resources at the International Institute for Sustainable Development (iisd.org).

- Establish a policy of transparency regarding your own business, production, and distribution policies. Make your policies available and easy to find on your website, and include the URL for the website on your packaging and other promotional materials.

- Become a certified B Corporation or green business through a recognized and reputable organization, such as B Lab (bcorporation.net) or Green America (greenbusinessnetwork.org). *Note:* This process can often take at least six months, so it's a long-term commitment.

- Re-evaluate the design of your product to see if you can improve its overall environmental footprint, and/or extend its lifecycle from production to disposal. If you need some help with the design process, explore IDEO's Human-centered Design Toolkit (ideo.com/work/human-centered design toolkit). If you're stymied by where to research materials that are more sustainable, visit Cradle to Cradle Products Innovation Institute (c2ccertified.org) as a starting point.

- Ensure that all staff and partners are educated about your sustainability policies. Invest in training, if needed. Better yet, include your employees and major partners in the process of designing those policies or putting together a training program.

- Reduce the number of days you use your car to get around, and encourage any employees to do the same. Make it more fun and doable by offering incentives such as bus passes, bike helmets, and the availability of a company bike.

- Encourage your local business community to learn about and apply some basic industrial ecology principles. Work together to create a business ecosystem in which waste is reduced or repurposed. In Chapter 3, we'll discuss a successful materials exchange program started by Saul Brown, owner of Saul Good Gift Co.

- Save for and invest in a professional energy and environmental audit.

- Consider switching to alternate energy sources to power your business.

Profits/Prosperity: Giving Back to the Community (Chapter 3)

Within 3 months

- Research and implement any financial or legal processes that need to be in place to allow your company to make a donation to a registered local or international nonprofit organization.

- Consider switching to a credit union or financial institution with a good reputation for supporting micro and small businesses and supporting economic development projects that yield positive social change. Alternatively, chat with your current bank's small business department and find ways to educate/encourage them to offer more community support.

- Join a business association that advocates for local, independently owned businesses and building local economies. If there's no such organization in your area, contact an organization like BALLE (livingeconomies.org) and research the feasibility of setting up a chapter in your area.

- Get involved with launching or supporting a "buy local" initiative in your community. Evaluate where you can shift up to 10% of your retail dollars to local businesses and suppliers.

- Invite staff or volunteers from a local nonprofit to set up at your business (if you operate out of commercial space) to raise awareness about any new campaigns they've just launched. Depending on the type of business you run, you could donate a portion of each sale to the organization, or you could invite the organization to a staff meeting and give your employees the option of donating time (volunteering) or money.

- Sponsor a charitable event in your local community. If you don't have the resources to actually sponsor events, find some other way of making a significant contribution to events.

Within 1 year

- Convene or sponsor an Action Circle (bethechangeearthalliance.org/circles), Jelly (workatjelly.com), or Meetup (meetup.com) group to explore how individuals and companies can adopt sustainable behaviors, or to make a tangible difference in solving a social or environmental problem at the community level.

- Collaborate with fellow socially responsible businesses to raise awareness of values-driven businesses and encourage other businesses to become values-driven. *Tip:* If you're a home-based business that provides an information-based product or service (e.g., editing, writing, web design, etc.), look into joining a coworking space (wiki.coworking.com) to expand both your network of like-minded individuals and your opportunities for collaborative projects.

- Offer to provide meeting space for an advocacy group that's aligned with your company's mission and vision.

- Set up a company-wide volunteer program (let your employees choose volunteer opportunities that are meaningful to them), or contribute your own time and skills to an organization.

- If your professional skills and personal passions include public speaking, teaching, motivating or inspiring action, or writing, offer to give a presentation or produce an engaging, reader-friendly document to raise awareness about a local issue.

- Support high school career exploration programs; be willing to give talks about your profession or socially responsible business practices, or provide information interviews.

Long term

- Inspire and encourage youth to step up to the S-R plate. Consider partnering with a community organization (e.g., Be the Change Earth Alliance) and the local school district to introduce (or support) a high school program on sustainable leadership skills.

- Be a diplomat and an advocate: Facilitate win-win connections between the various members of your networks.

- Support job-training programs for individuals with barriers to employment.

- Offer to mentor other micro or small business owners who are experiencing difficulties with trying to grow their businesses.

- Make a point of referring people in your network to other microentrepreneurs who are struggling to grow their business and might be facing additional barriers.

- Find out from your local community foundation, credit union, or regional small business development organization whether they have a small grant or partnership program to assist socially responsible for-profit microbusinesses and enterprising nonprofits (a.k.a. social enterprises). If you have the resources to do so, offer to work with these institutions to either set up a program or support an existing program.

- Make sure your sustainable purchasing policy includes a section on human rights and labor issues.

- Work with local and overseas suppliers to educate them about your policy and ensure that they take steps to comply with your policies.

- Consider relocating to an underserved area to help spark revitalization projects. Many big cities offer tax incentives for businesses to move in as part of their overall urban revitalization programs. *Note:* You may have to weigh this strategy in terms of easy access to public transportation and personal safety considerations for yourself, your employees, and your customers.

FURTHER READING

JUST as businesses don't operate in a vacuum, books are also not written in isolation and removed from influence. A small but invaluable selection of books on the subject of socially responsible business practices informed my ideas and deepened my understanding of social responsibility. Many of the strategies outlined in existing literature inspired me to come up with new and modified strategies designed for microbusinesses. In my research for *Small Business, Big Change*, I came across a remarkable body of reading that informed the guiding principles and content of this book. If you're interested in reading more about social responsibility (S-R), I highly recommend you check out these books to deepen your understanding, too.

Environment

Several books focused on the environmental dimension of S-R business practices and highlighted the business case for turning a business into a green one through strategies designed to save money and the planet by reducing energy and water use and the amount of waste produced. Two of the books in this category include *Green Your Work: Boost Your Bottom Line While Reducing Your Carbon Footprint* by Kim Carlson (2008) and *The Green Workplace: Sustainable Strategies that Benefit Employees, the Environment, and the Bottom Line* by Leah Stringer (2010). Both authors address the questions of why and how entrepreneurs should green their business. Both books walk the reader through the process of planning and implementing green strategies and identify some easy and inexpensive actions that produce quick "wins," and provide checklists and action plans at the end of each chapter.

Small Business, Big Change is similar to those books in that it, too, breaks down the process of integrating S-R practices into manageable steps, considers the challenges, as well as the triumphs of implementing S-R strategies, and offers checklists at the end of each chapter. *Small Business, Big Change*, however, goes beyond just looking at the environment and sees the decision to incorporate S-R practices being guided as much by core values as by the opportunity to boost the financial bottom line through cutting energy-related costs.

Books such as Kim McKay and Jenny Bonnin's *True Green at Work: 100 Ways You Can Make the Environment Your Business* (2008), Alex Shimo-Barry and Christopher Maron's *The Environment Equation: 100 Factors that Can Add to or Subtract from Your Total Carbon Footprint* (2008), and *David Suzuki's Green Guide* (2008) by David Suzuki and David R. Boyd provide useful strategies that can be implemented at work and at home (very handy if one has a home-based business). These three books also offer specific details about how much energy, water, or other resources we use for specific activities, what it actually costs for that energy or resource, and what we save (either in money or resources) just by making slight adjustments to our behaviors. If you want to align your professional and personal practices and are looking for ways to trim your household's carbon footprint, you might also be interested in consulting David Gershon's book, *Low Carbon Diet: A 30 Day Program to lose 5,000 Lbs* (2006).

Social Values

Books such as Tim Sanders' *Saving the World at Work: What Companies and Individuals Can Do to Go Beyond Making a Profit to Making a Difference* (2008) and Ben Cohen and Mal Warwick's *Values-driven Business: How to Change the World, Make Money, and Have Fun* (2006) focus on social values as well as environmental considerations. They are written from the perspective that the real driver for implementing S-R initiatives is a desire to align business practices with personal values that embrace the principles of cooperation, collaboration, equality, and respect.

While Sanders' book is intended more for employees and managers most likely employed by medium-sized businesses, Cohen and Warwick scale their approach to implementing S-R strategies to small businesses. *Small Business, Big Change* goes one step further than Cohen and Warwick's book and recognizes that microbusinesses of ten or fewer individuals, may still face unique challenges, both in terms of financial and other resources, when it comes to implementing S-R strategies.

Business Practices ("Value" and "Values")

John Ivanko and Lisa Kiviris' *Ecopreneuring: Putting Purpose and the Planet Before Profits* (2008) is a wonderful book tailored more toward guiding microbusinesses through the journey of incorporating S-R practices into their operational and strategic processes. Just as I have done with *Small Business, Big Change*, the authors recognize the importance of aligning business and personal values and practices as much as possible. In addition to walking microbusiness owners through the steps of setting up and running an S-R business, structuring finances and developing a sustainable approach to money management and personal finances, the authors of *Ecopreneuring* walk readers through the process of discovering their purpose and mission.

Unlike Ivanko and Kiviris' book, *Small Business, Big Change* speaks to microentrepreneurs who are clear on what they want to do but aren't sure about where to start with their S-R goals. It also addresses the concerns of microbusinesses that didn't necessarily start out with clear social/environmental missions. *Small Business, Big Change* also differs in that it advocates for a balanced approach and puts equal emphasis on people, the planet, and profits/prosperity. This three-pronged approach is less disconcerting for most microentrepreneurs who often worry that they might go broke in the quest to become a more socially responsible business.

AUTHOR'S NOTE

ANY guidebook—even as packed with ideas as this one—is never the final word on a topic. If you have other ideas or resources that I've missed here, I welcome you to share them with me. Similarly, if you can't find the answers to your burning questions on social responsibility, please contact me, and I'll do what I can to help you. You can contact me at susan_chambers@sdc-sage-editing.com.

ACKNOWLEDGMENTS

JUST as it takes a network of committed individuals and businesses to create a healthy, thriving community, it also takes a community of caring and dedicated people to transform an idea into a full-fledged book. The writing of *Small Business, Big Change* wouldn't have been possible without the direct and indirect help and encouragement from many individuals.

First and foremost, I'd like to thank Genevieve DeGuzman and Andrew Tang at Night Owls Press for providing me with the opportunity to reach out to socially responsible microentrepreneurs through this book. It has been my great pleasure and good fortune to work with an editor like Genevieve. Genevieve's attentiveness to the flow, tone, substance, and details in the text played an enormous role shaping the book you hold in your hands. Any remaining errors are a result of my oversight. As the Production Editor, Andrew has been exceedingly helpful and patient in navigating our way through the business process and details. Thanks also go to Andrew and Genevieve for doing a fantastic job of magically transforming pages and pages of text into a readable, user-friendly format. Thanks, also, to my sister and good friend, Jackie, for rolling up her sleeves and volunteering to help organize the almost overwhelming amount of rich details from the interviews into outlines for many of the case studies.

Thanks to Abhay Bhushan for generously agreeing to write the Foreword for the book and then further obliging Genevieve and me when we requested "just a few more details." It's an honor to have someone who's not only a pioneer in green business but also personally committed to a sustainable lifestyle lend his good name to this book.

Garth Yule, Program Manager of the Demonstrating Value project at the Vancity Community Foundation, has been incredibly supportive of this book project. Not only did he generously allow me to use their Performance Snapshot tool as a model for helping socially responsible microentrepreneurs track the impact of their actions, he also read through Chapter 1 and offered many helpful suggestions to further enhance the usefulness of this book.

To the microentrepreneurs featured in this book, my heartfelt gratitude. Not only did they take time out of their busy schedules to share their experiences for the book and graciously oblige my e-mails that started with

"Oh, just one more question…," they also made time to read through portions of the book and offer their feedback. Warm thanks particularly go to Linh Truong (The Soap Dispensary) for reading an early draft of Chapter 1, Kate Sutherland (Kate Sutherland & Associates) for reading through earlier drafts and the beta version of the Introduction and Chapter 1, and Lori Del Genis (Conscious Elegance) for reading through the beta version. A special thank you goes to Linh for allowing me to base the performance snapshot example in Chapter 1 on her store. Special thanks also go to Toby Barazzuol (Eclipse Awards) and Saul Brown (Saul Good Gifts Co.) for graciously allowing me to reference additional information about their S-R practices and philosophies from their excellent blogs, *Happiness Delivered* and *Stories from the Gift Box*, respectively.

I've also been blessed with friends who have been incredibly supportive throughout the writing of this book. Shoshana Allice and Karl Staib read through portions of the beta version and offered their insights and comments. Sharon Pendlington read through bits and pieces of the Introduction. My dear friends and fellow members of our "What's Your Tree" Action Circle (an action grove, really) have my thanks and appreciation for their encouragement.

Anne Thompson and Kate Sutherland generously referred me to their friends and contacts, many of whom ended up in this book as interviewees. Hilary Henegar (whom I indirectly met through Anne) also put me in touch with some amazing social entrepreneurs in Vancouver. Ladies, you all have my warmest thanks.

Thanks go to Maureen Jack-Lacroix, Founder of the Be the Change Earth Alliance and visionary organizer of "The Great Turning Un-Conference" in 2009 and 2011. Had she not been called to create both the Be the Change Earth Alliance and the "Un-Conference" I attended in 2009, I wouldn't have been exposed to a powerful means of transforming ordinary citizens into passionate social change agents. I also wouldn't have met the amazing people in my "What's Your Tree" Action Circle/grove, nor would the seed for this book have been sown.

Thanks also go to Mark Silver (Heart of Business, Inc.) whose teleseminar on heart-centered entrepreneurs and their relationships to money and power inadvertently served as the catalyst that shaped the topic of this book. More specifically, I'd like to thank Mark for graciously allowing me to make reference both to the discussion that happened at the end of the teleseminar and to his blog posts on the triple bottom line which helped to deepen my own understanding of corporate social responsibility as a set of two-way relationships rather than just numbers at the bottom of a page.

Finally, to all of those in my life who have encouraged me to pursue my love of writing over the years and served as my cheerleading squad while writing this book, a round of thanks and more thanks: my parents (Dorothy and John) and my sister (Jackie); Rajiv (my significant other) who listens patiently, encourages me both through words and by example to keep going when I feel like giving up, and makes me laugh when I start taking everything too seriously; the members of my "What's Your Tree" Action Circle—Kate, Anne, Greg, and Sharon—for encouraging me and reminding me that this book project epitomizes my purpose, and for serving as compassionate and wise sounding-boards on both the substance and writing process; and last, but definitely not least, an eternal thanks to Jeffrey Armstrong, my friend and Vedic teacher who delights in nurturing his students' creative talents. Jeffrey has only been telling me for nearly ten years that it was time I wrote a book. Well, that time has finally arrived.

Bibliography

Armstrong, Jeffrey. *Spiritual Teachings of the Avatar: Ancient Wisdom for a New World*. New York, NY: Atria Books/Beyond Words, Simon & Schuster, 2010.

Bonnin, Jenny, Kim McKay, and Tim Wallace. *True Green at Work: 100 Ways You Can Make the Environment Your Business*. Washington, D.C.: National Geographic, 2008.

Carlson, Kim. *Green Your Work. Boost Your Bottom Line While Reducing Your Carbon Footprint*. Avon, MA: Adams Business, 2008.

Carroll, A.B. and K.M. Shabana, "The Business Case for Corporate Social Responsibility: A Review of Concepts, Research and Practice," *International Journal of Management Reviews* 12 (2010): 85-105, accessed March 2, 2012, doi: 10.1111/j.1468-2370.2009.00275.x.

CHI Research, Inc., "Small Serial Innovators: The Small Firm Contribution to Technical Change," *Small Business Research Summary No. 225*, US Small Business Administration Office of Advocacy, 2003, http://archive.sba.gov/advo/research/rs225.pdf.

Christakis, Nicholas A., and James H. Fowler. *Connected: The Surprising Power of Our Social Networks and How They Shape Our Lives – How Your Friends' Friends' Friends Affect Everything You Feel, Think, and Do*. New York, NY: Back Bay Books, 2011.

Cohen, Ben, and Mal Warwick. *Values-Driven Business: How to Change the World, Make Money, and Have Fun*. San Francisco, CA: Berrett-Koehler Publishers, Inc., 2006.

Dear, Michael J., and Jennifer R. Wolch. *Landscapes of Despair: From Deinstitutionalization to Homelessness*. Princeton, NJ: Princeton University Press, 1987.

DeGuzman, Genevieve, and Andrew Tang. *Working in the UnOffice: A Guide for Indie Workers, Small Businesses, and Nonprofits*. San Francisco, CA: Night Owls Press, 2011.

Demonstrating Value Initiative. *Developing the Demonstrating Value Framework: Summary Report.* Vancouver, BC: Vancity Community Foundation, 2009.
De Waele, Martin. *Governing the World: the ethical imperative.* Bloomington, IN: Trafford Publishing, 2010.

Elkington, John. *Cannibals with Forks: the Triple Bottom Line of 21st Century Business.* New York, NY: Wiley, 1999.

Evanschitzky H., C. Groening, V. Mittal, and M. Wunderlich, "How Employer and Employee Satisfaction Affect Customer Satisfaction: An Application to Franchise Services," *Journal of Service Research*, 14, 2 (2010): 136. Available at http://jsr.sagepub.com/content/14/2/136.abstract, doi: 10.1177/1094670510390202.

Few, Stephen. *Show Me the Numbers: Designing Tables and Graphs to Enlighten.* Burlingame, CA: Analytics Press, 2004.

Gershon, David. *Low Carbon Diet: A 30 Day Program to Lose 5,000 Pounds.* Woodstock, NY: Empowerment Institute, 2006.

Hawken, Paul. *The Ecology of Commerce: A Declaration of Sustainability.* New York, NY: Harper Business, 1993.

Industry Canada. *Three Steps to Eco-Efficiency (Toolkit for SMEs).* Ottawa, ON: Government of Canada, 2001. (Downloadable tool available from http://www.ccnl.ca/greenerfutures/pdf/Unit%204%20-%20Information%20Sheet%20-%20Three%20Steps%20to%20Eco%20Efficiency.pdf.)

Ivanko, John, and Lisa Kiviris. *Ecopreneuring (Putting Purpose and the Planet before Profits).* Gabriola Island, BC: New Society Publishers, 2008.

Jack-Lacroix, Maureen, et al. *Be the Change Action Guide.* 4th ed. Vancouver, BC: Be the Change Earth Alliance, 2010.

Katsoulakos, P., M. Koutsodimo, A. Matraga, and L. Williams, "A Historic Perspective of the CSR Movement," White Paper produced for CSRQuest (www.csrquest.net), 2010 (accessed February 24, 2012).

Klein Jeff, *Working for Good: Making a Difference While Making a Living*. Boulder, CO: Sounds True, Inc., 2009.

Kobe, Kathryn, "The Small Business Share of GDP, 1998-2004," *Small Business Research Summary No. 299*, US Small Business Administration Office of Advocacy, 2007, http://www.sbaonline.sba.gov/advo/research/rs299.pdf.

McGuire, Judy and *Vancouver's Downtown East Side: A Community in Need of Balance*. Vancouver, BC: Strathcona Business Improvement Association, Ray-Cam Community Society and Inner City Safety Society, 2011.

Orlitzsky, Marc, F.L. Schmidt, and S.L. Rynes, "Corporate Social and Financial Performance: A Meta-Analysis," *Organization Studies* 24,3 (2003):403-441, doi: 10.1177/0170840603024003910.

Princic, Lisa. *Engaging Small Business in Corporate Social Responsibility: A Canadian Small Business Perspective on CSR*. Vancouver, BC: Canadian Business for Social Responsibility (CBSR), 2003.

Sadownik, Bryn. *The Demonstrating Value Workbook: An Activity Guide to Tracking and Expressing Your Organization's Success*. Vancouver, BC: Vancity Community Foundation, 2011.

Sanders, Tim. *Saving the World at Work: What Companies and Individuals Can Do to Go Beyond Making a Profit to Making a Difference.* New York, NY: Doubleday, 2008.

Shimo-Barry, Alex and Christopher Maron. *The Environment Equation: 100 Factors that Can Add to or Subtract from Your Total Carbon Footprint*. Avon, MA: Adams Media, 2008.

Stringer, Leah. *The Green Workplace: Sustainable Strategies that Benefit Employees, the Environment, and the Bottom Line.* New York, NY: Palgrave MacMillan (a division of St. Martin's Press), 2010.

Sutherland, Kate. *Make Light Work in Groups: 10 Tools to Transform Meetings, Companies and Communities.* Vancouver, BC: Incite Press, 2012.

Suzuki, David, and David R. Boyd. *David Suzuki's Green Guide.* Vancouver, BC: Greystone Books (A division of Douglas & McIntyre, Ltd.), 2008.

Suzuki, David. *David Suzuki at Work Toolkit* Vancouver, BC: The David Suzuki Foundation, 2009. (Toolkit can be downloaded from http://www.davidsuzuki.org/publications/downloads/2009/dsaw_toolkit_web.pdf.)

Ton, Zeynep, "Why 'Good Jobs' Are Good for Retailers," *Harvard Business Review (The Magazine)*, January-February 2012, http://hbr.org/2012/01/why-good-jobs-are-good-for-retailers (accessed April 15, 2012).

NOTES

FOREWORD

[1] Kathryn Kobe, "The Small Business Share of GDP, 1998-2004," Small Business Research Summary, April 2007, www.sba.gov/advo/research/rs299.pdf; CHI Research, "Small Serial Innovators: The Small Firm Contribution to Technical Change," February 2003, www.sba.gov/advo/research/rs225.pdf.

INTRODUCTION: Changing the World Through Your Business

[1] Heart of Business (heartofbusiness.com) offers a variety of resources, teleseminars, and home study courses designed to help heart-centered, "accidental" entrepreneurs figure out their business processes and an approach to marketing that feels authentic to these kinds of business owners.
[2] Heart-centered entrepreneurs are generally individuals in the field of complementary healing who are service-oriented and want to make a positive difference to the lives of others at both the personal and global level through work that is aligned with their values and lifestyles. Source: Joanna Scaparotti, "What is a Heart-centered Entrepreneur?" April 26, 2011, http://joannascaparotti.blogspot.com/2011/04/what-is-heart-centered-entrepreneur.html (accessed March 18, 2012).
[3] For the sake of expedience, the term "social responsibility" has been shortened to S-R when it refers to practices; for example: "A list of planet-friendly S-R actions are available in the next chapter."
[4] The *Action Guide* is organized into three levels: values related to major sustainability issues (environmental, social, spiritual, personal, and, indirectly, financial); intentions that set out a desire to make a change within one of the values areas; and actions that provide participants with small, manageable (but impactful!) changes they can make that support the intentions and values.
[5] The curricula and material for the "What's Your Tree" Action Circles were developed by Julia Butterfly Hill. The "What's Your Tree?" program is now part of the Engage Network. For more information, visit

http://whatsyourtree.it/wyt/THE_PROJECT.html. The curriculum was combined with major components from the "Be the Change" Action Circles.

[6] Susan Chambers, "Changing the World, One Business Owner at a Time, Part One," *Sage Wit* blog, June 6, 2011, http://sdc-sage-editing.com/sdc-sagewit/?p=144 (accessed March 18, 2012).

[7] The phrases, "people, planet, and profits" and the "triple bottom line," were coined by John Elkington in his book *Cannibals with Forks: the Triple Bottom Line of 21st Century Business* (New York, NY: Wiley, 1999). Source: International Institute for Sustainable Development, "The Triple Bottom Line," http://www.iisd.org/business/tools/principles_triple.asp (accessed March 18, 2012).

[8] Mark Silver, "Business Stability: The Triple Bottom Line," *Heart of Business*, March 11, 2004, http://www.heartofbusiness.com/2004/the-triple-bottom-line/ (accessed March 18, 2012).

[9] P. Katsoulakos, M. Koutsodimo, A. Matraga, and L. Williams, "A Historic Perspective of the CSR Movement," White Paper produced for CSRQuest (www.csrquest.net), 2010.

[10] A. B. Carroll and K. M. Shabana, "The Business Case for Corporate Social Responsibility: A Review of Concepts, Research and Practice," *International Journal of Management Reviews* 12 (2010): 85–105.

[11] For more details about the Natural Seal and the criteria it uses, refer to http://www.ecolabelindex.com/ecolabel/NaturalProductsStandard.

[12] Ben & Jerry's, "Activism," benjerry.com, http://www.benjerry.com/activism/ (accessed March 18, 2012).

[13] Angus Loten, "With new law, profits take a back seat," *The Wall Street Journal*, January 19, 2012, http://on.wsj.com/AjhIQ3 (accessed March 18, 2012).

[14] To learn more, visit http://www.naturespath.com/company/story.

[15] Ethical Consumer, "Successful Boycotts," http://www.ethicalconsumer.org/boycotts/successfulboycotts.aspx (accessed March 18, 2012); Sustainable Business Forum, "Top 10 CSR Stories of 2010," December 14, 2010, http://sustainablebusinessforum.com/craneandmatten/48685/top-10-corporate-responsibility-stories-2010 (accessed March 18, 2012).

[16] Kleercut, "Kimberly-Clark and Greenpeace agree to historic measures to protect forests," http://www.kleercut.net/en/ (accessed May 30, 2012).

[17] Vogel (2005), cited in A. B. Carroll and K. M. Shabana, "The Business Case for Corporate Social Responsibility: A Review of Concepts, Research and Practice," *International Journal of Management Reviews* 12 (2010): 85–105.

[18] A. B. Carroll and K. M. Shabana, "The Business Case for Corporate Social Responsibility: A Review of Concepts, Research and Practice," *International Journal of Management Reviews* 12 (2010): 85–105.

[19] Marc Orlitzsky, F.L. Schmidt, and S.L. Rynes, "Corporate Social and Financial Performance: A Meta-analysis," *Organization Studies* 24, 3 (2003): 403-441.

[20] These figures are estimates only. Data is extrapolated from the Corporate Register's CR Reporting Awards '10: Global Winners and Reporting Trends, April 2010 (available at http://www.corporateregister.com/pdf/CRRA10.pdf) and CR Reporting Awards '11: 2011 Global Winners and Reporting Trends, March 2011 (available at http://www.corporateregister.com/a10723/36941-11th-8607253C8215604518E-Gl.pdf).

[21] A. B. Carroll and K. M. Shabana, "The Business Case for Corporate Social Responsibility: A Review of Concepts, Research and Practice," *International Journal of Management Reviews*, 12 (2010): 85–105.

[22] Michael Mattis, "CSR-Washing is the new Greenwashing," CBS News.com, August 18, 2008, http://www.cbsnews.com/8301-505125_162-28440220/csr-washing-is-the-new-greenwashing/ (accessed March 18, 2012).

[23] Paul Hawken, *The Ecology of Commerce: A Declaration of Sustainability* (New York, NY: Harper Business, 1993).

[24] I first came across this story in Tim Sanders' *Saving the World at Work: What Companies and Individuals Can Do to Go Beyond Making a Profit to Making a Difference* (New York, NY: Crown Business, 2008).

[25] Not only does the company use sustainable, locally produced (or fairly traded) products, it also has a comprehensive code of conduct for its suppliers.

[26] Saul Brown, "How Paul Hawken Inspired the Creation of Saul Good Gift Co.," *Stories from the Gift Box* blog, November 16, 2011, http://www.itsaulgood.com/saul-blog/entry/how-paul-hawken-inspired-the-creation-of-the-saul-good-gift-co.html (accessed May 30, 2012).

ONE: Your Business as a Social Change Agent

[1] Nicholas A. Christakis and James H. Fowler, *Connected: The Surprising Power of Our Social Networks and How they Shape Our Lives - How Your Friends' Friends' Friends Affect Everything You Feel, Think, and Do* (New York, NY: Back Bay Books, 2011).

[2] Based on information on the *Demonstrating Value Worksheet: Identifying and Measuring Social Costs*. For more information see http://www.demonstratingvalue.org/tools-and-resources.

[3] The five-step process is outlined in a downloadable worksheet from the "Tools and Resources" page at http://www.demonstratingvalue.org/tools-and-resources. The worksheet was originally designed by Julie and Bernie Poznanski for Demonstrating Value in 2011.

[4] Bryn Sadownik, *The Demonstrating Value Workbook: An Activity Guide to Tracking and Expressing Your Organization's Success* (2011), 18. Download the workbook at http://www.demonstratingvalue.org/resources/demonstrating-value-workbook.

[5] Thanks to Garth Yule, Director of the Demonstrating Value Program, for bringing this matrix to my attention. This matrix was adapted from the Global Reporting Initiative's method for assessing materiality.

[6] Having said this, the Tiffin Project (thetiffinproject.com), which launched in Vancouver during the summer and fall of 2012, enables customers to use a specially designed takeout container (purchased through the nonprofit that oversees the project) at any of the restaurants participating in the project. The goals of the project are to: (1) reduce the amount of waste from disposable containers; and (2) use a portion of the proceeds from tiffin purchases to cultivate and support farm-to-table relationships between restaurants and local farmers.

[7] Lisa Princic, *Engaging Small Business in Corporate Social Responsibility: A Canadian Small Business Perspective on CSR* (Canadian Business for Social Responsibility, 2003). Download the report at http://info.worldbank.org/etools/docs/library/114189/Engaging%20SME%20in%20CSR%202003.pdf.

[8] Bryn Sadownik, *The Demonstrating Value Workbook: An Activity Guide to Tracking and Expressing Your Organization's Success* (2011), 18. Download the workbook at http://www.demonstratingvalue.org/resources/demonstrating-value-workbook.

[9] To learn more about the history and development of the Demonstrating Value Initiative, download http://www.demonstratingvalue.org/sites/default/files/basic-page-attachments/DV_research_initiative_summary_report.pdf.

[10] While both B Lab and Green America are located in the U.S., certification isn't limited to businesses located in the U.S.

[11] Bryn Sadownik, *The Demonstrating Value Workbook: An Activity Guide to Tracking and Expressing Your Organization's Success* (2011), 18. Download the workbook at http://www.demonstratingvalue.org/resources/demonstrating-value-workbook.

[12] An additional advantage with using the Demonstrating Value Project's toolkit and resources is that if you happen to be located in Vancouver, you also have the option of being referred to a consultant who is familiar with the framework and can walk you through the steps. (*Full disclosure:* I've worked with consulting clients through the Demonstrating Value project in the recent past, and most likely will continue to do so. Potential clients are generally

given the names of several consultants and it's up to the clients to choose which consultant they will work with.)

[13] While a broad library of downloadable templates isn't yet available, a template is available for social enterprises focused on providing employment skills training.

[14] Some of the snapshot examples have been designed as web-based, interactive snapshots using SAP Crystal Reporting software and Flash. To see an example of an interactive snapshot designed for a general audience (providing visitors information about an organization), visit http://www.demonstratingvalue.org/snapshots.

[15] For good design practices for charts and tables, Demonstrating Value recommends the following resources: Statistics Canada, "Using Graphs," www.statcan.gc.ca/edu/power-pouvoir/ch9/using-utilisation/5214829-eng.htm; Adobe Illustrator, "Put the Art in Charts," www.adobe.com/designcenter/illustrator/articles/illcs2at_chart_07.html; and Stephen Few's *Show Me the Numbers: Designing Tables and Graphs to Enlighten* (Burlingame, CA: Analytics Press, 2004).

[16] Genevieve DeGuzman and Andrew Tang, *Working in the UnOffice: A Guide for Indie Workers, Small Businesses, and Nonprofits* (San Francisco, CA: Night Owls Press, 2011). The book is available at http://www.nightowlspress.com/e-book-store/working-in-the-unoffice-a-guide-to-coworking/.

TWO: Treading Gently on the Planet

[1] For a great overview on consumerism and its inherent environmental problems, watch Annie Leonard's video, *The Story of Stuff* at http://www.storyofstuff.org/movies-all/story-of-stuff/.

[2] Jenny Bonnin, Kim McKay, and Tim Wallace, *True Green at Work: 100 Ways You Can Make the Environment Your Business* (Washington, D.C.: National Geographic, 2008), 46.

[3] Ibid., 82.

[4] See Seventh Generation's 2012 B Corporation rating for an overview of the company's other social responsibility measures that they have incorporated over the years at http://www.bcorporation.net/index.cfm/fuseaction/company.report/ID/ff4298a1-5da9-49ae-920d-435a93008899.

[5] Mike Berners-Lee, "What is a Carbon Footprint," *The Guardian* blog, June 10, 2010, http://www.guardian.co.uk/environment/blog/2010/jun/04/carbon-footprint-definition (accessed March 18, 2012).

[6] "Ecopreneur" is a term coined by John Ivanko and Lisa Kiviris in *Ecopreneuring: Putting Purpose and Planet Before Profits* (Gabriola Island, BC: New Society Publishers, 2008).

[7] To learn more about the "Two Block Diet," download http://www.vancouversun.com/pdf/Two-BlockDiet_Un-Manual.pdf.

[8] The Climate Smart program in BC is often hosted through municipal governments or large corporations that work with Climate Smart to provide grants that significantly reduce the fee for small businesses. See https://climatesmartbusiness.com/lowermainland/#cost for how this works.

[9] David Gershon, *Low Carbon Diet: A 30 Day Program to Lose 5,000 Lbs.* (Woodstock, NY: Empowerment Institute, 2006).

[10] For home-based businesses, depending on how and where your work space is set up within your home, you may find it more challenging to separate your business' eco-footprint from your household's footprint, overall.

[11] Alex Shimo-Barry and Christopher Maron, *The Environment Equation: 100 Factors that Can Add to or Subtract from Your Total Carbon Footprint* (Avon, MA: Adams Media, 2008).

[12] Many critics caution that the carbon footprint calculators available online fail to account for the true size of our carbon footprint. For example, see Mike Berners-Lee, "What is a Carbon Footprint," *The Guardian* blog, June 10, 2010, http://www.guardian.co.uk/environment/blog/2010/jun/04/carbon-footprintdefinition (accessed March 18, 2012). These calculators focus on the emissions we produce as a result of our lifestyles or work styles, and don't take into consideration the various goods and services we purchase—all of which come along with their own carbon footprints comprised of both direct and indirect emissions.

[13] Most of these ideas are standard recommendations for implementing socially responsible business practices and appeared in the following resources used in this book, including: Jenny Bonnin, Kim McKay, and Tim Wallace's *True Green at Work: 100 Ways You Can Make the Environment Your Business* (Washington, D.C.: National Geographic, 2008); Ben Cohen and Mal Warwick's *Values-driven Business: How to Change the World, Make Money, and Have Fun* (San Francisco, CA: Berrett-Koehler Publishers, Inc., 2006); Tim Sanders' *Saving the World at Work: What Companies and Individuals Can Do to Go Beyond Making a Profit to Making a Difference* (New York, NY: Doubleday, 2008); Alex Shimo-Barry and Christopher Maron's *The Environment Equation: 100 Factors that Can Add to or Subtract from Your Total Carbon Footprint* (Avon, MA: Adams Media, 2008); Leah Stringer's *The Green Workplace: Sustainable Strategies that Benefit Employees, the Environment, and the Bottom Line* (New York, NY:

Palgrave Macmillan, 2010); and David Suzuki and David R. Boyd's *David Suzuki's Green Guide* (Vancouver, BC: Greystone Books, 2008).

[14] This goal is inspired by Tom Van Camp's *Three Steps to Eco-Efficiency* (Ottawa: Industry Canada, Government of Canada, 2001). Download the information sheet at http://www.ccnl.ca/greenerfutures/pdf/Unit%204%20-%20Information%20Sheet%20-%20Three%20Steps%20to%20Eco%20Efficiency.pdf.

[15] For a comparison of the cost and energy performance for each type of bulb, check out Earth Easy's "Live LED Bulbs: Comparison Charts" at http://eartheasy.com/live_led_bulbs_comparison.html.

[16] For a list of screening questions for vendors and suppliers, consult the International Institute for Sustainable Development's tools at http://www.iisd.org/business/tools/.

[17] For more information on disclosing one's sustainability policies and practices, download Tom Van Camp's *Three Steps to Eco-Efficiency* (Ottawa: Industry Canada, Government of Canada, 2001) at http://www.ccnl.ca/greenerfutures/pdf/Unit%204%20-%20Information%20Sheet%20-%20Three%20Steps%20to%20Eco%20Efficiency.pdf.

[18] The cost-benefit analysis framework used here is a simple model that reflects the basic principles of what you need to consider. For some additional examples that use a more quantitative approach to ranking priorities and making decisions, see the following resources: Tom Van Camp's *Three Steps to Eco-Efficiency* (Ottawa: Industry Canada, Government of Canada, 2001), http://www.ccnl.ca/greenerfutures/pdf/Unit%204%20-%20Information%20Sheet%20-%20Three%20Steps%20to%20Eco%20Efficiency.pdf; Geoff Riley's "Cost-Benefit Analysis," Tutor2u.net, September 2006, http://www.tutor2u.net/economics/revision-notes/a2-micro-cost-benefit-analysis.html; and RIT Outreach Education and Training's "Cost Benefit Analysis," https://www.rit.edu/~w-outrea/training/Module5/M5_CostBenefitAnalysis.pdf.

[19] Alex Shimo-Barry and Christopher Maron, *The Environment Equation: 100 Factors that Can Add to or Subtract from Your Total Carbon Footprint* (Avon, MA: Adams Media, 2008).

[20] Environmental Protection Agency, "Paper Recycling: Basic Information Details," http://www.epa.gov/osw/conserve/materials/paper/basics/ (accessed September 25, 2012).

[21] The Water Project, "The Money Spent Can Be Better Used Elsewhere," http://thewaterproject.org/bottled_water_resources.asp (accessed September 25, 2012).

[22] Ibid.

[23] Pablo Päster, "What's the True Environmental Cost of Fiji Water?" Triple Pundit, February 5, 2007, http://www.triplepundit.com/2007/02/whats-the-true-environmental-cost-of-fiji-water/ (accessed September 25, 2012).

[24] For more information about the carbon-neutral shipping program at UPS, refer to http://www.ups.com/content/ca/en/resources/ship/carbonneutral/shipping.html.

[25] UPS (ups.com) is an example of a shipping company that provides its customers the option to purchase carbon offsets. To learn more about how UPS defines being carbon-neutral, see http://www.ups.com/content/us/en/bussol/browse/carbon_neutral_offset.html. More information about carbon offsets can be found at CarbonFund.org (http://www.carbonfund.org/offset).

[26] If, like The Soap Dispensary, your eco-friendly refill store not only reuses (refills) or repurposes its containers from its suppliers, but also sells the supplies to make your own cleaning products and offers workshops to show you how to make your own cleaning products—quadruple your bonus points and do the same for the business owner.

THREE: Social Capital and Social Impact on Your Community

[1] To learn more about Campbell Soup Company's latest CSR activities, read the Campbell 2011 Corporate Social Responsibility Report. The 2011 report can be downloaded at http://www.campbellsoupcompany.com/csr/resources_reports.asp.

[2] For more information about the Ford Foundation Fellowship program, see http://www.fordfoundation.org/.

[3] Vancity Savings Credit Union, "Streetohome Foundation Receives $1.2 Million From Vancity for Supportive Housing For Homeless People With Mental Illness and Addictions," Vancity.com, June 29, 2012, https://www.vancity.com/AboutUs/OurNews/AdditionalNews/jun292012/ (accessed December 8, 2012).

[4] The Great Bear region is a unique, environmentally sensitive ecosystem that will be destroyed if an oil pipeline is built through northern BC. For more information, see http://www.wwf.ca/conservation/oceans/greatbearsea/.

[5] These organizations are listed at http://www.meaningfultrip.com/about-meaningful-trips/affiliations/.

[6] More research on the impact of buying local can be found at Urban Conservancy and Civic Economics, "Thinking Outside the Box: A Report on Independent Merchants and the New Orleans Economy," September 2009, http://civiceconomics.com/app/download/5841600904/Magazine+Street+2009.pdf; and at Maine Center for Economic Policy, "Buying Locally Pays Big Dividends

for Maine's Economy," December 5, 2011,
http://www.mecep.org/view.asp?news=2002.

[7] Saul mentioned this analogy during our interview. For the full story, refer to the blog post, "The Vancity Movement: Local Banking as an Ecosystem," *Stories from the Gift Box* blog, March 22, 2012, http://www.itsaulgood.com/saul-blog/entry/the-vancity-movement-local-banking-as-an-ecosystem.html.

[8] Maine Center for Economic Policy, "Buying Locally Pays Big Dividends for Maine's Economy," December 5, 2011,
http://www.mecep.org/view.asp?news=2002 (accessed March 31, 2012).

[9] Ibid.

[10] Institute for Local Self-Reliance, "2011 Independent Business Survey," January 26, 2011, http://www.newrules.org/retail/news/survey-finds-buy-local-message-benefitting-independent-businesses (accessed March 31, 2012).

[11] Ibid.

[12] To learn more about the Strathcona Business Improvement Association's Materials Exchange program and the innovative exchanges that have occurred, read Saul Brown's blog post, "Strathcona Materials Exchange – adding value to waste," *Stories from the Gift Box* blog, June 16, 2009,
http://www.itsaulgood.com/saul-blog/entry/strathcona-materials-exchange-adding-value-to-waste.html (accessed April 15, 2012).

[13] Based on an analysis of median incomes by postal code (zip code) cited in Judy McGuire's 2011 report *Vancouver's Downtown East Side: A Community in Need of Balance*, prepared for the Strathcona Business Improvement Association, Ray-Cam Community Society and Inner City Safety Society.

[14] The phrase "landscape of despair" was coined by Michael J. Dear and Jennifer R. Wolch in *Landscapes of Despair: From Deinstitutionalization to Homelessness* (Princeton, New Jersey: Princeton University Press, 1987) to describe the inner city neighborhoods that often become the home for society's marginalized individuals and the service agencies that help them.

[15] Ben Cohen and Mal Warwick, *Values-driven Business: How to Change the World, Make Money, and Have Fun* (San Francisco, CA: Berrett-Koehler Publishers, Inc., 2006), 70-71.

[16] In addition to teaching Vedic wisdom and knowledge (a.k.a. the philosophy of yoga), Jeffrey Armstrong is also a widely published author. In his recent book *Spiritual Teachings of the Avatar: Ancient Wisdom for a New World* (New York, NY: Atria Books/Beyond Words, Simon & Schuster, 2010), he advocates strongly for a widespread socially responsible business model that is more people and planet friendly. The book is available at http://books.simonandschuster.ca/Spiritual-Teachings-of-the-Avatar/Jeffrey-Armstrong/9781582702810.

[17] Nicholas A. Christakis and James H. Fowler, *Connected: The Surprising Power of Our Social Networks and How they Shape Our Lives - How Your Friends' Friends' Friends Affect Everything You Feel, Think, and Do* (New York, NY: Back Bay Books, 2011).

[18] Greenpeace (greenpeace.org) was instrumental in launching a number of campaigns urging consumers to write letters and boycott Nestlé and other companies. To learn more about their campaign against Nestlé, read Stephanie Dearing's "Greenpeace boycotts Nestlé: 'Don't have a Kit Kat break today'," *Digital Journal*, March 23, 2010, http://digitaljournal.com/article/289481 (accessed April 15, 2012).

[19] Two books that I recommend as sources of inspiration and encouragement are Ben Cohen and Mal Warwick's *Values-driven Business: How to Change the World, Make money, and Have Fun* (San Francisco, CA: Berrett-Koehler Publishers, Inc., 2006) and Tim Sanders' *Saving the World at Work: What Companies and Individuals Can Do to Go Beyond Making a Profit to Making a Difference* (New York, NY: Crown Business, 2008).

[20] Your legal business structure will probably determine what you can or can't do regarding financial or in-kind donations. Consult a tax attorney or expert to make sure you follow the correct procedures for doing good through donations.

[21] Ben Cohen and Mal Warwick, *Values-driven Business: How to Change the World, Make money, and Have Fun* (San Francisco, CA: Berrett-Koehler Publishers, Inc., 2006), 116.

[22] Tim Sanders, *Saving the World at Work: What Companies and Individuals Can Do to Go Beyond Making a Profit to Making a Difference* (New York, NY: Doubleday, 2008), 167.

FOUR: People Power – Employees and Business Networks

[1] For an etymological definition and discussion of philanthropy, respectively, see http://www.etymonline.com/index.php?term=philanthropy and http://viktuliphilanthropy.blogspot.ca/2010/02/etymology-of-philanthropy.html.

[2] Jeff Klein's *Working for Good: Making a Difference while Making a Living* (Louisville, CO: Sounds True, Inc., 2009) offers a good overview of the skills needed to lead and encourage others to create positive changes through meaningful work and help shift the dominant business model from competitive to collaborative. Another great resource for understanding and enhancing group dynamics is Kate Sutherland's *Make Light Work in Groups: 10 Tools to Transform Meetings, Companies and Communities* (Vancouver, BC: Incite

Press, 2012). The book is available at http://www.katersutherland.com/kates-books/make-light-work-in-groups/.

[3] A few of these suggestions were mentioned in a blog post by Leslie Caccamese, "Five Ways to Make Your Employees Happier," *Great Place to Work* blog, February 13, 2012, http://www.greatplacetowork.com/publications-and-events/blogs-and-news/776 (accessed April 15, 2012).

[4] Stephen Thompson, "Minimum wage hike not enough, says B.C. Federation of Labour," *Straight.com*, May 1, 2012, http://www.straight.com/article-673546/vancouver/minimum-wage-hike-not-enough-says-bc-federation-labour (accessed April 15, 2012).

[5] Zeynep Ton, "Why 'Good Jobs' Are Good for Retailers," *Harvard Business Review*, http://hbr.org/2012/01/why-good-jobs-are-good-for-retailers (accessed April 15, 2012).

[6] Toby Barazzuol,"Eclipse Awards and the Living Wage Campaign," *Happiness Delivered* blog, August 27, 2010, http://www.eclipseawards.com/happinessdelivered.asp?ID=42 (accessed April 15, 2012).

[7] For example, see this study on the link between happy workers and better customer service: H. Evanschitzky, C. Groening, V. Mittal, and M. Wunderlich, "How Employer and Employee Satisfaction Affect Customer Satisfaction: An Application to Franchise Services," *Journal of Service Research*, 14, 2 (2010): 136. Download the paper at http://jsr.sagepub.com/content/14/2/136. Also, reported in the *Science Daily* (http://www.sciencedaily.com/releases/2011/06/110601131751.htm) and in the *Illinois Business Law Journal* (http://www.law.illinois.edu/bljournal/post/2010/04/25/Happiness-and-its-Effect-on-Economic-Development-and-Business-Profitability.aspx).

[8] John Sullivan, "The Death of the Cubicle — and the Killers Are Collaboration and Innovation," ERE.net, May 21, 2012, http://www.ere.net/2012/05/21/the-death-of-the-cubicle-and-the-killers-are-collaboration-and-innovation/ (accessed November 20, 2012).

[9] The conversation on optimal workspace design continues to evolve as proponents of open-plan spaces and cubicle advocates debate what types of spaces make workers happier and more productive. For an interesting chronicle of this debate, see John Tierney, "From Cubicles, Cry for Quiet Pierces Office Buzz," *The New York Times*, May 19, 2012, http://www.nytimes.com/2012/05/20/science/when-buzz-at-your-cubicle-is-too-loud-for-work.html (accessed November 20, 2012).

[10] Read about the Eclipse Awards team's adventures and find inspiring ideas for recognizing your people at the *Happiness Delivered* blog (http://www.eclipseawards.com/happinessdelivered.asp).

[11] Dr. Toni Yancey, a Public Health professor at University of California at Los Angeles (UCLA) and Co-Director of the UCLA Kaiser Permanente Center for Health Equity, recommends voluntary group exercise and breaks, and points out that they can reduce sick leave among employees. Source: As cited in Phyliss Korkki, "Communal Breaks: A Chance to Bond," *The New York Times*, July 14, 2012, http://www.nytimes.com/2012/07/15/jobs/group-breaks-can-raise-workplace-productivity.html (accessed November 20, 2012).

[12] Warwick shares this story in Chapter 3 of *Values-driven Business: How to Change the World, Make Money, and Have Fun* (San Francisco, CA: Berrett-Koehler Publishers, Inc., 2006) and notes that despite the objections from some board members, his decision prevailed and a profit-sharing program was put into place for the employees.

[13] Canadian Worker Co-Op Federation, "Statement of Co-operative Identity," http://www.canadianworker.coop/worker-co-op/principles (accessed April 15, 2012).

[14] Robert L. Masternak, "Gain sharing or Profit Sharing: The Right Tool for the Right Organization," http://www.hr-guide.com/data/G44301.htm (accessed March 1, 2012). Reprinted in the HR-Guide online, 2009.

[15] Tim Sanders, *Saving the World at Work: What Companies and Individuals Can Do to Go Beyond Making a Profit to Making a Difference* (New York, NY: Doubleday, 2008), 150.

[16] According to Susan Baka, historically underused businesses, or "supplier diversity"(defined as businesses owned by women, ethnic minorities, or Canadian Aboriginal persons) is a relatively new concept in Canada and there is currently no legislation in place to enforce implementation. Source: Susan Baka, "Supplier Diversity Takes Hold in Canada," *Minority Business Entrepreneur*, September/October 2012. Reprinted in the Canadian Aboriginal and Minority Supplier Council's (CAMSC) *Global Connections*, October 2012. Download the article at https://www.camsc.ca/uploads/File/Shared/Articles/Supplier-Diversity-takes-hold-in-Canada---MBE-magazine-article---Oct-2012.pdf.

[17] Tim Sanders, *Saving the World at Work: What Companies and Individuals Can Do to Go Beyond Making a Profit to Making a Difference* (New York, NY: Doubleday, 2008), 145.

[18] Ibid., 147.

[19] Ibid., 149.

[20] As with the other chapters in this book, these ideas are fairly standard S-R practices, and are a distillation of suggestions mentioned both by the entrepreneurs interviewed for this book and by authors such as Ben Cohen and Mal Warwick in *Values-driven Business: How to Change the World, Make Money, and Have Fun* (San Francisco, CA: Berrett-Koehler Publishers, Inc., 2006) and Tim Sanders in *Saving the World at Work: What Companies and Individuals Can Do to Go Beyond Making a Profit to Making a Difference* (New York, NY: Doubleday, 2008).

[21] In *Saving the World at Work: What Companies and Individuals Can Do to Go Beyond Making a Profit to Making a Difference* (New York, NY: Doubleday, 2008), author Tim Sanders recommends limiting computer time to less than five hours per day (139).

[22] Tim Sanders, *Saving the World at Work: What Companies and Individuals Can Do to Go Beyond Making a Profit to Making a Difference* (New York, NY: Doubleday, 2008), 154-155.

[23] Ibid., 150.

[24] Ibid., 146-147.

[25] Ibid., 147.

[26] Ibid., 148.

FIVE: Value, Values, and Valuing Your Customers

[1] MS&L Worldwide, *MS&L Global Values Study*, 2008, 18. Download the study at www.mslworldwide.com/annual-report/MS-L%20Global%20Core%20Values%20Study.pdf.

[2] Cone Communications, "2010 Shared Responsibility Study Fact Sheet." Download the fact sheet at http://www.coneinc.com/stuff/contentmgr/files/0/4b6d52e9ecfa4eb96b6ea2a801e48c c6/files/cone_2010_shared_responsibility_survey_fact_sheet.pdf.

[3] Ibid.

[4] According to Do Well Do Good's 2011 public survey, a public apology would win back 31% of customers and creating advertisements to inform people about its changes in policies and processes would win back 50% of consumers. Source: Do Well Do Good, "Second Annual Report on Sustainability," November 2011, http://dowelldogood.net/wp-content/uploads/2011/11/Second-Annual-Report-on-Sustainability-FINAL.pdf (accessed April 21, 2012).

[5] Ibid.

[6] As with the other chapters in this book, these suggestions are drawn from both the interviewees' practices and from the standard ideas about customer-related S-R practices mentioned in Tim Sanders' *Saving the World at Work: What*

Companies and Individuals Can Do to Go Beyond Making a Profit to Making a Difference (New York, NY: Doubleday, 2008) and Ben Cohen and Mal Warwick's *Values-driven Business: How to Change the World, Make Money, and Have Fun* (San Francisco, CA: Berrett-Koehler Publishers, Inc., 2006).

[7] Ben Cohen and Mal Warwick, *Values-driven Business: How to Change the World, Make Money, and Have Fun* (San Francisco, CA: Berrett-Koehler Publishers, Inc., 2006), 97.

[8] Ibid.

[9] Ibid., 98.

[10] Ibid., 86.

[11] Ibid., 90.

SIX: When Vision and Reality Collide – Unpacking the First-aid Kit

[1] Sheila Bonini and Jerry Oppenheimer, "Cultivating the Green Consumer," *Stanford Social Innovation Review*, Fall 2008, http://www.ssireview.org/articles/entry/cultivating_the_green_consumer (accessed April 15, 2012).

[2] Leah Stringer, *The Green Workplace: Sustainable Strategies that Benefit Employees, the Environment, and the Bottom Line* (New York, NY: Palgrave Macmillan, 2010), 152.

[3] Consult Leigh Stringer's *The Green Workplace: Sustainable Strategies that Benefit Employees, the Environment, and the Bottom Line* (New York, NY: Palgrave Macmillan, 2010) for additional ideas about how to implement this strategy.

[4] According to the Waterwonder Café (wonderwater.fi/projectsposts/wonderwater-cafe), it takes roughly twenty-seven liters of water to produce a glass of lemonade. A glass of wine, on the other hand, carries a water footprint of 110 liters. Source: Water Footprint, http://www.waterfootprint.org (accessed April 15, 2012).

[5] Jenny Bonnin, Kim McKay, and Tim Wallace, *True Green at Work: 100 Ways You Can Make the Environment Your Business* (Washington, D.C.: National Geographic, 2008), 21.

[6] BC Hydro Regeneration, "Turn Computers & Equipment Off When Not In Use," http://www.bchydro.com/guides_tips/green_your_business/office_guide/Turn_equipment_off_when_not_in_use_.html (accessed May 5, 2012).

ABOUT THE AUTHOR

SUSAN CHAMBERS is a writer, editor, and researcher who is passionate about empowering NGOs, nonprofits, social enterprises, and businesses alike to create positive change in the world. She has over twenty years of research experience and is the principal and creative force behind Sage Editing and Research (sdc-sage-editing.com). Susan volunteers for Oxfam and Be the Change Earth Alliance and does some consulting for a community foundation that is committed to social enterprise development and community change.

Susan's editorial passion is to help social change agents empower their message through clarity, strengthen their statements with facts, and captivate their audience. A long-time advocate for social justice and sustainable development issues, she has written for Be The Change Earth Alliance, an organization focused on community engagement on environmental issues, as well as spearheaded other independent projects.

Small Business, Big Change: A Microentrepreneur's Guide to Social Responsibility is her first book. For more about the book, visit www.smallbusinessbigchange.com.

ABOUT THE PUBLISHER

NIGHT OWLS PRESS (nightowlspress.com) is a small, independent press that publishes nonfiction books that challenge and re-imagine prevailing conventions about business, work, and life. Covering topics on entrepreneurship, education, innovation, and social responsibility, its focus is to turn big ideas into great books that inform and inspire.

For special orders and bulk purchases, contact admin@nightowlspress.com.

22196911R00150

Made in the USA
Charleston, SC
12 September 2013